D1528510

The Vietnam War on Film

The Vietnam War on Film

David Luhrssen

Hollywood History

An Imprint of ABC-CLIO, LLC
Santa Barbara, California • Denver, Colorado

Library of Congress Cataloging-in-Publication Data

Names: Luhrssen, David, author.
Title: The Vietnam War on film / David Luhrssen.
Description: Santa Barbara, California : ABC-CLIO, 2019. | Series:
  Hollywood history | Includes bibliographical references and index.
Identifiers: LCCN 2019009574 (print) | LCCN 2019010848 (ebook) | ISBN
  9781440866739 (eBook) | ISBN 9781440866722 (hardcopy :alk. paper)
Subjects: LCSH: Vietnam War, 1961–1975—Motion pictures and the war. | War
  films—United States—History and criticism.
Classification: LCC DS557.73 (ebook) | LCC DS557.73 .L84 2019 (print) | DDC
  791.43/658597043—dc23
LC record available at https://lccn.loc.gov/2019009574

ISBN: 978-1-4408-6672-2 (print)
      978-1-4408-6673-9 (ebook)

23 22 21 20 19   1 2 3 4 5

This book is also available as an eBook.

ABC-CLIO
An Imprint of ABC-CLIO, LLC

ABC-CLIO, LLC
147 Castilian Drive
Santa Barbara, California 93117
www.abc-clio.com

This book is printed on acid-free paper ∞

Manufactured in the United States of America

Contents

Series Foreword

Just exactly how accurate are Hollywood's film and television portrayals of American history? What do these portrayals of history tell us, not only about the events they depict but also the time in which they were made?

Each volume in this unique reference series is devoted to a single topic or key theme in American history, examining 10–12 major motion pictures or television productions. Substantial essays summarize each film, provide historical background of the event or period it depicts, and explain how accurate the film's depiction is, while also analyzing the cultural context in which the film was made. A final resources section provides a comprehensive annotated bibliography of print and electronic sources to aid students and teachers in further research.

The subjects of these Hollywood History volumes were chosen based on both curriculum relevance and inherent interest. Readers will find a wide array of subject choices, including American Slavery on Film, the Civil War on Film, the American West on Film, Vietnam on Film, and the 1960s on Film. Ideal for school assignments and student research, the length, format, and subject areas are designed to meet educators' needs and students' interests.

Preface

In the 20th century, eyewitness accounts of war began to merge with the imaginative re-creations projected on screens in movie theaters and, by the 1950s, on television. Long before smartphones, the popular imagination was refracted through screens and the stories seen there. Movies about wars became the way most of us remember those conflicts. As director Ingmar Bergman argued, "No art passes our conscience in the way film does, and goes directly to our feelings, deep down into the dark rooms of our souls" (Berger 1991). In worst cases, film can distort our memories. Essayist Geoffrey O'Brien called the impressions of real events left by the fictionalization of the movies "a colony of barnacles clinging to the underside of your visual memory" (O'Brien 1995, 24). Korea has been called the forgotten war. One reason may be the relative paucity of notable Korean War (1950–1953) movies produced during the fighting and after the armistice (Jeansonne and Luhrssen 2014, 84–85).

By contrast, the Vietnam War was never forgotten. *The Vietnam War on Film* examines how the war has been remembered—and, in one case, depicted during the time of the conflict—by Hollywood movies. It would have been a slender volume had it been published at the war's end in 1975. Before then, John Wayne's *The Green Berets* (1968) was the only major motion picture to address a war that raged not only on the battlefield but also in public debates and protests across the United States. As the only explicitly prowar entry, *The Green Berets* is an outlier in this book, yet, as Hollywood's first attempt at grappling with Vietnam, is a good place to begin.

Arranged chronologically, each of the 10 chapters of *The Vietnam War on Film* is devoted to a particular feature-length film that depicts the war through dramatization and storytelling as opposed to documentary footage and interviews. Each chapter will evaluate how closely those dramatizations reflected the actual truth, or how far from the truth they actually were. They were chosen in some cases for their role in defining the public memory and discourse about the war; some films were picked because of their popularity at the time of release; others were chosen for focusing on underappreciated aspects of the conflict and its aftermath.

A 10-year gap separates *The Green Berets* from the first wave of postwar Vietnam movies. For several years, with many Americans wanting only to put the war behind them, Hollywood was uncertain if a moviegoing audience existed for a conflict that had stirred such bitterness and controversy. The first postwar drama to reach theaters was Jane Fonda's *Coming Home* (1978), concerned with a paralyzed veteran who returned from combat in what he experienced as a dubious war. *The Boys in Company C* (1978) followed a group of marines from basic training through the hellfire of a mismanaged war. *The Deer Hunter* (1978) focused on a trio of soldiers from a Pennsylvania steel town and the psychological toll of their experience in Vietnam. It earned five Oscars and performed surprisingly well at the box office, but the Hollywood studios still worried that its success might be an anomaly.

Apocalypse Now (1979) represented the final breakthrough on the topic of Vietnam, commercially as well as cinematically. It drew large and returning audiences, became the subject of much discussion among critics and the general public, and was nominated for eight Oscars at the 1980 Academy Awards, winning two. The film's success was an important stimulus for reexamining a war that cost many lives, split Americans into warring camps, and ended in defeat. With the accolades and attention accrued by *Apocalypse Now*, Hollywood producers felt confident that audiences were ready for movies about Vietnam.

In the 1980s, as a strange sort of nostalgia began to settle over the subject of Vietnam, movies that addressed the war were no longer an unusual sight in movie theaters. The second half of the decade saw the release of six memorable movies included in *The Vietnam War on Film*. Five films from that period were set in part on the battlefield. Director Oliver Stone's *Platoon* (1986) was based on his experience of the war and was meant as a rebuke to *The Green Berets*. Stanley Kubrick's *Full Metal Jacket* (1987) recalled *The Boys in Company C* in its harrowing depiction of marines in combat.

While the 1980s will probably stand as the most prolific era for Vietnam War movies, the subject continued to inspire filmmakers in the 21st century. Starring Mel Gibson, *We Were Soldiers* (2002) dramatized ground combat between U.S. and North Vietnamese forces, as well as highlighted the introduction of the new, modern air cavalry, where soldiers "rode" into battle not on horseback, but in helicopters. Two other films from recent years are outstanding for portraying aspects of the conflict often overlooked in popular culture. Based on a novel by Graham Greene, *The Quiet American* (2002) examined the U.S. role in the first phase of the war when France struggled with communist forces for control over Vietnam. *Rescue Dawn* (2006) dramatized the trek of a downed American pilot who escaped from a prisoner of war camp.

Time is the ultimate judge of the value of art and entertainment. Many movies that achieved popularity in their day have faded with the passing of years. Film historians deem at least three of the films examined in *The Vietnam War on Film—The Deer Hunter*, *Apocalypse Now*, and *Full Metal Jacket*—as masterpieces. At least one selection, *The Green Berets*, is almost universally reviled by critics and historians. All, however, retain the ability to tell us something about how the war was received and interpreted at the time and in its aftermath. In many cases, they continue to inform a conversation that refuses to cease about America's most controversial war.

FURTHER READING

Berger, John. "Ev'ry Time We Say Goodbye." *Sight and Sound*, June 1991.

Jeansonne, Glen, and David Luhrssen. 2014. *War on the Silver Screen: Shaping America's Perception of History*. Lincoln, NE: Potomac Books.

O'Brien, Geoffrey. 1995. *The Phantom Empire: Movies in Mind of the Twentieth Century*. New York: W. W. Norton.

Radway, Janice A., Kevin K. Gaines, Barry Shank, and Penny Von Eschen, editors. 2009. *American Studies: An Anthology*. Chichester: Wiley-Blackwell.

Acknowledgments

The Vietnam War on Film isn't the book I might have written on the subject if left to my own devices, and that's probably just as well. I would like to thank Michael Millman at ABC-CLIO for proposing the project to me and my editor, Patrick Hall, who guided the manuscript along different avenues than I had in mind. With his input, *The Vietnam War on Film* became an interesting hybrid of film, military, and diplomatic history. There is no final word on a subject as large and complicated as Vietnam. As much as possible, I drew my narrative on various aspects of the war from the eyewitness accounts of servicemen and others, reports by journalists during the war, and reflections by historians during and after the conflict. My hope is that *The Vietnam War on Film* can contribute to the ongoing discussion of that war and America's role in the world as well as the ways in which reality is perceived through the medium of film.

I would also like to thank the late Glen Jeansonne, professor emeritus of history at the University of Wisconsin-Milwaukee, for introducing me to ABC-CLIO; Jamie Lee Rake for an engaging discussion on pro–Vietnam War sentiment in popular culture; and my lifelong companion, Mary Manion, who watched the movies included in this book with me and commented on my manuscript in progress.

Introduction

The Vietnam War remains the most divisive conflict in U.S. history since the Civil War (1861–1865). More than 58,000 Americans lost their lives in a war that ended by any reasonable measure in defeat. By the late 1960s, as the U.S. military commitment reached its peak, more Americans were in the streets protesting the war than were stationed in Vietnam. The battle for the hearts and minds of Americans was fought on college campuses and public spaces. There were casualties, including four dead at Kent State and two at Jackson State when the Ohio National Guard and Mississippi Highway Patrol fired on demonstrators, and one at the University of Wisconsin, where an antiwar radical blew up a defense research center.

Nearly 50 years have passed since Saigon, the capital of the U.S.-backed Republic of Vietnam (South Vietnam), fell to North Vietnamese–backed communists. Photographers captured unforgettable images of the last Americans in Saigon fleeing the U.S. embassy by helicopter with South Vietnamese allies desperately clinging to their sides. Debate over the war's outcome continues even today. While many Americans have concluded that the U.S. intervention was a mistake, others insist that the war could have been won with an even greater application of force coupled with the undivided support of the public.

There were two Vietnam wars in the 20th century, each pitting Western forces against the Vietnamese communists. France and its local allies fought the first with the aid of American guns and money. The United States and its allies fought the second. In both cases the Vietnamese communists triumphed through a combination of determined leadership, military strategy, knowledge of local geography and conditions, the relative weakness of anticommunist Vietnamese parties, and war fatigue on the home fronts of France and the United States. Unlike their opponents, the Vietnamese communists were committed unto death for their cause. "You may kill ten of my men for every one I kill of yours," Communist leader Ho Chi Minh (1890–1969) told a French negotiator, "but even at those odds you will lose and I will win" (Wintle 1991, 54).

The First Vietnam War, commonly known as the First Indochina War (1946–1954), began in the confused ending of World War II (1939–1945) in East Asia. Several months before Imperial Japan surrendered, Japanese forces, who had been stationed in Vietnam with the coerced consent of Vichy France, seized control and crushed the country's French colonial adminis-tration. At the same time, communist guerillas, the Vietminh under Ho Chi Minh, began sniping at the Japanese as well as French outposts with sup-port from the U.S. Office of Strategic Services (OSS), the forerunner of the Central Intelligence Agency (CIA) (Wintle 1991, 39). As the war ended, Ho seized major cities, including Hanoi and Haiphong, and declared Vietnam independent. The OSS watched as confused fighting broke out in Saigon, where British forces with rearmed Japanese prisoners of war (POWs) under their command vied with the Vietminh for control. An OSS agent, Lieutenant Colonel A. Peter Dewey, tried to broker talks but was killed by the Vietminh on September 26, 1945. He may have been mistaken for a Frenchman. He was the first American casualty in Vietnam (Ward 2017, 16–19).

Anyone inclined to sort the combatants of the First Vietnam War into heroes and villains will be frustrated by the facts. The Vietminh conducted its war of national liberation with as much brutality as the French Expedi-tionary Force, which arrived in 1945 with the mission of reasserting control (McAlister 1970, 164). "In the end cruelty was practiced on all sides," wrote an eyewitness, French journalist Lucien Bodard. "Often it happened that even the French were caught up in this intoxication of torture and death: it was in the air one breathed, it arose from the country itself, forming part of its ways and customs: from weariness, over-excitement and example" (Bodard 1967, 19–20). His words would apply equally well to the American experience in Vietnam.

The Vietnamese communists benefited from the remarkable leadership of Ho, who embodied his nation's traditions while calling for a new world based on the ideology of communism. The French had nothing to offer the Vietnamese but the continuation of a colonial regime whose back had been broken by the Japanese. Ho promised a new beginning within the context of Vietnamese culture. Lacking the resources to defeat Ho, France turned to the United States for help.

Before World War II, the United States had no stake in preserving the overseas empires of Europe, but by 1950, when U.S. military hardware, money, and military advisers began to arrive in Vietnam, the Cold War had changed America's perspective on the world. The Soviets liberated Eastern Europe from the Nazis in World War II and had no intention of loosening their grip; Mao Zedong's (1893–1976) communists had overrun mainland China; and a communist insurgency flared in Greece. According to U.S. diplomat George Kennan, "United States policy toward the Soviet Union must be that of a long-term, patient but firm and vigilant containment of Russian expansive tendencies" (Mr. X, 1947). Containment as it developed under the Harry S. Truman (1884–1972) and Dwight D. Eisenhower (1890–1969) administrations was understood as the middle ground between watching the nations of Europe and Asia fall to communism one by one, like dominoes in President Eisenhower's words, or risking a destructive war with the Soviet Union, a prospect that would become almost unthinkable once the Soviets detonated their first nuclear bomb in 1949. Containment came to mean drawing a boundary around the communist-controlled portions of the globe, fencing communism behind a network of U.S. military bases and alliances, and opposing it wherever it tried to expand.

The consensus favoring containment spanned the political spectrum and included the liberal intelligentsia. Columnist Max Lerner wrote that America had no choice but to build "positions of strength" across the globe in light of "this new power reality" and the realization that the Atlantic and Pacific Oceans, which had long served as America's moats, were no defense in the age of missiles and strategic bombers. He added that "the new colonial revolutions—often with Marxist slogans and leadership—have given Americans a more oppressive feeling than that of geographical encirclement, namely the sense of ideological encirclement" (Lerner 1957).

With the march of communism seen as a threat to America's values and even its existence, Vietnam ceased being simply a colonial war or even a civil war between local factions but a theater in the Cold War, the long struggle in which the United States and the Soviets confronted each other through proxy wars, espionage, subversion, and cultural competition but not direct combat. Eisenhower continued to support the French materially but, wary of another Asian war in light of the near debacle of the Korean War (1950–1953), refused to commit American troops or airpower in Vietnam.

After suffering a humiliating defeat when their fortress at Dien Bien Phu fell to the Vietminh in 1954, France participated in an international peace conference in Geneva, Switzerland. Under the Geneva Accords (1954), the French withdrew and Vietnam was divided at the 17th parallel with a demilitarized zone (DMZ) separating North Vietnam, controlled by Ho's communists, and South Vietnam, ruled by the pro-Western administration left behind by the French. An internationally supervised election was scheduled for 1956 for the purpose of reunifying the country under one government. The election never took place.

Ho rapidly consolidated his rule over the North according to his nationalistic understanding of Karl Marx by executing landlords, redistributing farmland to small holders, establishing labor camps, and killing or imprisoning all real or suspected dissidents.

The South was scarcely less oppressive. By 1955, the leadership of South Vietnam fell into the hands of American-backed president Ngo Dinh Diem (1901–1963). Roman Catholics in a predominantly Buddhist land, Diem's family antagonized the country while enriching themselves from its economy. Diem's narrow base of support left him vulnerable to Ho's ambitions. As the United States poured more guns and money into South Vietnam to train and grow its army, Ho encouraged the formation of the National Liberation Front, a procommunist party in the South whose armed wing, the Vietcong, began waging guerilla war against Diem. By 1959 they were winning battles and gaining control over rural areas.

The 1960 election of U.S. President John F. Kennedy, a Roman Catholic, seemed to bode well for Diem. However, Diem's autocratic and corrupt regime lost ground against the Vietcong and continued to lose popularity. In 1963, a Buddhist monk famously set himself on fire to protest Diem's prejudice and even persecution against non-Catholics. By August 1963, Washington lost confidence in Diem and signaled to his army officers that it would not oppose a military coup. On November 1, 1963, the army seized control; the following day, Diem and his brother were summarily executed, three weeks before Kennedy was assassinated in Dallas. By the time of Kennedy's death, there were 16,500 American advisers and Special Forces, the crack Green Berets, in South Vietnam to train its army in counterinsurgency.

Lyndon B. Johnson (1908–1973) assumed the presidency upon Kennedy's death, inheriting a war for which he saw only two plausible options: withdrawal or escalation. For Johnson, withdrawal would have spelled defeat, and defeat against a communist insurgency meant unraveling the policy of containment that was already fraying after Cuba, 90 miles from the Florida shore, fell to Fidel Castro (1926–2016) in 1959, and leftists of uncertain orientation seemed poised to control many emergent nations in Africa and the Near East. Unwilling to risk provoking the Soviet Union or communist China, which by then possessed its own atomic arsenal, Johnson chose the path of slow escalation, hoping at every step that American ground forces supported by airpower could crush the Vietcong and cow the North Vietnamese.

In August 1964, the Gulf of Tonkin incident provided Johnson with further rationale to escalate American involvement in the war. U.S. destroyers just outside North Vietnam's territorial waters, supporting a South Vietnamese naval operation against the North, were attacked by North Vietnamese torpedo boats. Johnson described the affair as an unprovoked attack and leveraged it to win congressional approval for the Gulf of Tonkin Resolution, authorizing the president to use force to "take all necessary measures to repel any armed attack against the forces of the United States" and to assist any member of SEATO, the Southeast Asian analog to NATO, "requesting assistance in defense of its freedom." It was not a constitutional declaration of war against North Vietnam but amounted to an authorization of war nonetheless.

Johnson began launching air strikes against North Vietnam in an effort to thwart its support for the Vietcong. U.S. ground troops landed in 1965, ostensibly to protect the airfields from where those raids were launched. Tons of bombs were dropped on the North, flattening wide swaths of its cities, yet the communist regime reassembled factories and relocated its population to the countryside; its ports continued to receive Soviet and Chinese ships loaded with fuel and weapons. As in World War II, the continual bombardment only seemed to stiffen civilian resolve. "Our lives were turned upside down by the bombing," said Vietnamese novelist Ba Ninh, 14 years old when the air raids began. "People were killed, their houses were destroyed. I couldn't go to school in Hanoi; I had to evacuate to rural areas. All of it aroused indignation" (Ward, 2017, 177–183). The air campaign was costly for the United States, which lost hundreds of planes from ground fire and dogfights with North Vietnamese jets. Many downed American pilots were held in hard conditions until the war's end.

The ground war was similarly inconclusive. U.S. Army infantry and Marines engaged in "search and destroy" missions, seeking out the Vietcong and, increasingly, North Vietnamese regulars in their jungle fastness. "Fire bases" were established to provide artillery support. The First Cavalry Division was mounted on helicopters and sent in flying columns to battle scenes, supported by the heavy fire of helicopter gunships. Still, conditions on the ground were always difficult. Private Jerry Johnson of the First Infantry Division recalled "mass hysteria and all I could do was hear them," he said of the unseen Vietcong, firing AK-47 assault rifles from the dark jungle. "No one knew what was going on. I didn't know what we were supposed to do. I just dropped down and gave supporting fire" (Ebert 1993, 135). Progress was always slow for U.S. forces, victory just beyond reach, so more reinforcements were sent. By 1966, troop levels climbed to 184,000; a year later their number increased to 485,000; by the start of 1968, 536,000 troops were stationed in Vietnam. The United States resorted to using Agent Orange, a chemical that defoliated the jungle but proved harmful when exposed to U.S. personnel and Vietnamese civilians alike.

Preoccupied with the calculus of war and convinced that technology could win the day, Secretary of Defense Robert McNamara (1916–2009) often overlooked reality on the ground and demanded statistics he could show to the president and Congress. The Pentagon obliged with "body counts" of enemy losses based on guesswork and high hopes. Meanwhile, the more accurate tally of American casualties grew by the day. Nevertheless, the U.S. commander in Vietnam, General William Westmoreland (1914–2005), insisted that victory was in sight.

His forecast was shattered on January 30, 1968, when the Vietcong and North Vietnamese army launched the Tet Offensive. Tet was the Lunar New

Year celebration, and the South Vietnamese were unprepared for the assault that struck cities, towns, and bases throughout the country, penetrating even the walls of the U.S. embassy. The scale and scope of the disruption caused by communist forces owed much to their network of spies and secret cadres woven through South Vietnam. They knew the routes of night patrols, the addresses of government officials, and the whereabouts of foreigners, and they drew up street-by-street target lists for the country's major cities (Oberdorfer, 2001, 560–564). American and South Vietnamese forces rallied and repelled the attacks, inflicting as many as 47,000 casualties on the communists while losing fewer than 5,000 of their own men. Yet, Ho's prophecy to the French was born out again. If Tet was a tactical victory for the United States, it was a Pyrrhic one. Television coverage of the Tet Offensive brought the chaos of war into American homes, and Americans did not like what they saw.

Perhaps the final blow to public support for the war effort was administered by the most trusted figure on television, "CBS Evening News" anchor Walter Cronkite. A World War II veteran and pillar of the consensus for containment, Cronkite supported the war in 1965, declaring, "The communist advance must be stopped in Asia." But after witnessing the fury of the Tet Offensive, he concluded that the Johnson administration and the military were lying about conditions in Vietnam. On February 27, 1968, 20 million Americans watched his "Report from Vietnam" and heard him predict "the bloody experience of Vietnam is to end in a stalemate" (Ward 2017, 290–291).

The antiwar movement had already been gathering strength, and its numbers swelled after Tet. For protestors at demonstrations, some of them numbering over 100,000 participants, Johnson was the villain. "LBJ, how many kids did you kill today?" they chanted. The protests were loose with the threat of unruliness. Most participants simply wanted the war to end, but a militant minority saw the demonstrations as rehearsal for a revolution against the existing order. "The majority of demonstrators," wrote novelist Norman Mailer, who took part in a march on the Pentagon, "had never marched in ranks; there were no leaders sufficiently well-known to command order easily" (Mailer, 1968, 112). The force of the movement was generated by conscription, the real fear among young men that the draft might send them to a losing war in a far country. A small number of men fled and found sanctuary in Canada. Many more evaded the draft through college deferments and medical exemptions. Most felt they had no choice but to comply when their number came up in the draft lottery. On the other hand, significant numbers of young men volunteered to fight, motivated by patriotism and memories of their parents' war, World War II. Their ranks thinned as the conflict dragged on.

Hollywood was slow to respond to Vietnam and was, in any event, still dominated by an older generation of executives with ties to Washington.

Only one major motion picture on Vietnam, *The Green Berets* (1968), was released during the war. The music industry, which had become dependent on the creativity and patronage of the generation confronted with serving in Vietnam, was more responsive. Even there, American rock bands recorded few explicit statements on the war, although Creedence Clearwater Revival songs such as "Run through the Jungle" and "Fortunate Son" resonated with anxiety and anger over Vietnam. The most pointed musical denunciation was Country Joe and The Fish's "I-Feel-Like-I'm-Fixin'-to-Die Rag" (originally released in 1965 but reissued in 1967 as opposition to the war grew). Band leader Country Joe McDonald, a navy veteran, claimed it was not a pacifist song but a soldier's song. He added, "The song attempts to address the horror of going to war with a dark sarcastic form of humor called 'GI humor.' GI humor is a way people have of complaining about their situation so it will not get them in trouble and keep them from going insane in an insane environment: war" (McDonald 2000).

The loss of public faith in the war's means and objectives was as much a war of attrition as the battlefields of Vietnam, and the Johnson administration was losing both. Aware he was in danger of losing the Democratic Party nomination for president to antiwar candidates, Johnson startled the country by announcing on March 31, 1968, that he wouldn't seek, or accept, the party's nomination. The nomination of his putative successor, Vice President Hubert H. Humphrey, was marred by violent clashes between police and antiwar protestors outside the Democratic National Convention that August. Most media accounts concurred with the description by novelist William Burroughs, covering the convention for *Esquire* magazine, of "the shocking ferocity" of the Chicago police (Burroughs 1968). It was an unsettling spectacle on television.

Capitalizing on the unrest, the Republican candidate, Richard M. Nixon, won the election in November and cryptically alluded to a "secret plan" for ending the war. Well aware that the war had stalled and of widespread discontent at home, Nixon spoke of "peace with honor" and proposed a plan to achieve an honorable withdrawal called "Vietnamization," which involved handing responsibility for the war over to South Vietnam. To diffuse the antiwar movement, he announced that the draft would end in 1973; in its place, the first all-volunteer army since prior to World War II in 1940.

As the U.S. pullout began, Nixon hoped to diminish the enemy by ordering the invasion of weakly governed, neutral Cambodia in May 1970. The military objective involved cutting the Ho Chi Minh Trail that funneled supplies to the Vietcong and smashing North Vietnamese sanctuaries across the border. The "incursion," as Nixon called it, proved a temporary setback at most for North Vietnam; it encouraged the spread of the militant Cambodian communists known as the Khmer Rouge, who turned their country into a graveyard after seizing power five years later, and it also sparked a new wave of protests in America. In the most publicized incident, on May 4, 1970, the Ohio National Guard opened fire on protestors at Kent State University, killing four students.

In 1971, Congress repealed the Gulf of Tonkin Resolution, yet Nixon continued his slow withdrawal of ground troops and his use of air strikes to keep pressure on North Vietnam. In June 1971, the *New York Times* began publishing the documents known as the Pentagon Papers, a top-secret report on the Vietnam conflict that chronicled a long record of government deception. The report was stolen by Daniel Ellsberg, a defense analyst, and given to the *Times*. Commissioned by McNamara, the Pentagon Papers revealed nothing that discredited Nixon's handling of the war. However, the president worried that other secrets might begin to leak into the media and obtained a court injunction halting further publication. Appealing to the U.S. Supreme Court, the *Times* argued that the First Amendment prohibited prior restraint on the press. The majority of justices agreed and permitted publication of the papers, which only confirmed what had already become the prevailing mood of public distrust over the conduct of the war.

In 1972, North Vietnam went on the offensive, overrunning South Vietnamese bases and attacking cities. The United States responded by increasing air raids on the North and mining the country's ports to block supply lines to China and the Soviet Union. The punishing air campaign and ongoing stalemate on the ground may have forced North Vietnam to the negotiating table in Paris, where sporadic talks had occurred since 1968. By October 1972, Secretary of State Henry Kissinger (1923–) and his North Vietnamese counterpart, Le Duc Tho (1911–1990), discussed a cease-fire that essentially left portions of South Vietnam under Vietcong control, a proposal that infuriated the country's embattled pro-American president, Nguyen Van Thieu (1923–2001). When the North remained slow to agree to concessions insisted on by Kissinger, Nixon unleased an unrelenting air assault that spared nothing. Tho resumed talks with Kissinger. Finally, on January 27, 1973, the United States, South Vietnam, the National Liberation Front (Vietcong), and North Vietnam signed the Paris Peace Accords. Although fighting never ceased despite the announced cease-fire, prisoners were exchanged, the United States withdrew, and to the outside world the treaty marked the end of the war. Kissinger and Tho were awarded the Nobel Peace Prize.

Nixon may have believed that he gave Thieu's regime the opportunity to survive. Even as the last U.S. forces withdrew, he threatened military retaliation if the North tried to overrun the South, a promise he was unable to keep as the Watergate scandal subsumed his administration and forced his resignation on August 9, 1974. Kissinger was more realistic, seeing the Paris Accords as providing only a "decent interval" between the U.S. withdrawal and North Vietnam's victory.

As one historian put it, "Obliged to stand on its own feet, the Saigon regime had neither the skill nor the temperament to survive" (Wintle 1991, 178).

Ho's dream of reuniting Vietnam under communism continued undimmed even after his death in 1969. The North's leaders wasted little time after the Paris Accords to muster their forces for the final assault.

By the end of 1974, the North Vietnamese army began occupying southern territory as Thieu's army deserted, surrendered, or retreated. The Ho Chi Minh Campaign, as the communists called it, moved with speed. Thieu fled to Taiwan, and on April 29, as North Vietnamese shells fell on Saigon, the United States mounted its final mission in Vietnam. Operation Frequent Wind brought a fleet of helicopters to Saigon for the evacuation of all remaining Americans and a few high-ranking South Vietnamese. The last helicopter left the embassy roof as North Vietnamese tanks rolled into the city.

The communist victory did not inaugurate a bloodbath comparable to the mass murder that would soon commence in neighboring Cambodia under the Khmer Rouge. Only a few executions occurred; 400,000 people with links to the Thieu regime were imprisoned under poor conditions in "reeducation camps," but most were released within two years. Saigon was renamed Ho Chi Minh City, albeit most Vietnamese preferred to call it by its old name.

If the war was traumatic for the United States, it was devastating for Vietnam, where the death toll may have passed 1.5 million. In the aftermath, Vietnam saw the exodus of hundreds of thousands of refugees, called "boat people" for the flimsy craft that carried them. Many had ties to the defeated South Vietnamese regime, but many others fled economic hardship or ethnic persecution. Most of the boat people who survived the perilous sea journey eventually settled in the United States, Australia, or Western Europe.

For a generation of American policy makers, the lesson of the Vietnam War was caution in foreign policy and a wariness of military intervention. The administrations of Gerald Ford (1913–2006) and Jimmy Carter (1924–) maintained a defensive posture in a world where communism was on the march. Dominoes fell not only on Vietnam's doorstep in Cambodia and Laos, but in Ethiopia and newly independent African states such as Angola and Mozambique. Carter responded to the 1979 Soviet invasion of Afghanistan not by sending troops and planes but by covertly supporting an array of rebels. Likewise, Ronald Reagan (1911–2004) sought to undermine the leftist government of Nicaragua by arming dissidents.

The United States returned to a more assertive posture after the September 11, 2001, terrorist attacks, starting with the occupation of Afghanistan, where terrorists planned the 9/11 attacks, but continuing with the 2003 invasion of Iraq, whose regime was hostile to Al Qaeda. The ambitious War on Terror proclaimed by President George W. Bush (1946–) led to a protracted struggle over the future of Iraq. In 2018, 17 years after the arrival of U.S. troops, Afghanistan resembles South Vietnam with a weak government beset by insurgents and propped up by American money, weapons, and troops.

The greatest irony of the Vietnam War occurred in Vietnam, where the communist regime, faced with economic stagnation and a restless population that no longer had a war of national liberation to inspire it, opened the gates to foreign investment and by 2001 had initiated trade relations with its old enemy, the United States. Luxury hotels and resorts opened. American tourists on bicycling and hiking trips reported no animosity from the Vietnamese.

At odds with China since 1979 when it turned back a Chinese invasion, Vietnam has been willing to turn to the United States for aid. In 2018, Vietnam welcomed the U.S. aircraft carrier *Carl Vinson* to Da Nang, the city that once served as the staging post for U.S. operations. "It's a pretty big and historic step, since a carrier has not been here for 40 years," said the *Carl Vinson*'s commander, Rear Admiral John V. Fuller (Beech 2018). For him, calling on Da Nang was something of a family milestone. His father had served in Vietnam.

FURTHER READING

Beech, Hannah. "U.S. Aircraft Carrier Arrives in Vietnam, With Message for China," *New York Times*, March 4, 2018.

Bodard, Lucien. 1967. *The Quicksand War: Prelude to Vietnam*. London: Faber and Faber.

Burroughs, William. "The Coming of the Purple Better One," *Esquire*, November 1968.

Ebert, James R. 1993. *A Life in a Year: The American Infantryman in Vietnam, 1965–1972*. Novato, CA: Presidio Press.

Lerner, Max. 1957. *American Civilization: Life and Thought in the United States Today*. New York: Simon and Schuster.

Mailer, Norman. 1968. *The Armies of the Night*. London: Weidenfeld & Nicholson.

McAlister, John T., and Paul Mus. 1970. *The Vietnamese and Their Revolution*. New York: Harper & Row.

McDonald, Country Joe. 2000. "How I Wrote the Rag." countryjoe.com.

Mr. X. "The Sources of Soviet Conduct." *Foreign Affairs*, July 1947.

Oberdorfer, Don. 2001. *Tet! The Turning Point in the Vietnam War*. Baltimore: Johns Hopkins University Press.

Ward, Geoffrey C., and Ken Burns. 2017. *The Vietnam War: An Intimate History*. New York: Alfred A. Knopf.

Wintle, Justin. 1991. *The Vietnam Wars*. New York: St. Martin's Press.

Chronology

September 22, 1940	Japan forces the Vichy French administration of Indochina to allow the stationing of Japanese troops in Vietnam.
May 1941	Communist leader Ho Chi Minh founds the Vietminh and begins an insurgency against the Japanese.
March 9, 1945	Japan seizes control of Indochina.
August 16, 1945	With Japan's defeat imminent, Ho and the Vietminh launch the "August Revolution," seizing control of Hanoi and other Vietnamese cities.
September 2, 1945	Quoting from the U.S. Declaration of Independence, Ho proclaims Vietnam an independent nation.
September 11, 1945	Agents from the U.S. Office of Strategic Services, the forerunner to the Central Intelligence Agency, arrive in Saigon to assess the situation.
September 26, 1945	Lt. Col. A. Peter Dewey is killed by the Vietminh in Saigon, becoming the first U.S. casualty in Vietnam.
October 4, 1945	French troops enter Saigon and begin to reassert French rule over Vietnam's cities.
June 5, 1948	France establishes the semi-independent State of Vietnam with Emperor Bao Dai as chief of state.

January 1950	Chinese communist leader Mao Zedong, now in control of mainland China, formally recognizes the Vietminh and supplies them with weapons.
June 25, 1950	North Korea invades South Korea, launching the Korean War and stiffening U.S. resolve to halt the spread of communism in Asia.
June 27, 1950	President Harry S. Truman approves $23 million in aid for the French in Vietnam and dispatches the Military Assistance and Advisory Group (MAAG) to the country.
October 10, 1950	MAAG establishes its headquarters in Saigon.
May 7, 1954	The French fortress at Dien Bien Phu, in North Vietnam, surrenders to the Vietminh, spelling the end of French suzerainty over Vietnam.
May 8–July 20, 1954	French, British, U.S., Soviet, and Chinese diplomats meet in Geneva, Switzerland, with representatives of several Vietnamese, Cambodian, and Laotian parties to negotiate the future of Indochina.
June 4, 1954	France grants full independence to Vietnam under Bao Dai.
June 26, 1954	Bao Dai appoints Ngo Dinh Diem as prime minister.
July 20, 1954	The Geneva Accords divide Vietnam in two, separated by a demilitarized zone, and promise an internationally supervised election to establish the government of united Vietnam.
February 12, 1955	MAAG assumes responsibility for training the South Vietnamese army.
October 23, 1955	The CIA helps depose Bao Dai as chief of state.
October 26, 1955	Diem proclaims himself president of the Republic of Vietnam (a.k.a. South Vietnam).
January 11, 1956	Diem issues a decree allowing the arrest of anyone deemed "dangerous to national defense" and imprisons suspects in concentration camps.
April 28, 1956	The last contingents of French troops leave Vietnam.

May 5–19, 1957	Diem visits the United States and receives a ticker-tape parade in New York; he addresses a joint session of Congress.
January 1959	The Central Committee of the Vietnam Workers Party (a.k.a. North Vietnam Communist Party) secretly approves the use of armed force to support rebellion against Diem.
May 1959	At Diem's request, the United States sends military advisers to work with South Vietnam's army at the battalion level.
May 6, 1959	Diem establishes military tribunals to execute anyone suspected of "offense to national security."
July 7, 1959	The *New York Times* salutes Diem and claims South Vietnam "is free and becoming stronger in defense of its freedom."
July 8, 1959	Communist guerillas attack U.S. advisers in their compound near Saigon, killing two.
May 5, 1960	The United States announces it will increase the strength of MAAG to 685 advisers by year's end.
October 1960	In a meeting with Diem, U.S. Ambassador Elbridge Durbrow warns that Diem's regime is in danger and encourages him to form a broader coalition. Diem rejects the advice.
November 10, 1960	A coup led by elements of South Vietnam's army fails to overthrow Diem.
December 20, 1960	Opposition groups under communist leadership secretly form the National Liberation Front (a.k.a. Vietcong) in South Vietnam, dedicated to overthrowing Diem, driving out the United States, and establishing a unified Vietnam.
January 20, 1961	In his inaugural address, President John F. Kennedy promises to "pay any price, bear any burden, meet any hardship, support any friend, oppose any foe" in the struggle against communism.
April 9, 1961	Diem is reelected president, claiming 89 percent of the vote.
June 30, 1961	For the first time, South Vietnam captures North Vietnamese troops within its territory.

November 16, 1961	Kennedy announces a plan to bolster South Vietnamese forces.
December 8, 1961	The United States publicly accuses North Vietnam of aggression and warns of a "clear and present danger" of communist victory.
February 7, 1962	U.S. forces in Vietnam are increased to 4,000 personnel.
May 8, 1963	Diem's police fire on a Buddhist demonstration, killing 12.
August 21, 1963	Martial law declared in South Vietnam as Diem's troops attack Buddhist temples.
September 2, 1963	Kennedy worries publicly that the Diem regime has "gotten out of touch with the people."
October 5, 1963	South Vietnamese officers meet with CIA operatives to sound out the United States' position on a coup against Diem.
November 1–2, 1963	A military coup overthrows and kills Diem.
November 22, 1963	At the time of Kennedy's assassination, 16,000 U.S. military personnel are stationed in Vietnam. Lyndon B. Johnson is sworn in as president.
January 30, 1964	A second military coup overthrows the leader of the previous coup.
August 2–4, 1964	The United States accuses North Vietnam of attacking American destroyers in international waters in the Gulf of Tonkin.
August 7, 1964	Congress passes the Gulf of Tonkin Resolution, authorizing greater use of military force in Vietnam.
August 27, 1964	A new military government installs itself in Saigon.
November 3, 1964	Johnson defeats Barry Goldwater in the presidential election.
January 1965	On January 7, under U.S. pressure, the military restores civilian rule in South Vietnam. However, on January 27, the military deposes the civilian administration.

February 7, 1965	Communist forces attack U.S. base, killing nine. Johnson responds with air strikes on North Vietnam.
March 9, 1965	Two battalions of U.S. Marines land in Da Nang, South Vietnam.
June 4, 1965	South Vietnamese air force general Nguyen Cao Ky heads a new military government.
June 8, 1965	The United States acknowledges that its ground troops are authorized for combat in Vietnam.
October 1965	The size of U.S. forces in Vietnam reaches 200,000 personnel.
October 15	A student organization coordinates nationwide protests against war in Vietnam.
November 27, 1965	The largest antiwar protest to date, a march for peace in Washington, DC, draws between 15,000 and 35,000 participants.
April 11, 1966	B-52 bombers raid North Vietnam for the first time.
June 1966	As public support for the war declines in the United States, Richard Russell, chairman of the Senate Armed Services Committee, says it is time to "get it over or get out."
June 23, 1967	At one of the first massive antiwar protests, thousands of demonstrators march on the Los Angeles hotel where President Johnson is speaking.
July 1967	American casualties in Vietnam reach nearly 70,000. A Gallup Poll shows 52 percent of Americans disapprove of Johnson's handling of the war.
September 3, 1967	In the first election under South Vietnam's new constitution, Nguyen Van Thieu is elected president and Ky chosen as vice president.
October 21, 1967	100,000 antiwar protestors march on the Pentagon in an event chronicled in Norman Mailer's book *Armies of the Night*.

November 21, 1967	In a speech at the National Press Club, General William Westmoreland, U.S. commander in Vietnam, says the end of the war "begins to come in view."
January 30, 1968	Timed to begin with the Lunar New Year, North Vietnamese troops support Vietcong guerillas in the Tet Offensive, a massive assault against U.S. and South Vietnamese positions in South Vietnam.
February 1968	A Gallup Poll shows only 35 percent of Americans support Johnson's policy in Vietnam.
February 24, 1968	U.S. forces recapture Hue, which fell to communist forces at the start of the Tet Offensive.
March 12, 1968	Antiwar presidential candidate Senator Eugene McCarthy surprises the nation by his strong showing against Johnson in the New Hampshire primary.
March 16, 1968	A second antiwar candidate, Senator Robert F. Kennedy, enters the Democratic presidential primary.
March 16, 1968	U.S. infantry under Lt. William Calley Jr. massacre hundreds of civilians in the village of My Lai.
March 31, 1968	With his popularity failing because of the war, Johnson announces he will not seek reelection or accept the Democratic Party's nomination. Johnson also orders a reduction in the bombing of North Vietnam.
May 10, 1968	The first Paris peace talks between the United States and Vietnam begin.
July 4, 1968	John Wayne's pro-war film, *The Green Berets*, is released.
August 26–29, 1968	The Democratic National Convention in Chicago is disrupted by violence between police and antiwar protestors. Vice President Hubert Humphrey becomes the Democratic nominee.
October 31, 1968	In the run-up to the U.S. presidential election, Johnson orders a halt to all attacks against North Vietnam.

November 5, 1968	Republican candidate Richard M. Nixon is elected president. He claims to have a "secret plan" to end the war in Vietnam.
January 16, 1969	U.S. and North Vietnam delegates resume meeting in Paris.
April 1969	U.S. forces in Vietnam reach their peak strength of 543,000 personnel.
September 3, 1969	Ho Chi Minh dies.
October 15, 1969	Antiwar activists declare the day a "National Moratorium," calling on students to stay away from class.
November 3, 1969	Nixon announces the "Vietnamization" project of turning over responsibility for the war to South Vietnam.
November 15, 1969	250,000 marchers assemble for an antiwar demonstration in Washington, DC.
April 30, 1970	Nixon announces a U.S. "incursion" into neutral Cambodia to destroy North Vietnamese bases and supply lines.
May 4, 1970	The Ohio National Guard opens fire into protestors at Kent State University, killing four students.
September 5, 1970	Operation Jefferson Glenn, the last U.S. ground offensive in Vietnam, begins.
November 20, 1970	U.S. commandos raid North Vietnamese prisoner of war camp hoping to free prisoners but find it empty.
December 31, 1970	U.S. troop level in Vietnam drops to 280,000.
March 29, 1971	Court-martial convicts Lt. William Calley for the murder of 22 civilians at My Lai. His life sentence is quickly reduced to 20 years.
April 1971	A demonstration organized by Vietnam Veterans Against the War takes place outside the White House and the Capitol.
May 8, 1971	Nixon orders the mining of North Vietnamese ports to disrupt Chinese and Soviet arms shipments.

June 13, 1971	The *New York Times* begins publishing the Pentagon Papers, a trove of classified documents leaked by defense analyst Daniel Ellsberg, which reveal the U.S. government's dishonesty in conducting the Vietnam War.
June 15, 1971	The Nixon administration obtains a court injunction against further publication of the Pentagon Papers.
June 30, 1971	The U.S. Supreme Court rules in favor of the *New York Times'* right to publish the Pentagon Papers.
December 17, 1971	U.S. troop level in Vietnam drops to 156,800.
December 28–30, 1971	U.S. bombers conduct five days of massive raids over North Vietnam, and Paris peace talks reach an impasse.
January 21–28, 1972	Nixon arrives in China for a historic meeting with Mao Zedong and the premier of the People's Republic of China, Zhou Enlai.
March 30, 1972	North Vietnamese army launches an attack across the DMZ, dubbed the Eastertide Offensive, its first major ground offensive since 1968.
April 26, 1972	Nixon announces the withdrawal of 10,000 troops per month from Vietnam.
May 8, 1972	In response to North Vietnamese Eastertide Offensive, Nixon steps up pressure on North Vietnam with Operation Linebacker, a series of air attacks on ports, railroads, and military bases.
July 18, 1972	Hollywood actress Jane Fonda broadcasts antiwar messages on Radio Hanoi.
August 23, 1972	The last U.S. combat troops withdraw from Vietnam.
October 8, 1972	North Vietnam presents a peace proposal that would allow the Vietcong to govern all parts of South Vietnam presently under its control, before nationwide elections can be held. Thieu later condemns the proposal.

December 18, 1972	With Paris peace talks stalled, Nixon launches Operation Linebacker II, a heavy bombing campaign over North Vietnam, hoping to force the communists to compromise.
January 8, 1973	Paris peace talks resume between Secretary of State Henry Kissinger and his North Vietnamese counterpart, Le Duc Tho.
January 25, 1973	U.S., North Vietnam, South Vietnam, and Vietcong representatives sign Paris Peace Accords.
February 12, 1973	North Vietnam begins releasing prisoners of war.
March 29–April 1, 1973	Under the Paris Peace Accords, North Vietnam releases remaining U.S. prisoners and the last U.S. contingents depart from South Vietnam.
February 1974	North Vietnam launches offensive against the South.
March 10, 1975	North Vietnam and the Vietcong launch a spring offensive.
April 29, 1975	The U.S. embassy evacuates from Saigon as South Vietnam collapses under the North Vietnamese assault.
May 16, 1975	Congress approves funds to help resettle over 100,000 refugees who fled South Vietnam as their country fell.
January 21, 1977	President Jimmy Carter pardons most Vietnam War draft dodgers.
February 2, 1978	The first Vietnam War film in 10 years, *The Boys in Company C*, is released.
February 15, 1978	Jane Fonda's film *Coming Home* is released.
December 8, 1978	Director Michael Cimino's Vietnam War film, *The Deer Hunter*, is released.
August 15, 1979	Francis Ford Coppola's film *Apocalypse Now* is released.
November 13, 1982	The Vietnam Veterans Memorial in Washington, DC, is dedicated.

December 19, 1986	Oliver Stone's *Platoon* is released.
June 17, 1987	Stanley Kubrick's film about U.S. marines in Vietnam, *Full Metal Jacket*, is released.
December 20, 1989	Oliver Stone releases another Vietnam War film, *Born on the Fourth of July*, based on antiwar activist and former U.S. Marine Corps Sgt. Ron Kovic's memoir.
August 2, 1991	U.S. Senate Committee on MIA/POW Affairs begins investigating claims that U.S. servicemen continue to be held by communist forces in Southeast Asia.
January 2, 1993	Senate Committee on MIA/POW Affairs concludes its investigation, finding no evidence that any servicemen were still held captive.
July 11, 1995	The United States establishes diplomatic relations with the Socialist Republic of Vietnam.
September 11, 2001	Terrorists fly hijacked passenger airliners into the World Trade Center in New York City and the Pentagon in Washington, DC, and a third plane crashes in Shanksville, Pennsylvania.
December 2001	The United States and Vietnam sign a trade agreement.
September 9, 2002	Director Phillip Nolan's *The Quiet American* is released.
January 2007	Congress approves Permanent Normal Trade Relations with Vietnam.
July 2007	Director Werner Herzog's *Rescue Dawn* is released.
December 22, 2017	Director Steven Spielberg's film on the Pentagon Papers, *The Post*, opens in theaters.

Chapter 1

The Green Berets (1968)

The Green Berets was released in the summer of 1968 in advance of the Fourth of July. It was the only major motion picture made about the Vietnam War while the war was ongoing and is unique for its resolutely pro–Vietnam War message. Given the growing controversy over the war at the time of its production, it was released with some reluctance by Warner Bros.-Seven Arts. *The Green Berets* was the personal project of John Wayne (1907–1979), who starred in the movie, codirected it with Ray Kellogg (1905–1976), and produced it through his own company, Batjac Productions. Screenwriter James Lee Barrett (1929–1989), an ex-marine with a long Hollywood career, wrote the picture based on the 1965 bestselling semifictional account of U.S. Special Forces in Vietnam, *The Green Berets*, by Robin Moore (1925–2008). The film version deviated substantially from the book and was produced with the full cooperation of the U.S. military. *The Green Berets* received few, if any, positive reviews by major film critics but found an audience nonetheless, becoming one of the top 10 box-office successes of 1968.

The Green Berets' premise is established in the opening scene as members of a Special Forces detachment make the case for U.S. intervention in Vietnam before an audience of journalists. After a testy exchange between Colonel Kirby (Wayne) and liberal antiwar journalist George Beckworth, played by David Janssen (1931–1980), Beckworth decides he will visit Vietnam and report on the war from the front lines. Although still skeptical about America's role, he is allowed to travel to Kirby's forward base, a remote jungle camp manned by Green Berets and their South Vietnamese counterparts commanded by Captain Nim, played by *Star Trek*'s George Takei (1937–), along with anticommunist Montagnard tribesmen.

Prominent among the small unit of Green Berets is Specialist Peterson, played by Jim Hutton (1934–1979), an actor whose career began a decade earlier in army training films. His character provides comic relief from his willingness to cut red tape by stealing supplies from other branches of the service, as well as sentimentality through his love for a Vietnamese orphan boy and his dog. Other stars include Western movie actor Edward Faulkner (1932–) as Captain MacDaniel, character actor Aldo Ray (1926–1991) as Master Sergeant Muldoon, onetime NFL linebacker Mike Henry (1936–) as Sergeant First Class Kowalski, and Rudy Robbins (1933–2011), who played a small role in Wayne's movie *The Alamo* (1960), as Sergeant Parks. The detachment is integrated through the presence of Sergeant First Class McGee, played by Raymond St. Jacques (1930–1990), a trailblazing African American actor for his previous role in the television Western *Rawhide*.

While on patrol with Kirby in the nearby hills, Beckworth witnesses the brutality of the enemy in the form of a Montagnard village whose men were slaughtered and whose women were raped before being killed. The scene represents the beginning of his change of mind on the war. *The Green Berets'* most memorable scenes occur during the long assault on the Special Forces camp by the Vietcong. By now an adherent to Kirby's view that the war is just and necessary, Beckworth picks up a rifle and helps defend the camp.

While Wayne edited *The Green Berets*, the Tet Offensive began on January 31, 1968. Confidence in the American war effort rapidly unraveled in the face of attacks on the U.S. Embassy in Saigon and cities across Vietnam. U.S. troops fought hard to regain ground lost to the enemy. The antiwar movement was no longer confined to college students and the counterculture but became a driving factor in American politics. As Wayne completed the film that spring, Eugene McCarthy and Robert Kennedy leaped into the Democratic presidential primary on antiwar platforms. Taken aback by their popularity, Lyndon Johnson surprised the nation by declaring he would not seek another term.

By the time it opened in theaters at the end of June 1968, *The Green Berets* drew widespread recrimination. "It is vile and insane. On top of that, it is dull," the *New York Times* thundered. "It is so full of its own caricature of patriotism that it cannot even find the right things to falsify" (Adler 1968). With its hackwork screenplay, thin characterizations, stiff performances, and transparent agenda, *The Green Berets* struck many observers as a B movie from an earlier war or a Western set in a jungle that looked suspiciously like the forests of North America. "At this moment in history," film critic Roger Ebert wrote, "what we certainly do not need is a movie depicting Vietnam in terms of cowboys and Indians." He continued, "Perhaps we could have believed this film in 1962 or 1963, when most of us didn't much care what was happening in Vietnam." He added, "Television has brought the reality of war to us" (Ebert 1968).

HO CHI MINH (CA. 1890–1969)

During the 1960s, the face of North Vietnam's leader, Ho Chi Minh, became familiar around the world as a picture of enigmatic calm in the face of overwhelming force. He was a man of mystery whose precise date of birth remains unknown. An exact chronology for most of his life has never been established. His real name was Nguyen Tat Thanh, and he used many aliases before settling on Ho.

Although educated in a French school, he became involved in protests against the high taxes and forced labor the French imposed on their Vietnamese subjects. He fled the country in 1911 and did not return for 30 years. Wearing a rented morning coat, he turned up at the 1919 Paris Peace Conference. Taking seriously the pledge by President Woodrow Wilson to ensure self-determination for all peoples, he tried to present the president with a petition calling for a democratic Vietnam within the French empire but was denied entry.

After embracing communism in 1920, he studied in Moscow, Russia, and became a Soviet agent in China. His manifesto, *The Revolutionary Path* (1927), blended Confucius with Karl Marx and Vladimir Lenin. He spoke in maxims throughout his career and often presented himself as a nationalist. The first Americans he encountered doubted that he was a communist.

Slipping into Vietnam during World War II, Ho allied with the United States in the struggle against Japan. After the war, he still hoped France would grant Vietnamese self-government and sought American support. He was disappointed and went to war, initially with little support from the Communist Bloc.

He defeated France with the strategy of striking at night from the jungle. Establishing himself as president of the Democratic Republic of Vietnam (North Vietnam) in 1954, he imposed communism on the North and proceeded to fight the pro-Western South Vietnamese government and its American backers with that same stealth and determination. The Vietnamese people called him Uncle Ho, but his benign facade concealed an iron will. By the time of his death in 1969, victory for his side was almost in sight.

Even the movie industry mouthpiece, the *Hollywood Reporter*, had no good words, calling *The Green Berets* "a cliché-ridden throw-back to the battlefield potboilers of World War II, its artifice readily exposed by the nightly actuality of TV news coverage" (*Hollywood Reporter* 1968). The premiere brought out protesters in Los Angeles and other cities. At the Warner Theater on New York's Times Square, angry demonstrators clashed with ticket buyers and police.

"I don't think he was prepared for the maelstrom of bad press that whipped up around him in the tumultuous summer of 1968," Wayne's daughter Aissa recalled. "Beneath his public bravado, his self-esteem was always tender, and this was an especially difficult time. Although he fired back at his critics, referring to them as a 'little clique back East,' of 'doctrinaire liberals,' 'not in touch with the American people,' at home my father privately brooded" (Wayne 1991, 127–128).

Despite the flak it drew, *The Green Berets* sold $20 million in tickets within 18 months of its release and ranked as a box-office hit. "The film's popularity was deeply rooted in both John Wayne's persona and in the pain his traditional audiences felt in 1968," wrote biographers Randy Roberts and James S. Olson. That "traditional audience" was working class, including the youths who volunteered or were drafted in disproportionate numbers. "Young men from working-class or poverty-level families were four times more likely than middle-class men to die in Vietnam" (Roberts 1995, 550). Class resentment against allegedly affluent war protesters and the "liberal intelligentsia" became a mobilizing force in American politics, identified by Richard Nixon with "the silent majority."

HISTORICAL BACKGROUND

In 1952, the U.S. Special Forces were established by army officers keenly aware of a new set of lessons in World War II (1939–1945) and the Korean War (1950–1953). During World War II, the traditional distaste shown by armies toward guerilla warfare came into question after the success enjoyed by partisans in Nazi-occupied Europe who pinned down German troops and assisted the advance of the Allies. During that war, the United States began to employ "unconventional warfare" through General William Donovan's Office of Strategic Services (OSS). Patterned after Britain's Special Operations Executive, the OSS sent parachute teams into enemy territory for sabotage and reconnaissance as well as support for local partisans. Unpopular with the regular military and banned from his theater of operations by General Douglas MacArthur, the OSS thrived only from Donovan's personal ties to President Franklin D. Roosevelt. With the war over and Roosevelt's death, the Pentagon moved swiftly to disband the OSS. Many of its members reappeared later in the Central Intelligence Agency (CIA), created in 1947. Some would eventually resurface in the Green Berets (Simpson 1983, 11–13).

The postwar army settled into a conventional mind-set with divisions hunkered down in West Germany for the Soviet invasion for which North Atlantic Treaty Organization (NATO) military planners prepared. On the other side of the world, in response to massive attacks from Chinese communist forces in Korea, the army cobbled together unconventional units to fight behind enemy lines. "Those efforts were not very successful," wrote Special Forces Colonel Charles Simpson III. "It eventually became apparent to all but the rigidly conservative military that in order to carry out special operations successfully, we have to prepare *before* the advent of war" (Simpson 1983, 16–17).

The Special Forces operated in secrecy in their early days, cloaked under the auspices of the Psychological Warfare Center at Fort Bragg, North

Carolina. The Pentagon regarded them as "a few maverick paratroopers" who were "playing around with something spooky." A tight esprit de corps was apparent from the outset. "They like each other, and they are constantly in one another's company, even after-duty hours, not going out of their way to be with non-SF," Simpson recalled (Simpson 1983, 21, 23–25). Each member was cross-trained with the other. As Moore found while embedded with the Green Berets, an unusual proportion of officers were refugees or foreign born, giving the Special Forces a Foreign Legion aspect. Little wonder they embraced the beret, a headgear common in foreign armies but rarely seen until then in the United States.

During the 1950s, the Special Forces prepared to operate in Eastern Europe during a war that never happened; they imagined their mission as sabotaging the advance of Warsaw Pact (Soviet allied) armies into Western Europe and organizing armed anticommunist partisans behind the lines. Other detachments were sent to several East Asian nations to train paramilitary units. With the inauguration of President John F. Kennedy, who admired their enthusiasm, the Green Berets were handed a new mission—counterinsurgency. Only weeks before Kennedy took office, Soviet Premier Nikita Khrueschev, (1894–1971) announced his support for "just wars of liberation and popular uprisings" around the world. Kennedy immediately recognized that a conventional military response was inadequate in populations whose deep-rooted dissatisfaction with the status quo left them vulnerable to the appeal of communism. He told the 1962 West Point graduating class that the army must find ways to "counter wars of liberation" with a "whole new kind of strategy, a wholly different kind of force" (Kennedy 1962).

The Special Forces became that different kind of force. Their numbers were increased and their responsibility widened to trouble spots around the globe, albeit Vietnam soon enough became their most storied mission. Aside from their extensive combat training, the Green Berets were more adept in cross-cultural relations and languages than most conventional troops. They brought sophistication to the battles they engaged.

Laos was the Special Forces' proving ground. They arrived in the country at Vietnam's border in 1959, bereft of berets and dressed in civilian clothes to conceal their covert mission. The regular army wanted its personnel to assist the Laotian army, but "since the Special Forces was trained to survive and operate in remote, undeveloped areas," they received the assignment instead. They were soon embroiled in a civil war leading a countercoup against forces they had only recently trained. According to military historian Shelby L. Stanton, a Vietnam veteran, "The wartime Special Forces was forged in the jagged Laotian mountains and forest plateaus," where "it fielded armed hill tribes," trained "remote, indigenous minorities" and cemented working relations with the CIA. "Valuable jungle warfare knowledge was gained," along with familiarity with terrain and climate similar to Vietnam's (Stanton 1985, 17, 21–22, 31–32).

As early as 1957, the 14th Special Forces Detachment was assigned to Vietnam, but its purpose was limited to training South Vietnam's nascent elite forces. In October 1957, Captain Harry G. Cramer, killed in a training accident, became the first Green Beret to die in Vietnam. The Special Forces still thought they were preparing for guerilla war against communist Chinese invaders during the expected World War III. They soon found themselves in a more complicated local situation as the corrupt regime of South Vietnam's president, Ngo Dinh Diem (1901–1963), fought an increasingly losing battle against its own citizens, only some of them with communist sympathies.

The Special Forces were drawn deeper into the conflict, partnering with the CIA in organizing illicit South Vietnamese commando raids into the North. They had reason to hold in low regard the Army of the Republic of Vietnam (ARVN), as the South Vietnamese military was called, and began casting for other allies against the Vietcong. By 1961, the CIA identified the potential of the Montagnards, a group of preliterate hill tribes speaking a variety of languages and dwelling in the hill country straddling Vietnam, Cambodia, and Laos. The Vietnamese called them "moi," meaning savages, and treated them accordingly. Relations between Montagnards and Vietnamese "have generally tended to be unpleasant," wrote the author of a manual intended for U.S. forces. He added, "The Montagnards, while composing a small percentage of Vietnam's total population, are of strategic significance inasmuch as they are the primary inhabitants of about 50% of Vietnam's land area" (Mole 1970, 5–7).

Diem triggered a Montagnard uprising with his scheme to resettle ethnic Vietnamese, many of them refugees from North Vietnam, on their lands. Montagnard rebels briefly seized a provincial capital, Pleiku, and at least one of their leaders joined the Vietcong after Diem retook the city. However, the Montagnards' hatred of all Vietnamese made them dubious accomplices for the Vietcong (Prados 1995, 73–74). The tribesmen admired the French, who treated them fairly, and the CIA grasped the idea that their allegiance—at least in the short run—could be transferred to the U.S. According to Americans on the ground, "the tribesmen liked Caucasian people" (Stanton 1985, 39).

The crucial objective of the small Special Forces detachments scattered across Vietnam's backcountry became organizing the jungle and hill country tribes, especially the Montagnards—whom the Green Berets affectionately called "the Yards"—into Civilian Irregular Defense Groups (CIDG), a project that began in 1962. The CIDGs were armed and trained by the Green Berets to secure their villages against the Vietcong and engage the enemy in the jungle. The Special Forces also dispensed medicine and other supplies. "Montagnards accepted only those who shared their lifestyles and dangers," and the Green Berets, along with their CIA colleagues, were willing to embrace the adventure of it all (Stanton 1985, 40). The regular army looked on with dismay, and the Diem regime complained about arming despised minority groups. However, by the end of 1963, the Green Berets had armed some 70,000 Montagnards.

Other groups aside from the Montagnards fought with the Special Forces, including the Nungs, a tribe that originated in southern China. "They had a reputation for being tough, fearless fighters, and they were very loyal," a Green Beret recalled. "Of course, they were pretty well paid, too. Nungs were paid better for their service than other Vietnamese minorities. But they earned it" (Adkins 2018, 59).

According to some military historians, "The success of the CIDG concept caused it to be altered by the high command in Saigon, to the program's detriment." The army decided that instead of securing populated areas in the countryside, the Green Berets should establish bases "in the most remote, dangerous parts of the country to block Communist movement" across the borders of Cambodia and Laos. Their camps "became isolated Fort Apaches near the border, under near constant attack" (Southworth 2002, 111).

The Special Forces were engaged in combat at least two years before U.S. combat troops were officially committed to the Vietnam War and found themselves in full-scale battles as early as July 1964, when the Vietcong nearly overran a camp at Nam Dong. Special Forces Captain Roger Donlon, wounded twice, rallied the troops and became the first Medal of Honor recipient in the Vietnam War. A year later in the Battle of Ia Drang Valley, the Special Forces became the first U.S. troops to fight—and defeat—the North Vietnamese regular army, whose divisions increasingly infiltrated the South in support of the Vietcong.

The Green Berets did not win every battle. In 1966, Vietcong and North Vietnamese troops overran their compound at A Shau Valley. In 1968, the Special Forces base at Lang Vei fell to North Vietnamese armored units. Lacking proper antitank weapons, the Green Berets fought back with grenades, prying open the hatches of tanks with bare hands. Their bravery was not enough and, according to observers, a nearby contingent of marines was "not overly quick to come to the Special Forces assistance" (Southworth 2002, 113).

By 1971, the Special Forces were withdrawn from Vietnam. They fought with exceptional courage and resourcefulness. Despite the attention of a best-selling novel, a hit song, and a Hollywood movie, they often operated beyond the sight lines of army commanders in Saigon and the American news media. During and immediately after the war, Green Berets who fought in Vietnam earned 17 Medals of Honor, 60 Distinguished Service Crosses, 814 Silver Stars, 13,234 Bronze Stars, and 2,658 Purple Hearts. The honor continued to expand. As recently as 2014, President Barack Obama awarded the Medal of Honor to Command Sergeant Bennie G. Adkins, who led to safety the survivors of the 1966 assault at A Shau.

DEPICTION AND CULTURAL CONTEXT

Even before the war became one of the most divisive issues in American society, Hollywood studios were disinterested in Vietnam and preferred to continue making nostalgic movies about the nation's most uncontroversial conflict, World War II. Prior to *The Green Berets*, only two American movies on the war appeared, both by little-known directors from insignificant studios with spotty distribution. One, *A Yank in Viet-Nam* (1964), was ostensibly filmed in the country with South Vietnamese and U.S. troops. The other, *To the Shores of Hell* (1966), was shot in the United States with the cooperation of the Marine Corps. Neither attracted much notice.

For Wayne, making a movie about Vietnam in support of his country's mission and the troops on the ground became a crusade. By one account, his passion for the project was triggered in 1965 by seeing a marine corporal, who had lost an arm in Vietnam, heckled by antiwar protesters at the University of Southern California (Roberts 1995, 536). Even so, Wayne's support for the Vietnam War was already a facet of his unmovable worldview, which saw America imperiled by the aggressive expansion of an alien ideology. "I can't believe that people in the U.S. don't realize that we are at war with international communism," he told a columnist. "I think somebody should take Senator [Robert F.] Kennedy and Senator [J. William] Fulbright to the forward areas of Vietnam to talk to the guys and see the kind of communist equipment they are getting wounded with" (Feinstein 1968). His comments on communist weaponry made their way into *The Green Berets* screenplay.

The origins of Wayne's superpatriotism and promilitary stance have been the subject of much analysis. Unlike most Hollywood stars eligible for military service, Wayne did not volunteer to fight in World War II, and took advantage of all possible deferments. He spent much of the war—and its long aftermath—playing a character that he repeated over and over until it culminated in his role as Colonel Mike Kirby in *The Green Berets*. Wayne, the cinematic soldier, embodied the rugged face of stoicism against danger and death. He wasted no words, resisted emotion, and expressed himself through action. His soldierly persona in movies such as *The Flying Tigers* (1942), *The Fighting Seabees* (1944), and *Sands of Iwo Jima* (1949) differed little from the cowboys in the Westerns on which his reputation was built, except that his war movies stressed tight-knit teamwork under the coaching of a paternal commander. Wayne continually played the officer who refused to stand on ceremony and was impatient with bureaucrats, red tape, and politicians. He was always the man with a job that had to get done. America depended on his success. Wayne "fulfilled the country's need for a hero" while resolutely refusing to become one in real life. "He achieved so much in the war years that he became virtually critic proof. Sadly, his greatest critic in the years ahead would be himself" (Roberts 1995, 262).

As a pro–Vietnam War picture, *The Green Berets* did not emerge from a vacuum and Wayne was not an outlier in his views, at least when the production began. American popular culture from the late 1940s through the mid-1960s was saturated with the assumption that communism was an existential threat not only to the United States but also to the freedom and dignity of humanity. It was not a naive proposition, given the tyranny of Joseph Stalin's (1878–1953) Soviet Union and the imposition of its system on Eastern Europe. Moscow-inspired communism appeared to be on the move with the fall of China to Mao Zedong and the North Korean invasion of South Korea.

However, not every anti-Western or anticolonial movement in the world was communist, much less controlled by Moscow, and the distinctions were often unclear in American politics and media. In countless magazine articles, South Vietnam was cast as a brave outpost of the free world, a role ill-suited to its succession of inept authoritarian presidents. According to a May 14, 1965, *Time* magazine editorial entitled "The Right War at the Right Time," "Lyndon Johnson will not allow the U.S. to be pushed out of Viet Nam. For if that were to happen, Americans would only have to make another stand against Asian Communism later, under worse conditions and in less tenable locations" (Rothman 1965). The networks and news magazines solemnly reported U.S. claims of progress against the resilient Vietcong guerillas, backed by shadowy puppet masters in North Vietnam and supplied by the Soviet Union and "Red China," as mainland China was universally called in those years.

The granite certainty of Wayne's screen persona defined patriotism and the struggle against communism for the first wave of baby boomers eligible to serve in Vietnam. Ron Kovic (1946–), author of *Born on the Fourth of July*, was not the only young man who enlisted in the Marine Corps and fought in Vietnam under the spell of Wayne's personification of American manhood. "John Wayne in *Sands of Iwo Jima* became one of my heroes," Kovic wrote. Meeting the Marine Corps recruiters at his high school, "I couldn't help but feel I was shaking hands with John Wayne" (Kovic 1976, 43, 61).

Support for the Vietnam War was also prevalent in country music. Johnnie Wright's "Hello Vietnam" spent 20 weeks near the top of the charts and reached number one for three weeks in 1965 (Whitburn, 2004, 398). Its message, "We must save freedom now at any cost," resonated with many Americans. Similar sentiments were heard in other country hits, including Dave Dudley's "What We're Fighting For" (1965) and Autry Inman's "Battle of Two Brothers" (1968). The most widely heard pro–Vietnam War song, Barry Sadler's "The Ballad of the Green Berets" (1966), extolled the valor of the elite force Wayne would depict. It was among the year's best-selling records. Sadler (1940–1989) was a Green Beret staff sergeant who cowrote the song with the author of the book on which Wayne's movie was based.

The author of *The Green Berets*, Robin Moore, was embedded with the Special Forces in Vietnam through much of 1963 and 1964. He underwent the full course of training in "unconventional warfare" at the Special Warfare School in Fort Bragg, North Carolina. The academy, later renamed the John F. Kennedy Special Warfare Center in honor of the president who championed the elite unit, trained Green Berets in weapons ranging from crossbows to AK-47s, as well as demolition and hand-to-hand combat. They were also drilled in "civil action" with the realization that an army dispensing medical aid, digging wells, and building schools might win support from civilians in contested areas. Moore was no ordinary war correspondent tagging along with the troops. He wore a Green Beret uniform complete with the silver wings of a paratrooper and was never without an automatic rifle. He took part in combat (Moore 1965, 16–17).

The book that resulted from his experiences was marketed as a novel, but in his foreword, Moore explained that it was only lightly fictionalized. "I changed details and names, but I did not change the basic truth," he wrote. "I saw too many things that weren't for my eyes—or any eyes other than the participants themselves" (Moore 1965, 11–12).

What he described was closer in some details to Marlon Brando's Colonel Kurtz in *Apocalypse Now* than Wayne's Colonel Kirby in the film adaptation of *The Green Berets*. Moore wrote of a Special Forces officer at a remote outpost who recruited Cambodians to conduct ambushes against the Vietcong across the border in Cambodia. "High command and the embassy have been asking some very strange questions about your operations out here," that officer's superior said (Moore 1965, 54). Eventually, the Special Forces in *The Green Berets* engage in kidnapping Vietcong suspects and battling a rogue Frenchman fighting with communist guerillas. Moore described a Captain Locke who "had no qualms when it came to getting an assignment accomplished. More than once he had boldly crossed the border into Laos to kill or capture a Viet Cong leader comfortably camped in privileged sanctuary" (Moore 1965, 282). Locke was in the process of "going native" and wore a Montagnard bracelet that showed he was an honorary member of the mountain tribe recruited to fight on the American side.

The success of *The Green Berets*, which sold 3 million copies after its publication in 1965, attracted adverse attention at the Pentagon. Despite valorizing the Special Forces, and its description of Vietnam as a "fight to keep the perimeter of the free world from shrinking further" (Moore 1965, 23), the *New York Times* reported that it "stirred up a fuss in Washington. The official objection to the book apparently is that it is too close to the facts," especially on Green Beret raids across international borders (Baldwin 1965). Interest in Hollywood was initially high; even before publication, Columbia Pictures took an option on the book and sought the military's assistance with the production. It was unable to present a screenplay scrubbed clean of elements objectionable to the Pentagon. At the end of 1965, Wayne purchased rights to the book and wrote President Lyndon B. Johnson for his support. Wayne told Johnson that his movie would "inspire a patriotic attitude on the part of fellow Americans—a feeling which we have always had in this country in the past during times of stress and trouble" (Roberts 1995, 539–540). Wayne readily admitted it would be propaganda. As a sympathetic biographer put it, "He believed it was for a just cause" (Shepherd 1985, 248).

Wayne was encouraged by his reception in South Vietnam during a three-week tour with the United Service Organizations (USO). Vietnamese civilians in Saigon cheered him and recognized him from his Western movies; he ducked Vietcong sniper fire while signing autographs for the marines at Chu Lai. He visited a Special Forces base at Pleiku, where his movie *Fort Apache* (1948) was screened for an audience of Green Berets and their Montagnard warrior allies. He merely shrugged when the Montagnards cheered the Indians, not the U.S. Cavalry (Roberts 1995, 541–542).

While Wayne toured Vietnam, Barrett submitted his draft of a screenplay for *The Green Berets* to the Pentagon. It was rejected for the same reasons the military disliked the book. "The development of the plot is not acceptable," a Pentagon spokesman said, because it depicted a raid into North Vietnam in which a North Vietnamese general was kidnapped. Barrett happily changed the setting to South Vietnam; the object of the kidnapping became a Vietcong general. With alterations in place, the Pentagon gave its blessing, telling Wayne that his film "promises to be a most worthwhile and, we trust, successful production" (Suid 1978, 224, 226).

Months before filming was set to begin, Universal Studios backed out of its agreement to release *The Green Berets*. Antiwar sentiment was growing, armies of protesters gathered in the streets, and public embrace of the project was no longer axiomatic. According to a Universal executive, "Nobody wants to see a guy getting killed in the Vietnam War when guys are actually getting killed in the Vietnam War," (Roberts 1995, 543–544). Undeterred, Wayne called in old favors and persuaded Warner Brothers to back the picture (Suid 1978, 229–230).

The Green Berets was shot at Fort Benning, Georgia, whose pine and leafy trees were a poor substitute for the jungles of Vietnam. The army was unable to secure a tropical setting for Wayne but was otherwise generous in its support. The army furnished *The Green Berets* with Huey helicopters, M16 assault rifles, and M60 machine guns, along with jeeps and trucks. When a scene called for wind, the army dispatched giant CH-53 Sikorsky helicopters to stir the foliage by hovering overhead. Servicemen were deployed as extras. "With the exception of documentaries, it was one of the most extensive cooperations of the armed services and Hollywood in history" (Roberts 1995, 544).

John Wayne's version of *The Green Berets* deviated considerably from the book as well as from reality. The movie captures only one aspect of the

Special Forces by depicting them as an elite and well-trained unit but barely hints at the outfit's unique ethos. In his memoir, a Green Beret sergeant emphasized how "everything about us is unconventional. The way we dress, the way we wear our hair, the way we train, and even the way we think." The Special Forces ate the same food as their indigenous allies, dining on *bok choy* and rice flavored with *nuoc mam* (fermented fish sauce) (Adkins 2018, 5, 39). The movie ignored that unconventionality and shoehorned the Special Forces into stereotypes from Wayne's previous movies about GIs on the front lines of World War II. They are depicted as tough but interchangeable with the marines, the infantry, and the fighting Seabees (United States Naval Construction Battalions).

In the opening scene at the John F. Kennedy Special Warfare Center, during brief presentations by members of the Special Forces detachment, many of the Green Berets speak German or Scandinavian languages, evidently to demonstrate their proficiency despite the limited uses for those tongues in Southeast Asia. This echoes the reality that the first wave of Green Berets in Vietnam included a surprising number of men born in northern Europe. Encountering a demolitions expert of Latino heritage in his book, Moore remarked, "I was surprised to see the olive-complexioned Rodriguez in this camp of Viking types." The Green Beret commander thought it necessary to explain that Rodriguez had "a Latin demon in the spirit of explosives" (Moore 1965, 47). An intelligence officer of Syrian-Armenian origin is identified, and the book—as well as the movie—shows a few African Americans. However, on screen, the Green Beret unit was depicted as consisting of mostly white soldiers (Captain MacDaniel was the only African American member of the main squad).

The book was crowded with characters, but the film is built around the interactions of two men, Wayne's Colonel Kirby and David Janssen's antiwar journalist George Beckworth. Wayne's persona was not entirely out of place in his role, given the laconic speech laced with irritable humor of some officers whose dialogue was recorded by Moore. Like a real Green Beret officer, Kirby does not want to be "desk bound" and looks forward to his posting at a forward camp. While one-dimensional, Kirby is at least a rough sketch of his real counterparts.

Beckworth, on the other hand, embodies Wayne's stereotype of the liberal media. He is not a longhaired protester, but a man of the East Coast establishment, articulate and smug in his pieties, disconnected from the brutal reality of the war. Deciding to "see for himself," Beckworth turns up in Vietnam wearing an expensive safari suit and with his preconceptions neatly packed in his luggage.

The story's arc concerns Beckworth's conversion from liberal critic of the war over to agreeing with Kirby's view that the war was just and necessary: "Why is the United States waging this useless war?" Beckworth demands at the outset. The journalist continues by declaring the war to be a conflict between the Vietnamese people. "Let them handle it," he says. The Green Berets at the Special Warfare Center answer him by pointing out the savage reality of the war—the Vietcong tactic of terrorizing or murdering anyone in the villages thought to oppose them. They point to the stack of captured Chinese, Soviet, and Czech weapons, tokens of support by communist nations for the Vietcong. From Kirby's standpoint, Vietnam is not a civil war but—in keeping with the U.S. Cold War doctrine of "containment"—the front line in a war between the free world and the communist bloc.

Beckworth is eventually persuaded by Kirby after witnessing the brutality of the Vietcong and even finds himself fighting (like Moore) with the Green Berets. His change of heart is entirely opposite to the actual direction of the American news media and its Vietnam correspondents as the 1960s developed. In the early years, the press largely supported the U.S. mission in the war and the fiction of progress against the enemy, even if questions were raised about South Vietnam's regime or American tactics. In 1962, the *New York Times* asserted "the war isn't going badly" and "the fact remains that security seems better in most parts of Vietnam." The correspondent worried that the war could drag on for years but cautioned "it is too late to disengage; our prestige has been committed" (Bigart 1962).

The ineptitude of South Vietnam's government was often reported. "Really important things often have to go all the way to Saigon (which does not work nights or on weekends)," as was the mayhem of communists who hacked off the heads of government supporters and planted their flag among mutilated corpses (Browne 1965, 1–8). If the war's objectives remained sacrosanct, doubts about victory grew more prevalent. David Halberstam, reporting on an especially capable U.S. Army officer, wrote that the officer represented "the best kind of optimism; it was not the automatic we-are-winning push-button chant of Saigon, but a careful analysis of the problems on both sides, and a hope that there was still time and human resources enough to turn the tide" (Halberstam 1965, 117–124).

But by 1967, the tide of coverage changed. "The summer's events in Vietnam have generated a major conflict between the American Government and the press. It is a conflict over the course of the war," the *Washington Post* reported (Harwood 1967). Weeks after Wayne completed the final edit of *The Green Berets*, America's most respected journalist, CBS News anchor Walter Cronkite, drove the final stake into the media's acceptance of the war. On February 27, 1968, he announced that he no longer shared "the optimism of the American leaders" and pronounced that "the bloody experience of Vietnam is to end in stalemate" (Ward 2017, 290–291).

A critical flaw in Wayne's movie was its depiction of the army of the Republic of Vietnam, whose Green Beret–trained elite, the Luc-Luong Dac-Biet (LLDB), operated in tandem with the Special Forces at forward bases and commanded the CIDG under Green Beret guidance. The movie shows the LLDB as capable allies and plucky fighters in the vein of how Chinese nationalists and Free French were represented in World War II Hollywood. In reality, the Green Berets seemed to despise their allies. "If I wanted a patrol to leave early in the morning, say about six, I would be lucky to even get an LLDB leader up, much less have the patrol ready," a Green Beret veteran recalled. "Even though the LLDB commanders were supposed to be commanding them and we were only supposed to be advising, most of the time we Americans were doing their work for them." When the going got tough, the LLDB, "our friendlies" as the Green Berets contemptuously called them, shot at each other as they raced for the U.S. evacuation helicopters (Adkins 2018, 21, 46).

In his book, Moore maintained that the Special Forces' mission "was made far more difficult and dangerous because [South Vietnamese President] Diem saddled them with the untrained, combat-shy, and by U.S. standards, corrupt LLDB." The South Vietnamese officers often "seemed allergic to firefights." After Diem was overthrown and then assassinated in 1963 with U.S. connivance, Moore observed some progress, yet, "The yo-yo that is Vietnamese politics isn't much help in establishing permanent improvements" (Moore 1965, 22–23).

The LLDB's appetite for torturing Vietcong prisoners and suspects is recognized in the movie. As torture is about to begin, Kirby simply leaves the room and lets his LLDB counterpart go about his painful interrogation, to the outrage of Beckworth, who shouts, "There's still such a thing as due process!" In the book, Moore described the situation in greater detail. "Captured VC usually talked after two days without water in the cage," he wrote, referring to the wire mesh cages where they were held (Moore 1965, 48). He witnessed the LLDB beating and thrusting pins under the fingernails of prisoners. A Green Beret colonel shrugged and told the author, "Those methods work on some of these people, but I do not like torture," and added that the LLDB commander's prisoners will "say anything they think he wants to hear. The lie detector is best" (Moore 1965, 51). Moore described the Special Forces injecting prisoners with sodium pentothal ("truth serum") and strapping them to polygraph machines (Moore 1965, 51). The Special Forces also extracted information from wounded Vietcong prisoners "by making them think they were not going to receive medical attention unless they did talk. Of course, sometimes what they told us was valuable and sometimes it was not" (Adkins 2018, 49).

The Green Berets movie acknowledged that Vietcong infiltrators were present among the Special Forces' Vietnamese allies but underrepresents the extent of the duplicity faced by American forces. A Green Beret recalled the value of intuition in ferreting out traitors. "If one of the individuals I was training was a little too good at what we were doing or was learning a little bit too fast, especially if I was showing him something new, I could be pretty sure he was getting training elsewhere." He called them "doubtfuls" and suspected they were Vietcong infiltrators (Adkins 2018, 28).

The movie portrays the Montagnards, the Green Berets' best comrades-in-arms, with some accuracy. Their village of bamboo long houses on stilts conformed to reality, as did the village elder who did not understand the concept of money. He and the terrible fate of his community at the hands of the Vietcong were based on a passage from the book. "The old chief who had wanted nothing for his people but to live unmolested by either side in this war they couldn't understand and which offered them nothing no matter which side won, lay dead" (Moore 1965, 242). However, the film entirely ignored the Montagnards' hatred of South Vietnam. In 1964, the tribal CIDG contingents "whose loyalty extended only to their Montagnard leaders and Special Forces advisors" revolted and killed their LLDB commanders and any ARVN troops they could find. The Green Berets mediated the dispute and brought it to an uneasy conclusion (Stanton 1985, 79–81).

The Special Forces engaged in covert operations involving the kidnapping or assassination of Vietcong leaders and even officials inside North Vietnam. The cross-border raids depicted by Moore were nonstarters if Wayne hoped to gain the U.S. Army's assistance in making the movie. As a result, several scenes from the book were condensed and rewritten into a ridiculous scenario set in a vague South Vietnamese location. A beautiful temptress who hated communism is dispatched to assist in kidnapping an unwary Vietcong general shown driving through the jungle in an expensive Peugeot sedan with flags flapping on the front bumpers as if on a diplomatic mission. The bedchamber of his elegant mansion was furnished with caviar and chilled champagne for the tryst.

The most realistic aspects of *The Green Berets* movie involved the layout of the forward operating base and the Vietcong assault on the camp. Such bases often held as many as 400 people. Fewer than 20 of them were Green Berets. Aside from a small LLDB detachment, most of the base's occupants were either civilian laborers or CIDG fighters. The camps were usually surrounded by a free-fire zone of open fields cleared of jungle and were defined by a barbed wire perimeter laced with broken glass and steel spikes. The field inside the outer fence was sown with remote-triggered Claymore mines and wooden punji stakes. Inside the inner fence were trenches and, beyond that, a sandbagged mud wall studded with machine gun emplacements. An airfield stretched out at the edge of the compound.

The movie's battle scene replicates a central episode from the book as well as numerous other accounts of nocturnal assaults against remote Special Forces bases in which the Vietcong, and sometimes North Vietnamese regulars, attacked in unrelenting human waves. The communist forces apparently numbered in the thousands and assembled for their assault under cover of the dense jungle foliage. The sheer numbers and unrelenting discipline of the attackers, aided by South Vietnamese traitors, breached the perimeter and caused confusion and casualties inside the base. Several of the movie's leading characters are killed or wounded. Helicopters evacuate the camp before it briefly falls to the enemy. After the sun rises, an air strike annihilates the communists. The surviving Green Berets and their allies retake the camp and rip down the Vietcong flag.

The film acknowledges the subversive role of communist infiltrators but does not represent the war's worst-case scenarios. In 1963, hit by mortars from outside and traitors from within, Camp Hiep Hoa fell. Infiltrators manning one of the wall's machine gun emplacements turned their fire on loyal troops. The Vietcong scaled the walls with ladders shouting in Vietnamese, "Don't shoot! All we want is the Americans and the weapons." The surviving South Vietnamese troops honored that request by ceasing fire. ARVN contingents in nearby villages remained in place and offered no assistance. In the 1965 battle of Camp Plei Mrong, the Vietcong poured through a 12-foot gap in the outer fence that had been prepared by communist sympathizers inside the base. The Special Forces' howitzers had been disabled and the radio antenna had been cut, yet the Green Berets managed to send out signals for assistance and repelled the attack by sunrise. Many Special Forces bases "had been placed in convenient but militarily unsound locations by Vietnamese officials," a veteran complained. The Vietcong often controlled the surrounding villages. "Each camp was on its own during the night, as the ARVN was reluctant to move during darkness for fear of ambush" (Stanton 1985, 56–57, 68–70).

Although they captured the imagination of the American public and fought with courage and unusual resourcefulness, the Green Berets were thrust into a war they could not win. Their numbers were small and their mission was often hampered by a variety of factors, including corrupt South Vietnamese officials, unreliable units of the ARVN, and mixed signals from the U.S. Army command in Saigon.

CONCLUSION

The Green Berets accurately depicted the visual appearance of Special Forces camps and the brutality of the Vietcong, while largely overlooking the abuses of the South Vietnamese military. Some scenes were pure fantasy. The movie not only presented an incomplete understanding of the Special Forces but also a false picture of the U.S. situation in Vietnam in 1968. By underestimating the weakness of the South Vietnamese regime and its military, the movie played on the fading hope that victory could still be achieved. As history, *The Green Berets* is valuable only as a record of the attitude of prowar American conservatives who continued to believe that Vietnam was strategically valuable to the United States and that the war was winnable.

FURTHER READING

Adkins, Bennie G. 2018. *A Tiger Among Us: A Story of Valor in Vietnam's A Shau Valley*. Cambridge, MA: Da Capo Press.

Adler, Renata. "'Green Berets' as Viewed by John Wayne." *New York Times*, June 20, 1968.

Baldwin, Hanson. "Book on U.S. Forces in Vietnam Stirs Army Ire." *New York Times*, May 29, 1965.

Bigart, Homer. "A 'Very Real War' in Vietnam—and the Deep U.S. Commitment." *New York Times*, February 25, 1962.

Browne, Malcolm W. 1965. *The New Face of War*. New York: Bobbs-Merrill.

Ebert, Roger. "The Green Berets." *Chicago Sun-Times*, June 26, 1968.

Feinstein, Phyllis. "Some Guys Never Learn." *Movie Life*, February 1968.

"The Green Berets." *Hollywood Reporter*, June 17, 1968.

Halberstam, David. 1965. *The Making of a Quagmire*. New York: Random House.

Harwood, Richard. "The War Just Doesn't Add Up." *Washington Post*, September 3, 1967.

Kennedy, John F. "Remarks at West Point to the Graduating Class of the U.S. Military Academy," June 6, 1962. Online by Gerhard Peters and John T. Woolley, The American Presidency Project. https://www.presidency.ucsb.edu/node/235775

Kovic, Ron. 1976. *Born on the Fourth of July*. New York: McGraw-Hill.

Mole, Robert L. 1970. *The Montagnards of South Vietnam: A Story of Nine Tribes*. Rutland, Vermont: Charles E. Tuttle.

Moore, Robin. 1965. *The Green Berets*. New York: Crown.

Prados, John. 1995. *The Hidden History of the Vietnam War*. Chicago: Ivan R. Dee.

Roberts, Randy, and James S. Olson. 1995. *John Wayne American*. New York: Free Press.

Rothman, Lily. "Read the TIME Essay That Advocated for the Vietnam War." *TIME*, May 14, 1965. http://time.com/3850301/the-right-war-vietnam-history

Shepherd, Donald, and Robert Slatzer, with Dave Grayson. 1985. *Duke: The Life and Times of John Wayne*. New York: Doubleday.

Simpson III, Charles M. 1983. *Inside the Green Berets: The First Thirty Years*. Novato, CA: Presidio Press.

Southworth, Samuel A., and Stephen Tanner. 2002. *U.S. Special Forces: A Guide to America's Special Operations Units*. Cambridge, MA: Da Capo Press.

Stanton, Shelby L. 1985. *Green Berets at War: U.S. Special Forces in Southeast Asia 1956–1975*. Novato, CA: Presidio Press.

Suid, Lawrence H. 1978. *Guts & Glory: The Making of the American Military Image in Film*. Reading, MA: Addison-Wesley.

Ward, Geoffrey C., and Ken Burns. 2017. *The Vietnam War: An Intimate History*. New York: Alfred A. Knopf.

Wayne, Aissa, with Steve Delsohn. 1991. *John Wayne: My Father*. New York: Random House.

Whitburn, Joel. 2004. *The Billboard Book of Top 40 Country Hits: 1944–2006*. Menomonee Falls, WI: Record Research.

Chapter 2

Coming Home (1978)

Coming Home opened in U.S. theaters in February 1978. The first commercially successful and widely screened movie on the Vietnam War since *The Green Berets* (1968) a decade earlier, *Coming Home* earned critical acclaim (the first Vietnam War film to do so). Actress Jane Fonda (1937–), who starred in the film, also produced it through her own company, IPC Films; United Artists released the film. Nancy Dowd (1945–) wrote the original story after discussions with Bruce Gilbert (1947–), Fonda's partner in IPC. As antiwar activists, Fonda, Dowd, and Gilbert wanted to make a statement about the moral and physical cost of the Vietnam War.

Producer Jerome Hellman (1928–) ordered an extensive rewrite by Waldo Salt (1914–1987), a screenwriter blacklisted during the McCarthy era for his membership in the Communist Party, but who regained stature in the industry for writing *Midnight Cowboy* (1969). When Salt suffered a heart attack during the production, *Coming Home*'s director, Hal Ashby (1929–1988), whose prior successes included *Shampoo* (1975) and *Bound for Glory* (1976), brought in his friend Robert C. Jones (1937–) to finish the screenplay (Fonda 2005, 367). Cinematographer Haskell Wexler (1922–2015), who filmed Fonda's seldom-seen documentary on North Vietnam, *Introduction to the Enemy* (1974), photographed *Coming Home* in natural light in an effort to underscore the realism of the story's setting.

Given Fonda's notorious opposition to the war and her work to organize antiwar veterans, the U.S. military and Veterans Administration refused to cooperate in the production. The crew filmed the story of a Marine Corps officer's wife who volunteers at a VA hospital and falls in love with a paraplegic Vietnam veteran in a civilian hospital for spinal cord injuries in Downey, California (Davidson 1990, 171). Fonda initially experienced difficulty in

NEW LEFT

While it had roots in America's Marxist and social democratic parties from earlier in the 20th century, the New Left was populated by a generation born after the Great Depression and World War II and infused with a new sense of self-confidence. The movement began on a hopeful note with the revitalization of a largely dormant organization, Students for a Democratic Society (SDS), and the inspiration derived from SDS's Port Huron Statement (1962). Cowritten by Tom Hayden, the declaration described the generation as one uncomfortable with the world they inherited from the previous generation. Hayden's generation would later be called the baby boom, and SDS and the New Left generally drew support from middle-class baby boomers on college campuses.

SDS was not the only New Left organization but represented its vanguard and rose to 100,000 members nationwide. Growing opposition to the Vietnam War swelled the ranks of the New Left and provided it with a large milieu of youthful dissent in which to operate. However, most antiwar protesters never formally joined the New Left, and organizations such as SDS had larger agendas involving the transformation of American society in ways most Americans found unpalatable. The overtly Marxist, Maoist, and pro-Vietcong elements of the New Left eventually isolated it from mainstream society and the majority of young people.

The New Left affiliated itself in often uneasy alliances with groups drawn from other demographics such as the Black Panthers, Vietnam Veterans Against the War, and Hispanic and Native American activists. Opposition to the status quo was the common bond but proved insufficient to sustain common strategies and agendas. By the mid-1970s, the end of the Vietnam War and widespread disgust over the terrorism of extreme New Left offshoots brought the New Left's dissolution. However, many of its leaders went on to careers in politics and activism.

VIETNAM VETERANS AGAINST THE WAR

On paper, Vietnam Veterans Against the War (VVAW) had as many as 30,000 members. Even if many individuals on their mailing lists expressed support but never marched in the streets under their banner, the VVAW established chapters across the country and became a high-profile advocate for ending the Vietnam War and improving the facilities maintained by the Veterans Administration and enhancing services such as drug counseling. Aside from their primary focus on the war and veterans' issues, the VVAW criticized the American status quo, especially the corporate capitalism that dominated the economy and exerted undue influence on politics.

Unlike many groups associated with the political protests of the New Left in the 1960s and early 1970s, VVAW's members were largely working class and formed their political views in combat, not in classrooms. Inspired by the April 15, 1967, speech by Martin Luther King Jr. in which opposition to the Vietnam War was equated with the struggle for civil rights in America, six veterans formed VVAW. They quickly caught the attention of the Federal Bureau of Investigation and gained members, becoming a sizable contingent among protesters. VVAW members often marched in uniform with a military discipline that gave pause to the riot police assigned to halt the marches.

The VVAW gathered force through 1973 and staged several memorable events, including a 1971 Washington, DC, protest in which veterans hurled their medals onto the Capitol steps. However, VVAW suffered from many of the problems that plagued other New Left groups, including personality clashes and differing agendas that led to splintering. The radical left wing of VVAW broke away to form the Winter Soldiers Organization. The most prominent VVAW member, Ron Kovic, wrote a best-selling memoir, *Born on the Fourth of July* (1976), that director Oliver Stone turned into a popular film in 1989 about the Vietnam War and its veterans.

finding financing for *Coming Home*. The commercial failure of films such as *Introduction to the Enemy* and the little-known movie starring Fonda's brother, Peter, *Two People* (1978), made Hollywood wary of another Vietnam movie. When Fonda first proposed the project, her strident activism had diminished her star power. However, she persisted, and by the time the production began, her star rose again through her role in the award-winning *Julia* (1977) (Guiles 1982, 244). U.S. involvement in Vietnam ended three years before *Coming Home*'s release, when the last Americans evacuated Saigon by helicopter. It was time, many felt, to begin a painful process of assessment.

Not every critic, or audience, universally admired *Coming Home*. The *New Yorker*'s Pauline Kael (1919–2001), virtually the dean of serious film critics in the 1970s, commented that Fonda played not a character but "an abstraction—a woman being radicalized." Fonda starred as Sally, the proper wife of gung-ho Captain Bob Hyde, played by Bruce Dern (1936–), who is transformed by encountering the paraplegic Luke Martin, played by Jon Voigt (1938–). Categorizing Sally as little more than a stand-in for Fonda's evolution from naive starlet to political activist, Kael wrote that the character "develops only to the level of doctrinaire awareness which has been reached by the people who put *Coming Home* together." She praised Voigt's performance but derided his role, calling it "a parody of the new sanctimoniousness." Kael pointed to the lack of "imaginative sympathy" for Captain Hyde and the screenplay's overall "pettiness of spirit" and "self-admiration," as if *Coming Home* was a political pamphlet dressed up as a bad romance novel (Kael 1978).

However, most critics offered kinder assessments. Writing in the *Chicago Sun-Times*, Roger Ebert (1942–2013) called it "an extraordinarily moving film" whose protagonist, Sally, "is no longer able to accept anything simply because her husband, or anybody else, says it's true" (Ebert 1978). The trade magazine *Variety*, in an unsigned December 31, 1977, review, remarked that it was "in general an excellent Hal Ashby film" that "reigned in any tendencies to be smug or pedantic."

Coming Home grossed $36 million worldwide against a modest $3 million budget. By any measure, it was a hit. Audiences were drawn to it perhaps less from what it said about the Vietnam War than for its unconventional but affecting love story and the resonance of the screenplay for issues having nothing to do with the war. Voigt's performance as Luke was touching at a moment when consciousness over the difficulties of the disabled began to swell into a movement that eventually won passage of the Americans with Disabilities Act (1990). Before its public release, Hellman screened *Coming Home* for a representative of the President's Committee on Employment of the Handicapped, who told the producer that it was the first time she had "seen a disabled person on the screen dealt with as a complete human being" (Davidson 1990, 174). *Coming Home* demanded greater male emotional sensitivity, a forward-thinking position at the time. Fonda said, "I saw the fledgling film that Bruce Gilbert, Nancy Dowd and I had been developing as a way to help redefine masculinity" (Fonda 2005, 360). Fonda's Sally represented a larger transformation that had taken place as women shed previously accepted roles and explored new possibilities. Feminism did not emerge from the Vietnam War, but the women's liberation movement sprang up alongside the protests against the war, and many middle-class women became active in the antiwar movement.

The movie industry quickly heaped honors on *Coming Home*. Voigt received the Best Actor prize at the Cannes Film Festival, where the film screened in May 1978. *Coming Home* received eight nominations at the 1979 Academy Awards and won for Best Original Screenplay (Salt, Jones, and Dowd), Best Actor (Voigt), and Best Actress (Fonda). However, it lost for Best Picture to another film on the Vietnam War, *The Deer Hunter*, a picture Fonda wrongly condemned as prowar (Guiles 1982, 248).

HISTORICAL BACKGROUND

Jane Fonda was the only filmmaker or actor responsible for a major Vietnam War movie who played a significant role in that war's history. She did not serve in the war, and her closest brush with the military before joining the antiwar movement was as Miss Army Recruiter 1959 (Hershberger 2006, 56). As the daughter of beloved actor Henry Fonda, she had easy entry to Hollywood and enjoyed a bankable career in a varied roster of movies such as *Walk on the Wild Side* (1962) and *Barefoot in the Park* (1967) before starring in the science-fiction sex fantasy *Barbarella* (1968), directed by her French husband, Roger Vadim (1928–2000). The notoriety she earned from that film by playing a kittenish sex object made her an unlikely political agitator. She publicly espoused no opinions on American society or its foreign entanglements until well into her sojourn in France.

"I'm a latecomer to the peace movement," she admitted. She was far from the first Hollywood actor to take up the cause. Paul Newman from the younger ranks of stars and Robert Ryan from the older generation preceded her. Her opposition to the Vietnam War began while watching a French television newscast with footage showing "tens of thousands of American people in the streets protesting the war" (Fonda 1972). The realization that the Vietnam War was a doubtful enterprise shocked her and, as with thousands of middle-class youth, triggered a shift from acceptance of the status quo to an embrace of the political left. "Part of my identity had been that I was a citizen of a country that, in spite of its internal paradoxes, represented moral integrity, justice, and a desire for peace," she said. "I had always assumed that wherever our flag was flying, that was the side of the angels" (Hershberger 2006, 55–56).

Encountering U.S. troops stationed in West Germany whose dissident movement, RITA (Resistance Inside the Army), covertly spread antiwar messages in the ranks of the military partly shaped her perceptions. "I wanted to act on what I was learning," she said, adding that she knew this would mean leaving France and her husband (Fonda 2005, 197).

She wasted no time upon returning to the United States in 1970. Her fame drew media attention to the antiwar left and to herself, threatening to eclipse the work of longtime activists. Some of those activists were not amused. Community organizer Saul Alinsky (1909–1972) called her "a hitchhiker on the highway of causes" (Guiles 1982, 182). She hurled herself into virtually every left-of-center cause, including the militant Black Panther Party and the struggles of Native Americans. She signed letters to her friends "Power to the People." "Almost from the get-go we were swept up in the tumultuous events of 1970—the invasion of Cambodia, the killing of students at Kent State University in Ohio and Jackson State University in Mississippi and a series of campus uprisings," Fonda recalled (Fonda 2005, 231). Radical leader Abbie Hoffman (1936–1989) said Fonda "was too earnest, and too naive. She thought she could lump all the world's ills into one overall cause, and that doesn't work" (Davidson 1990, 110). According to a biographer, "Jane was a prize plum, ready for plucking by any resourceful militant" (Guiles 1982, 162).

The light of Fonda's stardom drew radicals to her side, such as lawyer Mark Lane (1927–2016), a prominent proponent of John F. Kennedy assassination conspiracy theories, and leftist screenwriter Fred Gardner. Fonda and Lane were instrumental in organizing the Legal Clearing House, which provided free attorney services for troops in trouble for their views on the war. Gardner opened a string of "GI coffeehouses" near army bases in the United States and called on friends to tour this circuit as members of the satirical Free the Army revue. Participants in the revue included comedian Dick Gregory (1932–2017), actor Donald Sutherland (1935–), singer Country Joe McDonald (1942–), and Fonda. For much of 1970 and 1971, Fonda constantly moved around the country, flying from one coffeehouse revue and campus antiwar rally to another, traveling light and catching naps on planes (Guiles 1982, 163–164). The GI revues were well attended, albeit some soldiers gave full reports to army intelligence after they returned to base. What Fonda actually said at the coffeehouses was often a matter of dispute. "The more conservative the informant, the more radical the portrait of Jane" (Guiles 1982, 169).

Free the Army suffered from the same divisiveness that splintered most radical groups from the late 1960s and early 1970s. McDonald eventually attacked Fonda and Sutherland, charging, "The movement has been duped by them. Their place in the hierarchy is much lower than they think it is," adding, "I'm not going to be part of their ego trip." Gardner also turned on Fonda and Sutherland. He told an underground paper that under their leadership, "The show does not fight imperialism. It does nothing but advertise organizations and projects that have utter contempt for the soldiers" (Guiles 1982, 191–192).

Leftists may have been divided in their view of Fonda, but the right united in its hatred for the actress. The editor of the conservative magazine *National Review*, William F. Buckley Jr., equated her with Chinese communist leader Mao Zedong (Buckley 1972). Her fame as well as her activity attracted the eyes of FBI Director J. Edgar Hoover, whose agents followed her through airports and into talks she gave at private homes as well as public rallies. The FBI spent thousands of dollars on informants who recorded her words, while office-bound agents amassed clipping files of her mentions in newspapers. The FBI spread disinformation claiming she had called for the assassination of President Richard M. Nixon when, in reality, she did no more than denounce him as a criminal. Her ties with foreigners, leading up to her much-publicized 1972 trip to North Vietnam, brought the attention of the CIA and the National Security Agency. The agencies tapped Fonda's phones. A biographer filing a Freedom of Information Act request on Fonda received, in return, a file of 763 pages with many lines redacted in black magic marker decades later for reasons of national security. FBI memos inaccurately classified her as an anarchist (Davidson 1990, 1).

Whether loved or hated, Fonda continued to draw attention. When a reporter asked about her status as a "glamour girl" activist, she condemned the categorization and the "chauvinism" it implied, but added, "I think a lot of people come to hear me because I'm an actress. Certainly. I don't care. What I care about is what they leave with" (Hershberger 2006, 39).

While campaigning for the war to end, she fell in love with a fellow traveler, Tom Hayden, president of Students for a Democratic Society. The radical left considered him a hero, as a member of the Chicago Seven tried for their role in the disturbances outside the 1968 Democratic National Convention in Chicago. Fonda and Hayden married in 1973 and worked together closely for several years on various causes.

However, Hayden did not accompany Fonda on her first trip to North Vietnam. A French lawyer with contacts at the North Vietnamese embassy in Paris made arrangements for Fonda's journey. As the United States had no diplomatic representatives in North Vietnam, Americans could seldom travel to that country, but other U.S. citizens did visit Hanoi after the war began. Some 200 people preceded her, many of them affiliated with organizations such as the Women Strike for Peace and the American Friends Service Committee, as well as churches and synagogues concerned with halting nuclear testing, curbing the Cold War, and promoting international solidarity. Most felt a strong affinity between the struggle for civil rights in the United States and for self-determination by formerly colonized people around the world. Many of them published or presented accounts of their trip upon returning home (Hershberger 1998, xv–xvii). The *New York Times*' Harrison Salisbury, the first mainstream American correspondent allowed into North Vietnam, wrote of witnessing civilian casualties and damage from air strikes on Hanoi at a time when the United States denied bombing the country's capital or targeting civilians. The Pentagon made "a suggestion, widely reported in the press, that Salisbury and the *Times* were serving as propaganda agents for the enemy" (Hersh 2018, 55).

However, only Fonda attracted the full glare of the American media, angry conservative protesters, and threats of reprisals by the U.S. government. The communist regime was well aware of her value. "In Hanoi she was a showpiece and their best propaganda tool to date" (Guiles 1982, 201). Without exaggeration, the Vietnamese people greeted her as "the great progressive American actress" (Davidson 1990, 144).

Like all visitors to North Vietnam, Fonda was impressed by the remarkable resilience of the Vietnamese people, who in the words of Ho Chi Minh, could bend like bamboo without breaking. Fonda accurately related the wartime situation endured by North Vietnam's people. However, she bought into the political interpretations given to her by her North Vietnamese handlers. Especially in her carefully stage-managed visits with American prisoners of war (POWs), Fonda was unwilling to look beneath surface appearances. As her biographer put it, describing her undiscerning embrace of radical causes after returning to the United States, she repeated everything the Black Panthers and others told her. "Jane lacked the ability to detect a lie or an exaggeration if it came from a friend" (Guiles 1982, 195). She regarded the North Vietnamese as her friends.

Fonda brought back touching, even cinematic stories, especially when her party came under an American air attack. "I was told I had to get out of the car and run because the bombers were coming," she recalled. "All along the side of this road at regular intervals were these manholes for individual people that had thick straw lids that you pull over to protect you from the bombs and shrapnel." She ran, "and suddenly a young Vietnamese girl comes up behind me and pulls me down into one of those holes. She was a school girl, she had her books wrapped up in a belt. She dropped them and pushed me down into this hole and then got into the hole with me and pulled the top on." Fonda was not the only visitor to observe that North Vietnamese civilians bore no apparent anger toward Americans, at least for those not in uniform (Hershberger 2006, 14).

Fonda brought a tape recorder and a camera with her while investigating reports that the United States bombed a network of dikes that held back the Red River. The destruction of those dikes would flood the lowlands and could cause tens of thousands of deaths. The Nixon administration denied bombing the dikes, and Fonda maintained that the footage she took showing damage from air strikes mysteriously disappeared after she returned to the United States. Her claim was not improbable given the FBI's aggressive tactics against left-wing radicals (Hershberger 2006, xv). The truth of her allegations about the dikes was complicated. "In fact it was the anti-aircraft sites built on top of the dikes that were the targets," wrote Seymour Hersh, the *New York Times*' antiwar Vietnam War correspondent (Hersh 2018, 168). And in fact, the Nixon administration contemplated the full-scale destruction of the dikes, but when plans were leaked to the press, Secretary of State William P. Rogers (1913–2001) and Defense Secretary Melvin Laird (1922–2016) pleaded with Nixon to drop a scheme that would only inflame the antiwar movement and tarnish America's standing overseas (Ward 2017, 425).

Fonda's criticism of the targets chosen by the U.S. military and the cost of civilian lives from bombing raids might have received a respectful hearing had she not opted to give a series of fervent broadcasts on Radio Hanoi, a decision that stirred unpleasant World War II–era memories of Axis Sally and Tokyo Rose, U.S. citizens who broadcast propaganda from Nazi Germany and Imperial Japan with the objective of demoralizing American forces. Fonda's July 14, 1972, broadcast was directed toward U.S. pilots. "I beg you to consider what you are doing," she began. "In the area where I went yesterday it was easy to see that there are no military targets, there is no important highway, there is no communication network, there is no heavy industry." She went on to compare Vietnam's peasants to the hard-working farmers of the American Midwest. "Are these the enemy?" she demanded. "What will you say to your children years from now who may ask you why you fought the war? What words will you now be able to say to them?" (Hershberger 2006, 24).

Fonda was not the only American guest of the North Vietnamese who was invited to speak on Radio Hanoi, but most of the visitors confined themselves to measured statements promoting peace and understanding. Hersh recalled meeting the famous folksinger and antiwar activist Pete Seeger in Hanoi. The singer told him that he "had been asked to discuss his feelings about the war in a radio interview that day. He asked for my advice. I told him his critical views on the Vietnam War, and all wars, in fact, were well known, and if he wanted to do a sing-along on the radio, he should go right ahead." Lacking Seeger's talent for music, Hersh refused several invitations to appear on Radio Hanoi (Hersh 2018, 154).

Not content with a single broadcast, Fonda returned to the studios of Radio Hanoi on July 19 to describe the bombing of Nam Dinh, the center of North Vietnam's textile industry, where homes, schools, cinemas, and pagodas were destroyed. "What are your commanders telling you? How are they justifying this to you?" she demanded. Fonda went on to praise "the resistance and determination to resist that has spread to every district, to every hamlet, to every house and to every Vietnamese heart." She concluded with a distorted history lesson, claiming the Vietnamese had "been fighting for four thousand years" for "freedom and democracy" (Hershberger 2006, 26).

Her most controversial broadcasts aired on July 20 after her meeting with seven U.S. POWs, fliers shot down during air raids. "They are all in good health," she declared. "We had a very long talk. We exchanged ideas feely." To a man, they seemed to concur with Fonda's views. "They asked me to bring back to the American people their sense of disgust of the war and their shame for what they have been asked to do." She added, "They have all assured me that they had been well cared for. They listen to the radio. They receive letters. They are in good health" (Hershberger 2006, 28).

Fonda's assessment had little to do with reality. The American POWs held in North Vietnam were never kept in comfort but at first were treated relatively well. They were kept in isolation but tapped Morse code messages to each other. Rats were everywhere, and food was austere, yet they received letters from home and packages from the International Red Cross. As the air raids continued, destruction became more widespread, and Vietnamese casualties mounted, their treatment worsened. The North Vietnamese withdrew mail privileges, withheld Red Cross packages, and subjected prisoners to harsh interrogations, beatings, and torture. "The manacles, the ropes, the beatings, they broke bones," recalled Lieutenant Everett Alvarez, the first U.S. pilot shot down over North Vietnam (1966). "They did everything. My arms turned black from the cuffs that cut off all circulation. And they didn't let me die. They just kept the pain going" (Ward 2017, 178).

Fonda remained committed to her view of the "good health" of the POWs for several years. When North Vietnam released prisoners in 1973 after the Paris Accords that ended American involvement in the Vietnam War, she denounced the gaunt, pale, and sometimes disabled men who came home from the prisons. "History will judge them severely," she said, calling them "hypocrites" and "criminals." She was widely denounced for her remarks (Guiles 1982, 227). She later conceded: "I firmly believe that the POWs I met with had not been tortured. But what I didn't know at the time was that prior to 1969 there had in fact been systematic torture of POWs. I was wrong and I am sorry" (Fonda 2005, 327).

An incident from her 1972 excursion to North Vietnam that sparked even greater controversy than her remarks over the POWs was her decision to be photographed at an antiaircraft battery near Hanoi, wearing a steel helmet and appearing as if she was ready for action should a U.S. plane fly overhead.

When questioned by the press about the incident after returning to the United States, Fonda insisted she had done nothing wrong. "I asked to see an antiaircraft gun and I was taken there, needless to say, when there were no American planes around." She explained that it was a matter of curiosity on her part. "I went there because I wanted to see who the men are who are firing these guns, what do they have to say for themselves." She described it as a joyous outing. "They sang me a song and they showed me the gun and I looked at the gun and a lot of people have misunderstood that. I applauded the singing . . . They were singing praises to the blue skies of Hanoi and hoping the war would end so there wouldn't have to be any more silver planes in the blue skies of Hanoi" (Hershberger 2006, 35).

Years later she expressed regret, admitting to "a terrible lapse of judgment on my last day there. I sat on an anti-aircraft gun. A group of soldiers had sung me a song, I had sung one back, everyone was laughing and clapping." After someone asked her to sit down, "Pictures were taken by reporters and I didn't realize until a moment after I got up what the implication of that images would mean." She insisted that the gun was "inactive" and no U.S. planes were overhead. "I simply wasn't thinking about what I was doing, only what I was feeling—innocent of what the photo implies. Yet the photo exists, delivering its message, regardless of what I was really doing or feeling" (Hershberger 2006, 61). The incident followed her for decades, and she continued to issue explanations. "My only regret about the trip was that I was photographed sitting on a North Vietnamese antiaircraft gun site" (Fonda 2005, 291).

The broadcasts and the antiaircraft photographs were enough for the U.S. Department of Justice to consider indicting her for treason. They never proceeded because the charge would have been difficult to substantiate, given that the United States waged war against North Vietnam without a declaration of war. The DOJ also contemplated sedition charges, but Fonda's remarks fell short of calling on U.S. troops to disobey orders. Although never charged, a Democratic congressman from Missouri, Richard Ichord (1926–1992), and a Republican colleague from Georgia, Fletcher Thompson (1925–), demanded she be tried for treason. Other Americans already determined the outcome of such a trial and proposed punishment. New Hampshire's leading newspaper, the *Manchester Union Leader*, called for her to be shot. The Maryland legislature debated whether she should be hanged or her tongue cut out. Bumper stickers proclaimed: "I'm not Fonda Hanoi Jane." Through the 1980s, her conduct in North Vietnam made her a target for Republican recrimination. In 1988, presidential candidate George H. W. Bush attacked his Democratic rival, Michael Dukakis, by saying: "I will not be surprised if my opponent thinks a naval exercise is something you find in the *Jane Fonda Workout Book*," referring to her best-selling exercise manual (Davidson 1990, 6–7).

Even after the United States ended its combat role in Vietnam, Fonda continued to visit and support North Vietnam. While in the country filming her 1974 documentary, *Introduction to the Enemy*, she wrote a laudatory essay for *Rolling Stone* magazine looking back on the war, describing "teams of young school girls devising ways to defuse time bombs that have been dropped at night, soldiers walking for months with dismantled tank parts on their backs" and teams of women filling "a bomb crater with their hands in a few days to keep the traffic going" along with men who "sink their ferry during the day to hide it from the planes and pump it out every night" so it could carry freight under cover of darkness (Fonda 1974). However, by 1975, she decided to focus her attention on the plight of wounded American veterans coming home from the war who faced uncertain futures.

Depiction and Cultural Context

Coming Home was the capstone of Fonda's anti–Vietnam War activism and grew out of her experiences working with veterans who shared her opposition to the war. Their numbers were not inconsiderable, and the leaders of one of the movement's key organizations, Vietnam Veterans Against the War (VVAW), had been speaking out on the issues addressed by *Coming Home* through demanding "an immediate increase in Veterans Administration funds to correct the deplorable inhumane conditions that prevail in VA hospitals, and to facilitate the initiation of rehabilitative programs responsive to the needs of wounded Vietnam Veterans" (Nicosia 2001, 62).

Fonda eagerly addressed veterans at VVAW rallies, telling the crowd that Nixon "can't ignore the sound of his own troops marching against his own policies," adding, "The rest of us can be accused of being reds, hippies, unpatriotic what-have-you, but the guys who have been there can't be ignored." A historian of the antiwar movement noted that her remarks on that occasion were greeted "with great cheers—more than she would ever hear from American veterans again" (Nicosia 2001, 68–69). She alienated many veterans' activists soon enough with her moral certainty, high-handedness, and willingness to use the funds she raised as leverage (Nicosia 2001, 82–85), but she eventually apologized, realizing that the experiences of actual war veterans possessed an authenticity greater than her ideological abstractions.

"I had spent over two years working with GIs and Vietnam veterans and had spoken before hundreds of thousands of antiwar protesters telling them that our men in uniform *aren't* the enemy. I went to support GIs at their bases and overseas," Fonda recalled. "In the years ahead I would make *Coming Home* so Americans could understand how the wounded were treated in veterans hospitals" (Hershberger 2006, 61).

As Fonda admitted, she conceived *Coming Home* at a time when her career was at loose ends and her box-office draw was uncertain, given her unpopularity among segments of the public. "I thought, it takes three months to make a feature film and I just couldn't imagine spending three months making a film just for the money," she added. "And I thought, well how am I ever going to make movies that speak to my heart and to my values?" (Hershberger 2006, 13). The answer came when Fonda encountered a leading figure among Vietnam veterans in the antiwar movement, Ron Kovic (1946–).

In 1973, Kovic and Bill Unger, both disabled ex-marines, led a VVAW chapter and invited Fonda to speak at one of their rallies outside the Long Beach, California, VA hospital. According to a historian of the veterans' movement, "Most of the vets were impressed by her deep concern, and even more significantly, she was deeply affected by them. Kovic recalls that she looked 'stunned,' as if 'she had walked into hell,' and that it was obvious she had never witnessed anything like this before" (Nicosia 2001, 320–321).

Fonda described Kovic as "very fiery, very charismatic, had been real gung-ho; he reenlisted for three terms in Vietnam, had been shot and was paralyzed from the waist down and was in a wheelchair." She heard him say, "'I may have lost my body but I've gained my mind.' That, I don't know, that just kind of pierced me, entered me." As she saw it, "He had come to shed the traditional warrior ethic to become a full human being. And I said, we could make a movie about that, and that's what evolved into *Coming Home*" (Hershberger 2006, 13). Within days of that rally, Fonda sent business partner-producer Bruce Gilbert and screenwriter Nancy Dowd to begin research for the screenplay.

To prepare for her role as the wife of a Marine Corps captain, Fonda made a study of military officers' wives. Admittedly, they were a class of people who were not interested in being studied by her. "How does a woman like Sally move, dress, talk? That's what I want to know," she said. "The degree to which I can render that woman real has a whole political implication for me—because those are the kinds of people who hate me, who thought I was a traitor" (Davidson 1990, 173).

Screenwriter Waldo Salt, who despite his political sympathies toned down the overt political rhetoric of the screenplay's first draft in the interest of good storytelling, was eager to meet the men he was hired to describe. He "threw himself into his research with the gusto one would expect from a man with his history, visiting VA hospitals, talking with veterans." Salt also encouraged Kovic to write the memoir that became *Born on the Fourth of July*, which became the basis for a hit film starring Tom Cruise (Fonda 2005, 360–361).

The wider effect of the Vietnam War on American society rather than the war itself informs the messages Fonda put across in *Coming Home*. "Maybe this is a way to redefine sexuality, sensuality," she said (Hershberger 2006, 14). The movie's hero is not Sally's husband, Captain Bob Hyde, who sought to prove his manhood on the battlefield. "We're going there, pal, Nam, combat city," Bob tells his buddy, excited by the prospect of experiencing warfare. The hero is Luke, who found his identity after losing many of his body functions to war. Many also recognized *Coming Home* at the time of its release as a statement on the women's movement. Although not a mother, Sally was in all other respects a conventional military wife as the film begins. The opening is probably set in February 1968, given Bob's optimism that with the recently ended Tet Offensive, the rest of the war will be merely "a mop-up operation." Wedded to the idea that a husband must be the provider, he had problems with Sally taking a job while he was away. "I am afraid, but I'm proud of you," Sally dutifully tells Bob as he departs for Vietnam. However, she glimpses wider horizons under the influence of her new friend Vi Munson, the girlfriend of Bob's buddy. Penelope Milford (1948–) plays Vi like a streetwise character from 1940s Hollywood, but the flowers painted on her van and the beaded curtains in her attic identify her as a bohemian, if not quite a hippie.

Vi becomes the bridge to *Coming Home*'s main theme when she mentions her brother Billy. Played by Robert Carradine (1954–), Billy is home from Vietnam but confined to the psych ward of the nearby Veterans Administration hospital. Impulsively, Sally volunteers at the hospital and is tasked with wheeling trays of juice and coffee through the day rooms and helping feed veterans confined to bed and unable to lift their forks.

She meets Luke, a stand-in for Kovic and other antiwar Vietnam vets. Although *Coming Home* never mentions VVAW or any organization, a discussion involving Luke and other vets confined to the VA hospital, condemning those who try to justify the war, hints at the solidarity Kovic and his colleagues worked toward. Having grown up in Hollywood, Fonda had no illusion over reaching the widest audience with a gritty portrayal of wounded men in an inhospitable hospital. "Somewhere along in there . . . it was becoming clear that this was becoming a love story, a triangle," she said, an affair that would make a statement about the war and social values in a way that would stir audience interest and emotional involvement (Hershberger 2006, 14).

Coming Home accurately depicts the squalid conditions of many VA hospitals and the situations many Vietnam veterans faced in the late 1960s and 1970s. The influx of casualties overwhelmed facilities at a time when Congress and the White House bickered over budget priorities. Appropriate funding increases for the VA were not always forthcoming, and the situation only worsened for a time in the years following the 1968 setting of *Coming Home*. In 1972, Richard Nixon vetoed a bill to increase the VA's budget, and a year later, Congress slashed the agency's budget by $65 million. VVAW leader John Musgrave, an ex-marine who walked with a limp after receiving three Purple Hearts, declared: "The VA's the enemy of the veterans, not the friend" (Nicosia 2001, 299, 302).

Ironically, improvements in medical care partly contributed to the crowded and inadequate conditions. Unlike previous wars, where soldiers with spinal cord injuries usually died shortly after being wounded, in Vietnam helicopters rapidly evacuated them from the battlefield to well-equipped forward hospitals. As a result, paralyzed men in wheelchairs filled the VA wards. Like Luke, some waited many weeks for a wheelchair and propelled themselves from place to place while lying on their backs on gurneys.

While VA administrators tried to downplay the problems, word of bad conditions faced by returning veterans drew significant media coverage in the years leading up to *Coming Home*'s release. The cover story of the May 22, 1970, issue of *Life* magazine, "Our Forgotten Wounded," stared at shoppers in supermarket checkout lines across the country. It included a set of disturbing photos taken inside VA hospitals by Dutch photojournalist Co Rentmeester, who had been wounded while covering the war. According to the photo essay's captions, "One out of every six men wounded in Vietnam ends up in an understaffed, overcrowded VA hospital." Ex-marine Marke Dumpert, paralyzed from the neck down, said of the Bronx VA hospital: "It's like you've been put in jail or been punished for something." He described worse conditions than those shown in *Coming Home*. For example, Luke didn't have to contend with rats in the hospital in the film. Bad publicity continued after VVAW activist Skip Roberts organized a series of "hospital zaps," inviting reporters, TV cameramen, and politicians on surprise visits that pushed into VA wards to expose the poor conditions endured by patients.

The problems of returning veterans became a political issue as early as 1969 when Senator Alan Cranston (1914–2000), a Democrat from California, initiated oversight hearings on understaffed, overcrowded VA hospitals. In his much-publicized testimony before the Senate Foreign Relations Committee, future Secretary of State John Kerry, then a veteran recently returned from Vietnam, told senators that 57 percent of Vietnam vets entering VA hospitals talked of suicide and that those facilities "won't or can't meet" their needs (Thorne 1971, 24).

Suicide is the fate of two of *Coming Home*'s veterans. Vi's brother Billy acts happy when prescribed "uppers" by VA staff, but his erratic mental state eventually leads him to kill himself in the hospital by injecting himself with an empty syringe, triggering heart failure. Bob is disturbed by things he witnessed in Vietnam. Emotionally bottled up, he will say only that after taking a certain hamlet, his second lieutenant asked, "Would it be okay if we put the heads on poles?" to frighten the Vietcong. "My men were chopping heads off!" he admits to Sally. After returning home, limping after having sustained a wound he doesn't care to discuss, Bob becomes understandably upset upon learning of the affair between Sally and Luke. His reaction when confronting them with a bayonet in combat pose suggests a flashback to Vietnam. It's a symptom of what is now called post-traumatic stress disorder, which the American Psychiatric Association added to its diagnostic manual in 1980 in response to mental health problems among Vietnam veterans. Bob takes his own life in the film's closing scene.

Like Luke, Kovic complained that his urine bags were not emptied often enough and overspilled onto the floors. He pointed to other vets left for hours in their own excrement. The casual illegal drug use occurring in VA hospitals is noticed in the film but underplayed. As shown in *Coming Home*, vets who became unruly because of their ill treatment were administered Thorazine and placed in restraints. Although the movie doesn't say so, a few veterans were even subjected to lobotomies (Nicosia 2001, 319).

Kovic's description of the Long Beach, California, VA hospital adheres to the movie. He wrote of "the awful bedsores that never seemed to go away." He called it a "hideous place" with "depressing and sickening green walls, the windows that were always locked." *Coming Home* could only suggest "the putrid, stifling air that always hung like death, the stink of that place always in your nostrils, in your clothing, your oversize shirts with the government label that always reminded you of Auschwitz, the constant screaming, the absurdity of bingo games in the midst of so much suffering" (Nicosia 2001, 317).

Coming Home illustrated the gap between veterans of World War II and Vietnam by the Fourth of July celebration in which older members of the American Legion droned on from the podium about "defending freedom" while younger vets smoked marijuana and carried on. The scene reflected Kovic's experiences as well as Fonda's first visit to his VA hospital, where counterprotesters, World War II veterans, tried to disrupt her speech by singing "God Bless America" (Nicosia 2001, 320).

Although *Coming Home* steers clear of showing organized resistance by Vietnam vets, Luke is depicted in an act of protest when he is arrested for chaining himself to the gate of a Marine Corps base. This leads to the wiretapping and continual surveillance of Luke and Sally by a pair of FBI agents. Film critic Pauline Kael took issue with this as an unrealistic plot element (Kael 1978). While the FBI subplot reflected the surveillance and harassment Fonda and Kovic experienced for their activism in the early 1970s, some wondered if relatively unimportant people such as Sally and Luke would merit the attention of the federal government. Since the film's release, information on the FBI's covert COINTELPRO (Counter Intelligence Program), revealing the extent to which the agency spied and tried to discredit individuals deemed "subversive" by exposing embarrassing details from their private lives, adds credibility to the film and belies accusations of political paranoia.

CONCLUSION

Coming Home accurately depicted the problems faced by disabled Vietnam veterans in VA hospitals and registered the dissatisfaction that found a voice in real life through organizations such as VVAW. With the wounds of Vietnam fresh in everyone's mind, Fonda was an even more polarizing figure in 1978 than she is today, and Hollywood questioned how veterans would respond to the film. Shortly before its public release, *Coming Home*'s producer, Jerome Hellman, arranged a private screening in Washington, DC, for representatives of various veterans groups. "I deliberately invited people who were not too well disposed to Jane Fonda," he recalled. "I flew in from LA for the screening and wanted to see what the reaction would be. I could sense nothing but rapt attention when the film was running." He added, "That toughest of audiences was overwhelmed" (Davidson 1990, 174).

FURTHER READING

Buckley, William F., Jr. "Secretary Fonda." *National Review*, August 18, 1972.

Davidson, Bill. 1990. *Jane Fonda: An Intimate Biography*. London: Sidgwick & Jackson.

Ebert, Roger. "Coming Home." *Chicago Sun-Times*, January 1, 1978.

Fonda, Jane. "Why Famous Actress Became a Peace Activist." *Philadelphia Bulletin*, October 1, 1972.

Fonda, Jane. "A Vietnam Journal: Birth of a Nation," *Rolling Stone*, July 4, 1974.

Fonda, Jane. 2005. *My Life So Far*. New York: Random House.

Guiles, Fred Lawrence. 1982. *Jane Fonda: The Actress in Her Time*. Garden City, NY: Doubleday.

Hersh, Seymour M. 2018. *Reporter: A Memoir*. New York: Alfred P. Knopf.

Hershberger, Mary. 1998. *Traveling to Vietnam: American Peace Activists and the War*. Syracuse, NY: Syracuse University Press.

Hershberger, Mary. 2006. *Jane Fonda's Words of Politics and Passion*. New York: New Press.

Kael, Pauline. "Coming Home: Mythologizing the Sixties." *New Yorker*, February 20, 1978.

Nicosia, Gerald. 2001. *Home to War: A History of the Vietnam Veterans Movement*. New York: Crown Publishers.

Thorne, David, and George Butler. 1971. *The New Soldier*. New York: Collier.

Ward, Geoffrey C., and Ken Burns. 2017. *The Vietnam War: An Intimate History*. New York: Alfred P. Knopf.

Chapter 3

The Boys in Company C (1978)

In February 1978, the Hollywood taboo against Vietnam War movies lifted
with the release of two films, *Coming Home*, which became one of the year's
greatest hits, and the modestly successful *The Boys in Company C. The Boys
in Company C* was the first widely seen movie set in Vietnam since *The
Green Berets* (1968). It also was the first film to grapple realistically with
men in combat during the Vietnam War and broke ground for a raft of movies such as *Platoon* (1986) and *Hamburger Hill* (1987).

The film's director, Sidney J. Furie (1933–), was a Canadian whose career
began with gritty adolescent dramas before moving to London in the 1960s.
While in Great Britain, he produced a checkered body of work suggesting
sensitivity to the human condition, visual acumen, and a willingness to work
in virtually any genre. Furie's British successes led him to Hollywood, where
he enjoyed a similarly eclectic career.

The Boys in Company C follows a group of young men from their arrival
at a U.S. Marine Corps induction center through basic training and combat in Vietnam. They experience the war not as a glorious opportunity for
valor but as a series of incidents revealing the bureaucratic incompetence
of the military and the uncertainty of their mission in Vietnam. In the climactic scene, the squad is given the opportunity to avoid future combat by
"throwing" a soccer game with a South Vietnamese unit, a scheme devised
to improve morale among the Vietnamese allies. The boys refuse, and those
who survive a sneak attack on the playing field by the Vietcong are sent to
Khe Sanh, where for six months in 1968, marines engaged North Vietnamese troops in an ultimately unsuccessful battle to keep the strategic base
from falling to the enemy.

FROM THE HALLS OF MONTEZUMA

The U.S. Marine Corps was the vanguard of American intervention in many conflicts before the Vietnam War. From the early years of the republic, marines were dispatched to protect American interests in foreign lands and to seize strategic points through their specialty, amphibious assault. As seagoing soldiers attached to the U.S. Navy, they fought in the Barbary Wars (1801–1806) on "the shores of Tripoli," as the "Marines' Hymn" proclaims, and "the Halls of Montezuma" in the Mexican-American War (1846–1848).

As the United States gained status as a world power, marines were dispatched across Latin America and to the far corners of the globe. Before the end of the 19th century, marines were sent to Formosa, Korea, Samoa, Uruguay, Panama, Argentina, and Chile. War correspondent Richard Harding Davis, a witness to the marines' storming ashore to put down a rebellion in Panama (1903), coined a phrase that became part of the corps' lore: "The Marines have landed and they have the situation well in hand." They took part in the occupation of Cuba, Puerto Rico, and the Philippines during the Spanish-American War (1898) and in the overthrow of the Kingdom of Hawaii.

Marines were sent to China to protect American interests during the Boxer Rebellion (1899–1901) and remained in the country through the beginning of World War II. During the early 20th century, Marines engaged in the "Banana Wars," a series of engagements throughout the Caribbean and Central America where the corps gained experience in modern counterinsurgency. Marines occupied the Dominican Republic from 1916–1924 and Haiti from 1915 through 1934. During World War I, they fought as conventional infantry on the Western Front, but during World War II, they resumed their traditional role as amphibious assault forces in the Pacific. They were prominent in the Korean War amphibious attack on Inchon (1950) and saw action during the Cold War across the world in Lebanon, Thailand, and the Dominican Republic.

Revisiting a formula familiar from many World War II movies, the squad of marines represents a cross-section of the era's servicemen. They include Dave Brisbee, a draft dodger brought to the training center in handcuffs by the Federal Bureau of Investigation; Tyrone Washington, an African American with a tough attitude steeled by the racism he has experienced; Billy Ray Pike, a Southerner who transcends stereotypes through his reluctance to join the service; Vinnie Fazio, who provides comic relief as the streetwise Italian American kid from Brooklyn; and Alvin Foster, a budding author seeking inspiration and experience through war.

Columbia Pictures released *The Boys in Company C*, which was produced by Golden Harvest, a Hong Kong firm previously known for martial arts movies. Furie and an unknown 19-year-old Yale student, Rick Natkin (1958–), wrote the script. A pair of memoirs written by men who served in Vietnam influenced Furie: Ronald J. Glasser's *365 Days* (1971) and Tim

O'Brien's *If I Die in a Combat Zone* (1973). Natkin was inspired by stories told by returning war veterans. Furie shopped their screenplay to Hollywood's major production houses and studios without success. When Golden Harvest contacted him with the idea of directing a crime caper, he convinced them to make *The Boys in Company C* instead (Kremer 2015, 237).

Filming an American-oriented war picture in Vietnam was impossible due to the hostility of the country's communist regime, but finding a location with similar terrain was essential for the sake of realism. Furie hoped to shoot *The Boys in Company C* in Thailand, where Michael Cimino (1939–2016) was working on another Vietnam film that saw release in 1978, *The Deer Hunter*. He settled instead on the Philippines after Golden Harvest convinced him that it was easier to do business there than in Thailand. At the same time, Francis Ford Coppola (1939–) was already in the country laboring on *Apocalypse Now*. Furie visited Coppola on his set (Kremer 2015, 240–241).

Unlike the headache-inducing budget overruns and the sprawling storyline that threatened to sink Coppola's project, Furie focused on modest ambitions within a tight budget. And yet he had a fierce determination to show the lives of ordinary servicemen in Vietnam without softening the sense of reality to gain a larger audience. When John Travolta (1954–), a rising star from the success of his television comedy *Welcome Back, Kotter*, offered to play a lead role in *The Boys of Company C*, Furie turned him down. According to Golden Harvest producer Andre Morgan, Travolta wanted the job because "the notion of a Vietnam War movie was fresh and exciting." He recalls Furie rejecting Travolta by telling the actor, "You're sitcom! I cannot have a sitcom going to Vietnam!" (Kremer 2015, 241).

The five actors eventually cast in the roles of the Marine Corps recruits at the heart of Furie's story were little known with only short résumés. They were Stan Shaw (1952–) as Tyrone Washington, Andrew Stevens (1955–) as Billy Ray Pike, James Canning (1946–) as Alvin Foster, Michael Lembeck (1948–) as Vinnie Fazio, and Craig Wasson (1954–) as Dave Bisbee. Conditions during the filming of *The Boys in Company C* were squalid with cast members suffering noxious insects, food poisoning, and rat-infested quarters. "And we had bat attacks every night—we had to wear helmets," Shaw said (Berry 1978).

An ex-marine staff sergeant and drill instructor, R. Lee Ermey (1944–2018), was already in the Philippines as technical adviser for *Apocalypse Now*. During downtime in Coppola's production, Ermey played Sergeant Loyce, one of the drill instructors in *The Boys in Company C*. Breaking with Hollywood production norms, Furie filmed his story in sequence, scene by scene, allowing the actors to grow together as characters. "We did a lot of improvising," Shaw said, noting that the screenplay was reworked as their characterizations developed. "And it was truly an ensemble effort" (Berry 1978).

The actors in *The Boys in Company C* and *Apocalypse Now* spent many off-hours together. When Martin Sheen suffered a heart attack while in his role as Captain Willard, Furie's cast visited him in the hospital. "There was a lot of criss-cross going on," Morgan said. "We were borrowing stuff from their sets, we were helping them out" (Kremer 2015, 245). As in *Apocalypse Now*, the Philippine military loaned helicopters and weaponry used in *The Boys in Company C* and the military often pulled the supplies away for use in actual combat with nearby communist rebels. Unlike Coppola, Furie continued work unfazed by difficulties. "Uniformly, *The Boys in Company C* proved to be the reverse mirror image of *Apocalypse Now*," Furie's biographer commented (Kremer 2015, 246). Furie completed his movie on time and under budget.

After final editing in Los Angeles, Morgan shopped the film to studios for distribution. Paramount Pictures, United Artists, and Universal Studios turned him down, ostensibly because of its rough language. Only Columbia was willing to accept the picture as it was (Kremer 2015, 247). At screenings for veterans, Shaw recalled audiences cheering and talking back to the screen. "It was incredible. They went crazy, because they saw reality on the screen, and because they didn't think that anyone would film the things that actually happened" (Berry 1978).

The film drew positive as well as negative reviews. *New York Times* critic Janet Maslin (1949–) attacked *The Boys in Company C* for its "cute camaraderie," its "stereotypical" depiction of the marines, and the film's "failure to take any stand on Vietnam" (Maslin 1978). However, Roger Ebert (1942–2013) mounted a spirited defense in the *Chicago Sun-Times*, calling the movie "a thrilling entertainment that starts by being funny and ends by being very deeply moving," adding that it "reflects an attitude about Vietnam that wouldn't have been possible in a war movie of the early 1940s" for showing how the insanity of the war came to seem "strangely, almost logical" in its own context (R. Ebert 1978).

The Boys in Company C performed well at the box office early in its theatrical release and later on VHS, but the Academy of Motion Picture Arts and Sciences ignored the film and presented Oscars to the year's other Vietnam movies, *Coming Home* and *The Deer Hunter*. Although it may have served as a template for Stanley Kubrick's Vietnam War film, *Full Metal Jacket* (1987), the Kubrick film's greater technical sophistication, buoyed by his reputation as a director, also helped obscure memories of *The Boys in Company C*.

However, Furie continued to find inspiration and movie contracts in the material he first explored in *The Boys in Company C*. He went on to direct two more Vietnam War movies, *Under Heavy Fire* (a.k.a. *Going Back*) (2001) and *The Veteran* (2006). Both were concerned with veterans returning to the scene of the war. *Under Heavy Fire* had an advantage Furie was denied in the 1970s. He was able to film portions of it in Vietnam.

HISTORICAL BACKGROUND

Prior to the spring of 1965, U.S. air and naval units undertook operations against North Vietnam, and Special Forces (Green Berets) were drawn into fighting against the Vietcong in the guise of advising South Vietnamese irregulars. But when President Lyndon B. Johnson (1908–1973) finally decided to commit combat ground forces to the Vietnam War, the U.S. Marines arrived first. On March 8, 1965, elements of the Third Marine Division, whose honors included defeating the Japanese at Guam and Iwo Jima during World War II, waded ashore at Da Nang. The Pentagon arranged for photographers to meet them at the beach. Pictures were taken of combat-helmeted marines with fixed bayonets advancing through the surf from their landing craft in a scene meant to evoke the amphibious assaults of previous wars. The First Marine Division soon joined the Third.

The U.S. ambassador to South Vietnam, General Maxwell Taylor (1901–1987), opposed the landing. "Once you put that first soldier ashore, you never know how many others are going to follow him," he wrote prophetically. Despite his opposition, General William Westmoreland (1914–2005), who commanded the U.S. military in Vietnam, asked Johnson for marines to guard the vulnerable air base at Da Nang, the launch point for an increasing number of air raids against North Vietnam. Johnson agreed, worried that "the security provided by the Vietnamese [is] not enough." However, Johnson was aware of the danger of escalating the war by sending the Marine Corps. "I guess we've got no choice, but it scares the hell out of me," he said (Ward 2017, 115–116).

The marines soon realized that protecting Da Nang involved missions beyond the perimeter of the air base. "You've got to spread out because the enemy's going to mortar it, they're going to shoot rockets," recalled United Press International correspondent Joseph Lee Galloway (1941–), assigned to cover the marines. "So you've got to reach out fifteen or twenty miles. And once you're doing that you're no longer guarding an air base, you're operating in hostile territory" (Ward 2017, 124).

During their first year in South Vietnam, the marines increased in number and were largely confined to fighting Vietcong guerillas in the country's central provinces. During a series of engagements called Operation Deckhouse (1966–1967), the marines deployed in their traditional role as amphibious assault troops in actions directed against Vietcong strongholds in the Mekong Delta. They conducted similar landings in the coastal province of Binh Dinh (Nolan 1991, 1, 6). In many early operations, they encountered only scattered resistance from the enemy. "It wasn't so much the Viet Cong that were intimidating at that point as it was the terrain," recalled marine Philip Caputo. "It was terribly hot. There were snakes and bugs all over the place" (Ward 2017, 124).

The marines were forced to adjust to an increasingly stubborn guerilla war where the enemy could be anyone and everywhere. They referred to their patrols as "humping" and called the jungle "Indian country" after the Hollywood Westerns they grew up with (Nolan 1991, 12). "They told us if you receive one round from the village, you level it," recalled rifleman Reginald "Malik" Edwards (1946–). "See, we didn't go into the village and look. We would just shoot first. You fired and go in. So in case there was somebody there, you want to kill them first" (Terry 1984, 3–4). The Marine Corps' tradition of never leaving behind dead or wounded comrades resulted in greater casualties.

Starting on July 15, 1966, elements of the First and Third Marine divisions were sent north toward the demilitarized zone (DMZ), a five-kilometer-wide band stretching across the border of North and South Vietnam established by the Geneva Conference of 1954 to separate the hostile halves of newly independent Vietnam. The July mission, Operation Hastings, stopped a North Vietnamese army division from crossing into South Vietnam. Thus began a series of missions whose names evoked the American Revolution and the Indian Wars: Operation Prairie, Operation Beacon Hill, Operation Hickory, Operation Cimarron, and Operation Buffalo—all of them intended to thwart North Vietnamese infiltration into South Vietnam.

The marines became bogged down in American defensive positions along the DMZ, dubbed "McNamara's Wall" or the "McNamara Line" after Defense Secretary Robert McNamara (1916–2009). A six-mile strip of farmland running westward from the South China Sea was bulldozed and at least 15,000 Vietnamese villagers were driven out to create a "free fire zone" where any intruder was deemed the enemy and could be shot. The McNamara Line was strung with barbed wire and planted with minefields and sonic and seismic sensors designed to betray enemy troop movements at night. It was studded with strongpoints. Manning the McNamara Line was considered dangerous duty; the marines insisted that DMZ stood for Dead Marine Zone. A North Vietnamese veteran, Le Van Cho, recalled that the McNamara Line "was nothing to us. Every night, we would go across it" (Nolan 1991, 6). The confrontations were continual and deadly for both sides. Between March 1967 through February 1969, 1,419 marines and navy corpsmen died within a four-mile rectangle around the town of Con Thien dubbed "Leatherneck Square" by the marines.

At the west end of the DMZ, surrounded by jungled mountains and valleys whose terrain could not be leveled, the marines established a base at Khe Sanh, a strategically important juncture of the Vietnamese and Laotian borders, near North Vietnamese supply routes into the South. Dense foliage and swirling mountain fog that rendered air support difficult left the base especially vulnerable to attack. At Khe Sanh and all along the DMZ, the marines were put into an uncomfortable defensive posture that left the initiative to the North Vietnamese. As General John H. Cushman complained, "Digging [in] is not the Marine way" (Herr 1978, 105).

Given the "political shackles" that prevented him from invading North Vietnam and fighting the enemy on their home ground, Westmoreland positioned the marines at the DMZ hoping to draw the North Vietnamese army into the open and grind them "into bone dust with overwhelming U.S. fire power." He overestimated the ability of South Vietnam's forces to maintain security in the rear and "underestimated the punishment" the North Vietnamese could absorb (Nolan 1991, 16).

Khe Sanh came to remind observers of Dien Bien Phu, the doomed French base in a similarly remote corner of Vietnam whose fall in 1954 spelled victory for the communists at the end of the First Indochina War (1946–1954). Unlike the well-designed Green Beret advance bases, Khe Sanh included haphazard dugouts and hovels with inadequate overhead cover. As war correspondent Michael Herr (1940–2016) wrote, "The defenses were a scandal, and everywhere you could smell that sour reek of obsolescence that followed the Marines all over Vietnam" (Herr 1978, 106). Marine veteran and military historian Keith William Nolan (1964–2009) was forced to agree with the general thrust of Herr's remark. Nolan described "undermanned, underequipped, undersupplied, undertested, and undertrained Marine companies" confronted by "numerically superior North Vietnamese regulars in nose-to-nose fights." He added that Marine Corps leadership "was not as inspired" as in World War II or Korea, "nor did the units on the DMZ (having no rear to pull back to for group training and refurbishment) operate with the same cohesion as their counterparts on Iwo Jima or in the Chosin Reservoir." However, Nolan stressed that "on a man-to-man, platoon-to-platoon level, those Vietnam Marines performed with a bravery and endurance that would have made their forebears proud" (Nolan 1991, ix).

Lance Corporal J. Larry Stuckey was not alone in his complaints about the tactics he was forced to execute. "Our company movements in the field were very routine, noisy, and much too predictable," he recalled. "My fireteam set up many ambushes trying to hit the NVA [North Vietnamese Army]. Not once did we ever ambush an NVA unit" (Nolan 1991, 13). Weaponry was also a problem. By the time they arrived at the DMZ, the marines' reliable M14 automatic rifle was replaced by the M16, lighter in weight but shorter in range and whose early models were plagued by jamming while in combat. Some marines cleaned the M16 as many as five times a day hoping it would fire when the enemy attacked.

Along with the durable AK-47 assault rifle, the North Vietnamese were armed with an array of Soviet-made artillery pieces plus the less destructive but highly mobile Katyusha rocket launchers. North Vietnam's army operated with great sophistication, often firing their guns in late afternoon when muzzle flashes were difficult to detect and moving artillery between well-constructed emplacements. They built phony gun sites and set off charges to simulate muzzle flashes to further confuse American forces and draw fire. Antiaircraft batteries and Soviet surface-to-air missiles protected their emplacements.

The fight for Khe Sanh, which became the most publicized of the battles along the DMZ, began in 1967 when marines repelled North Vietnamese attempts to seize summits overlooking the base. Undeterred by early losses, the North Vietnamese persisted, building roads under the jungle canopy and massing as many as 40,000 troops in the hills and valleys near Khe Sanh, held by only 6,000 marines and a few hundred South Vietnamese rangers.

On January 21, 1968, the North Vietnamese launched a determined assault, destroying Khe Sanh's munitions dump and rendering the landing strip impassable. The siege of Khe Sanh lasted for 77 days. Associated Press correspondent John T. Wheeler was with the marines at the besieged base and filed vivid reports as 1,500 rounds of rockets, artillery, and mortar shells rained down on U.S. positions each day. "Inside the bunkers the Marines hugged their legs and bowed their heads, unconsciously trying to make themselves as small as possible" as explosions "sent thousands of pounds of shrapnel tearing into sandbags and battering already damaged messhalls (sic) and tent areas long ago destroyed and abandoned for a life of fear and filth underground." Wheeler saw signs of "the beginning of combat fatigue" in the eyes of the troops, the "1,000 yard stare" as he described it. Yet, the marines remained at battle stations, "frightened but uncowed" (Wheeler 1998, 576–577).

Worried about loss of morale should the base fall, Westmoreland recommended the use of atomic and chemical weapons to clear the jungle of enemy troops. Johnson refused to authorize such drastic tactics. The siege finally broke after B-52s dropped 110,000 tons of bombs on suspected North Vietnamese positions (Ward 2017, 256–264).

As Khe Sanh held on, the marines were engaged throughout South Vietnam during the Tet Offensive (January–February 1968) and spearheaded the assault that retook Vietnam's former imperial capital of Hue. The marines continued to operate in tandem with U.S. Army and South Vietnamese units in difficult fighting.

In the early months of 1969, the marines' combat role continued with units taking the lead in the war's largest amphibious assault, Operation Bold Mariner, on the Bantangan Peninsula, and Operation Dewey Canyon, an offensive against North Vietnamese supply lines in Laos. But the marines' role in the war began winding down. Between July and November 1969, President Richard M. Nixon (1913–1994) withdrew the Third Marine Division as part of his program of Vietnamization, which gradually turned over combat responsibility to South Vietnamese forces. From October 1970 through May 1971, the First Marine Division followed them out of Vietnam. The Vietnam War proved to be the costliest conflict in the history of the Marine Corps. In their six years of combat in Vietnam, the Marines suffered 103,324 casualties, 14,691 of them fatal. This compares with 86,940 marines killed or wounded in World War II and 30,544 in Korea. Altogether 450,000 marines served in Vietnam.

DEPICTION AND CULTURAL CONTEXT

The Marine Corps has always been composed almost entirely of volunteers. Marine veterans have declared the draft as "anathema to the U.S. Marine Corps and its history, traditions, mindset and culture." However, during World War II, the Korean War, and the Vietnam War, the corps accepted conscripts drafted by the army. Those "recruitment referrals" were sometimes punitive, as is the case with the draft dodger, Dave, brought to San Diego's Camp Pendleton, one of the corps' two recruit depots (training centers), in the opening scene of *The Boys in Company C.*

Although Dave is alone among the movie's central characters for questioning the war, no one in his squad appeared to be motivated by the gung-ho spirit that led many young men to enlist in the U.S. Marines during the first years of the corps' deployment in the Vietnam War. Not everyone joined out of a desire to see action. For some it seemed the best option among limited choices. "My parents were split up and I was sort of just going on my own," recalled James Stanton, who joined the Marine Corps in 1967, the year in which *The Boys in Company C* begins. "I ran out of places to live, so I joined the service. The only people that would take me was the Marine Corps because I never had a high school education" (J. R. Ebert 1993, 8).

Some young men considered highly eligible for conscription decided to volunteer for the Marine Corps before being drafted. Perhaps Tyrone's motivations were similar to those of real-life marine Vince Olson, who joined the corps ahead of the draft because marines were "just a little tougher, and I thought I could do a little better and better myself" (J. R. Ebert 1993, 13).

The movie's early sequences represented well the Marine Corps' reputation for brutal basic training. The drill instructors hurl verbal and physical abuse at the recruits, intending to break their individuality and remold them into a unit that will obey orders and react quickly when under fire. "Are you a bunch of old ladies? I still can't hear you!" shouts Sergeant Aquilla, played by Santos Morales (1942–2012). His objective is to train the men to snap to attention and obey without question the commands they are given. He is not the company's only drill instructor and works in tandem with Sergeant Loyce, who calls the recruits "civilian scum." Their heads shaven to underscore the demand for uniformity, those recruits who make it through basic training will have to shed many habits of their former life in favor of the esprit de corps summed up in the Marine Corps' motto, *Semper Fidelis,* Latin for "Always Faithful."

Reports confirming the depiction of drill camp at Camp Pendleton are numerous. Rifleman Edwards described "these guys with these Smoky the Bear hats and big hands on their hips" confronting the arrivals. "And everybody starts cursing and yelling and screaming at you." His first instinct was to laugh. "But then they get right up in your face. That's when I started getting scared" (Terry 1984, 5). According to marine recruit Gwynne Dyer, basic training had less to do with learning skills than changing people "so that they can do things they wouldn't have dreamt of otherwise. It works by applying enormous physical and mental pressure to men who have been isolated from their normal civilian environment" (J. R. Ebert 1993, 26). Physical abuse was carefully calibrated by most drill instructors. "I was hit once the whole time I was there," said Stanton, who did his training at the corps' other recruit depot at South Carolina's Parris Island. "The rest was browbeating—screaming at you constantly from sunup 'til sundown. But after a couple of weeks they started to soften up a little." He concluded: "By then you were starting to listen to what they had to say" (J. R. Ebert 1993, 36).

The details of the training course marine recruits were run through is sketched accurately, including the rifle training, the bayonet drill, hand-to-hand combat practice, and crawling under barbed wire while under live fire. Said Stanton, "They taught you everything they knew about killing a person—whether it was with a rifle or a bayonet, a knife, a piece of rope, anything—they instilled in you that you were going to have to do it" (J. R. Ebert 1993, 36). To further build teamwork and discipline, the recruits were given hard and sometimes arbitrary physical work. In *The Boys in Company C*, the task of loading crates of body bags destined for Vietnam proved prophetic.

In the film, Tyrone Washington represents the experience of African Americans in the Vietnam-era Marine Corps, where attitudes toward minorities underwent a rapid shift. Blacks had not been allowed to join the Marine Corps until 1942, and then only in small segregated units. Despite the 1948 executive order by President Harry S. Truman (1884–1972) that integrated the services, the Marines Corps dragged its boots and did not fully desegregate until 1960 (Morris 1969). Edwards, an African American, joined the corps in 1963, a few years before the opening of *The Boys in Company C*, and found old attitudes in place with blacks and Hispanics receiving especially rough treatment (Terry 1984, 7).

In the movie, Tyrone suffers racial insults early on from bigoted fellow recruits but is supported by Sergeant Loyce, who recognizes and promotes his potential as a squad leader. This adheres to the shift in attitude within Marine Corps leadership, which would have been apparent by 1967. The *New York Times* described military life in Vietnam as "like a speeded up film of recent racial progress at home" (Johnson 1968). As an African American marine, Adolphus Stuart recalled that he endured an occasional bigoted remark, but "once we were in the field, there was not trouble. There was no color." He added, "I put my life on the line many times trying to stop a white fool from doing something" (Stuart, 1985, 138).

Company C's arrival in South Vietnam mirrors the experience of many marines who sailed in on troop ships. It was not the entry to the war they had expected. As Edwards recalled, he anticipated that his company would land on the beach, as in World War II movies or the photographs taken of the first Marines at Da Nang. He was disappointed when "we pulled into this area like a harbor almost and just walked off the ship" at a pier crowded with children asking for cigarettes (Terry 1984, 8).

Unlike the obviously North American backdrop for *The Green Berets*, the rice paddy terrain of *The Boys in Company C* was a convincing stand-in for Vietnam, and the Vietnamese scenes depict a number of realistic and commonplace situations encountered by marines. The ever-present danger of stepping on mines or booby traps was dramatically represented when Tyrone realizes he has set his foot lightly on a mine and needs help to extricate himself. His position in the formation of the marine patrol is accurately described as "on point," Marine Corps jargon for the man in the lead. While the soldier on point was liable to be first into a minefield, the Vietcong seldom shot at him. "You learned that the point usually survived. It was the people behind you who got killed," Edwards recalled (Terry 1984, 9).

The movie also portrays the danger of being killed or maimed by U.S. military actions. Tyrone is angered when shelling by American gunners falls on U.S. troops and by the glib response of his incompetent commanding officer, Captain Collins, played by Canadian actor Scott Hylands (1943–). "The colonel knows what he's doing," Collins insisted, despite evidence to the contrary. Stuart recounted similar incidents from his tour of Vietnam. "We lost our fair share of people from 'short rounds'—friendly fire," he recalled. "A guy calls artillery on the wrong place and we get hit while the enemy is getting away" (Stuart 1985, 136). The situation seen in *The Boys in Company C* recalled Herr's remarks on "patrols that came back either contactless [with enemy forces] or chewed over by ambushes and quick, deft mortar-rocket attacks, some from other Marine units" (Herr 1978, 47–48).

The character of Captain Collins embodies the failure of those officers with a weak grasp of the tactical situation but a strong desire to please their superiors at any cost. The movie's characteristic scene involves a punishing ambush of the company as it escorts a convoy deemed essential to the war effort. They lose two dead to protect a load of whiskey, cigarettes, frozen steaks, televisions, and rattan furniture destined for the general's headquarters. Collins, like most every officer in Vietnam from General Westmoreland down to the company level, was obsessed with "body count," the preferably real but often fabricated tabulation of enemy casualties whose sums were displayed as evidence that the Vietcong and North Vietnamese army were collapsing under the weight of American firepower. The evidence was often elusive. Communist troops, not unlike the marines, usually carried the bodies of their fallen comrades from the battlefield. After a firefight he had witnessed, a correspondent reported "only two bodies were left behind, but the [U.S.] artillery men were confident many, many more had died. No one knew how many" (Just 1968, 166). Edwards recalled killing a guerilla who charged at him and being forced to drag the body back to camp. "We had a real kill. We had one we could prove. We didn't have to make this one up" (Terry 1984, 11).

The movie shows the results of troops deranged by combat fatigue and drugs through the destruction of the general's prefabricated residence by a bomb blast. Herr reported a comparable incident, a marine who "opened the door of a latrine and was killed by a grenade that had been rigged on the door. The Command tried to blame it on a North Vietnamese infiltrator," he continued, "but the grunts knew what had happened . . . Some guy just flipped out is all" (Herr 1978, 58).

Drug use was common, especially marijuana, but according to Herr, marines in combat situations usually kept their joints for rest and recreation. They "didn't want to be stoned" when the inevitable attack came (Herr 1978, 88). A more serious problem resulted from drug trafficking orchestrated by GIs in Southeast Asia, their connections back home, and corrupt South Vietnamese authorities. In *The Boys in Company C*, Tyrone sets out to organize a drug smuggling ring but turns his back on the fortune he could have made. He becomes disgusted with the South Vietnamese police he would have collaborated with after they summarily execute a villager with whom the marines had just played baseball. Tyrone's change of heart is necessary in the storyline for sustaining his status as the movie's main hero. Assertions for the "Vietnamese connection" were spelled out in an Associated Press report, published in the December 17, 1972, *New York Times* under the headline "Drug Feared Sent in Bodies of G.I.'s." The article described a conspiracy dating back eight years to smuggle heroin into the United States by hiding it within bodies of soldiers killed in action, according to testimony by military officers and customs agents in federal court.

If *The Boys in Company C* falls short of reality, it is in underestimating the psychological toll of the war on many marines. According to Herr, the eyes of the marines at Khe Sanh were "always either strained or blazed-out or simply blank, they had nothing to do with what the rest of the face was doing, and it gave every one the look of extreme fatigue or even a glancing madness" (Herr 1978, 87).

The climactic scene of *The Boys in Company C* concerns a soccer game between the marines and a South Vietnamese team. The marines are promised a safe posting far from "the meat grinder" of Khe Sanh if they lose the game. But the marines have been drilled to never lose and are disgusted by the conduct of the war. As they trounce the Vietnamese players, the soccer stadium falls under enemy attack. Alvin, recording the adventures of his comrades for the book he will never write, is killed in the barrage along with the feckless Captain Collins.

CONCLUSION

At the conclusion of *The Boys in Company C*, an epilogue details the unit's fate. According to it, of the company's original 110 members, 43 were killed in action, 51 were wounded, and two are listed as missing in action. The epilogue also states the fate of the surviving protagonists and represents a cross-section of real-life outcomes for many marines. Billy Ray deserted and escaped to Canada, which would have been a difficult trek to make from Vietnam. However, as many as 420,000 Vietnam-era desertions from the U.S. military have been reported. Many deserters were quickly apprehended, but "some were able to change their names and keep a low profile to avoid detection in the U.S., while still others disappeared into the black market economy of Southeast Asia" (Giraldi 2014). Tyrone received the Navy Cross, one of the highest honors for a marine, before perishing in battle, and Vinnie, seriously wounded, is confined for life to a Veterans Administration hospital.

Although the Company C of the movie was fictional, the numbers reflect the reality of combat in Vietnam. The 26th Marine Regiment suffered a casualty rate of 40 percent in just one day of battle; it was common for Marine Corps companies to lose at least 75 percent of their original members in casualties (Herr 1978, 86). However, they fought well despite all the losses. As marine veteran Thomas Lindenmeyer explained, "Every man knew what he had to do, and every man knew that he had to do that thing for the group, and if he didn't, everybody in the group was in jeopardy. And every man owed every other man in the group the loyalty of doing his job and doing it the best he could. And that crossed all lines. It crossed wealth, it crossed education, it crossed race" (Nolan 1991, 10).

FURTHER READING

Berry, Jeff. "Two of the 'Boys in (and out of) Company C.'" *UCLA Daily Bruin*, May 19, 1978.

Ebert, James R. 1993. *A Life in a Year: The American Infantryman in Vietnam, 1965–1972*. Novato, CA: Presidio Press.

Ebert, Roger. "The Boys in Company C." *Chicago Sun-Times*, February 24, 1978.

Giraldi, Philip. "Deserters, Traitors and Resisters: A Long Tradition of Those Who Walked Away from War." *Huffington Post*, September 2, 2014.

Herr, Michael. 1978. *Dispatches*. New York: Alfred A. Knopf.

Johnson, Thomas A. "The U.S. Negro in Vietnam." *New York Times*, April 29, 1968.

Just, Ward S. 1968. *To What End: Report from Vietnam*. Boston: Houghton Mifflin.

Kremer, Daniel. 2015. *Sidney J. Furie: Life and Films*. Lexington, KY: University Press of Kentucky.

Maslin, Janet. "The Boys in Company C." *New York Times*, February 2, 1978.

Morris, Steven. "How Blacks Upset the Marine Corps: 'New Breed' Leathernecks are Tackling Racist Vestiges." *Ebony*, December 1969.

Nolan, Keith William. 1991. *Operation Buffalo: USMC Fight for the DMZ*. Novato, California: Presidio Press.

Stuart, Adolphus. 1985. "Leatherneck Square." In *To Bear Any Burden: The Vietnam War and Its Aftermath in the Words of Americans and Southeast Asians*, edited by Al Santoli. New York: E. P. Dutton.

Terry, Wallace. 1984. *Bloods: An Oral History of the Vietnam War by Black Veterans*. New York: Random House.

Ward, Geoffrey C., and Ken Burns. 2017. *The Vietnam War: An Intimate History*. New York: Alfred A. Knopf.

Wheeler, John T. 1998. "Life in the V Ring: Khe Sanh under Siege." In *Reporting Vietnam Part One: American Journalism 1959–1969*. New York: Library of America.

Chapter 4

The Deer Hunter (1978)

The Deer Hunter screened briefly in New York and Los Angeles in December 1978 to meet the deadline for consideration in the 1979 Academy Awards and opened in several cities across the United States in February 1979. Following its success on Oscar night, it opened more widely. Director Michael Cimino (1939–2016) had previously directed only a single film, but Universal Studios gambled on him because the artistic community considered him part of the rising generation of filmmakers whose ranks included Francis Ford Coppola and Martin Scorsese. Freely inventing his own life story, Cimino implied he had been in Vietnam "attached to a Green Beret medical unit" (Deeley 2009, 197), when in reality, he enlisted in the Army Reserves in 1962 and received one month of medical training at Fort Sam Houston, Texas (Bach 1985, 170).

Unhappy with the film's length, Universal trimmed *The Deer Hunter* from three and a half hours to three hours and four minutes and released it in the hope of recovering expenses despite the dissatisfaction of studio executives. Although completed over budget and behind schedule, *The Deer Hunter* grossed $48.9 million in the United States and earned favorable reviews from many critics. *The Deer Hunter*'s profitability was considered remarkable, given that a film of its length inevitably enjoys fewer screenings per day at cinemas than a standard two-hour movie.

The Deer Hunter originated in a screenplay by Hollywood veterans Louis Garfinkle (1928–2005) and Quinn K. Redeker (1936–). *The Man Who Came to Play* concerned the ultimate high-stakes gamble, Russian roulette, and showed a dark and illicit side of Las Vegas gambling. The original protagonist was a Vietnam veteran damaged psychologically by his wartime experience. British producer Michael Deeley (1932–) and his company, EMI

SELECTIVE SERVICE

The Selective Service System administering the draft classified potential inductees in 18 categories headed by I-A ("Available for military service") and ending with V-A ("Registrant over the age of liability for military service"). Certain civilian and public service occupations were exempted from service. Despite changing definitions of eligibility, many college students were II-S ("Registrant deferred because of activity in study").

There were no less than three conscientious objector categories determining which tasks were suitable to a draftee depending on the nature of his beliefs. The definition of conscientious objector was argued in the federal courts. According to the 1965 U.S. Supreme Court decision in *United States v. Seeger* (380 U.S. 163), "a sincere and meaningful belief" could constitute conscientious objection, yet local draft boards continued to allow or disallow claims. Only 50,000 men were classified as conscientious objectors during the Vietnam War.

A far larger number of men, estimated at 3.5 million, were exempted from service under the classification IV-F ("Registrant not qualified for any military service"). The system favored affluent draftees with access to private physicians or psychiatrists willing to write them a note claiming a medical exemption. Most of those "doctor's notes" went unquestioned at understaffed induction centers. Exemptions were granted for flat feet, skin rashes, asthma, trick knees, emotional disturbances, being gay, and even dental braces.

Films, purchased the screenplay and hired Cimino to direct. With Deric Washburn (1937–), Cimino rewrote it extensively, shifting the Russian roulette episodes to Vietnam and casting the protagonists as steelworkers from a small town in Pennsylvania.

The Deer Hunter follows a group of friends from that town who were affected by the Vietnam War. Three of them, Mike, Nick, and Steve, are headed for a tour of duty in Vietnam as the film begins. Steve marries a local woman only days before their departure. The friends find time for a final hunting trip before they leave. While fighting in Vietnam, Mike, Nick, and Steve are captured by the Vietcong, held in harsh captivity, and tortured by being forced to play Russian roulette. They escape their captors, but their lives are forever changed. Mike, the strongest among the trio, engineers their escape and eventually returns home a decorated war hero, yet he is emotionally unsettled. Nick never comes home but deserts the army and stays in Saigon, where he becomes the center of a Russian roulette gambling ring. Mike returns to Saigon to rescue Nick as the city is about to fall to communist forces but is unable to save him. Steve is psychologically damaged from his experience as a POW and prefers the certainty of a Veterans Administration hospital to the challenge of facing life outside.

Concerned over the new screenplay's "gruesome-sounding storyline" coupled with "a barely known director," Deeley sought star power and pursued

Robert De Niro (1943–), who established himself as one of the era's prominent male actors for his role as an emotionally disturbed Vietnam veteran in Martin Scorsese's *Taxi Driver* (1976). De Niro's presence became crucial to financing *The Deer Hunter* and gaining distribution through Universal. As Deeley put it, to "convince our markets around the world that they should buy it before it was finished. I *needed* someone with the caliber of Robert De Niro" (Deeley 2009, 167–168).

De Niro starred as Green Beret Sergeant Mike Vronsky, who served in Vietnam alongside his friends from Pennsylvania, Corporal Nick Chevotarevich, played by Christopher Walken (1943–), and Corporal Steve Pushkov, played by John Savage (1949–). Meryl Streep (1949–) played the primary female character, Linda. De Niro introduced Cimino to Streep, who improvised much of her role at the director's suggestion. The cast also included two friends of the protagonists who stayed home instead of serving in Vietnam, John Cazale (1935–1978) as Stan and George Dzundza (1945–) as John. Cazale was dying of cancer during the production of *The Deer Hunter* and didn't live to see the film's release. De Niro took charge of rehearsals, turning them into a bonding process for the male actors that made them buddies in real life as well as onscreen. Their friendship seemed palpable in the movie (Deeley 2009, 170–171).

Not unlike *Apocalypse Now*, released one year later, *The Deer Hunter* experienced a troubled production. Deeley claimed Cimino "had always intended to ignore his contractual commitment" to keep the film under two and a half hours long (Deeley 2009, 173). Cimino and Washburn had previously collaborated on the screenplay for the science-fiction film *Silent Running* (1972), but they fell into recriminations over who was responsible for *The Deer Hunter*. Denouncing Washburn as "mentally deranged," Cimino claimed to have written the final version himself. Washburn rejected his claims (Biskind 2008). The Writers Guild sided with Washburn, awarding him sole screenwriting credit and forcing Cimino to share a "story by" credit with Washburn, Garfinkle, and Redeker.

The film's production costs before editing rose to a large sum for the 1970s, $13 million, in part from Cimino's decision to shoot the Vietnam scenes in nearby Thailand for sake of an authentic-looking jungle terrain. Vietnam's victorious communist government remained hostile to the United States, and the country was off-limits to Hollywood filmmakers. According to Deeley's coproducer, Barry Spikings, Universal executives Lew Wasserman and Sid Sheinberg were "shocked" by the film and appalled by its length, and they denounced it as "anti-American." Universal's president, Thom Mount, called it a "continuing nightmare," adding, "The movie was endless. It was *The Deer Hunter and the Hunter and the Hunter*" (Biskind 2008).

Cimino quarreled with the editing, which fell to Peter Zinner, and eventually claimed that he trimmed *The Deer Hunter* himself (Griffin 2002). The Academy of Motion Picture Arts and Sciences disagreed, giving Zimmer the Oscar for Best Editing.

Despite fears that the film would fail with audiences over its Vietnam theme, its shocking violence, and its length, favorable reviews generated momentum for *The Deer Hunter*'s popularity. Writing in the *Chicago Sun-Times*, Roger Ebert called it "one of the most emotionally shattering films ever made" and deemed the first of the movie's Russian roulette scenes "one of the most horrifying sequences ever created in fiction" (R. Ebert 1979). His counterpart from the *Chicago Tribune*, Gene Siskel, praised it as "a big film, dealing with big issues, made on a grand scale. Much of it, including some casting decisions, suggest inspiration by 'The Godfather'" (Siskel 1979).

Dissenting from the chorus of approval, the *New Yorker*'s Pauline Kael called *The Deer Hunter* "a small-minded film with greatness in it" and a triumph of technique over substance. "At times, we feel that we're there to be awed rather than to understand." She criticized Cimino for his "xenophobic yellow peril imagination" but conceded that *The Deer Hunter* takes no political position for or against American involvement in the Vietnam War (Kael 1978).

Communist Vietnam's allies in the Soviet Bloc railed against *The Deer Hunter* and stormed out of its screening at the 1979 Berlin Film Festival. Left-leaning Hollywood celebrities Jane Fonda and Warren Beatty condemned the film, but their motivations may have been mixed: Fonda's Vietnam War film, *Coming Home*, and Beatty's *Heaven Can Wait* were in competition with *The Deer Hunter* at the 1979 Academy Awards. On Oscar night, members of Vietnam Veterans Against the War protested *The Deer Hunter* outside the ceremony and clashed with police, accusing the movie of racism (Harmetz 1979).

Despite the uproar, *The Deer Hunter* earned five Academy Awards, including Best Picture, Best Director, Best Actor in a Supporting Role (Walken), Best Film Editing, and Best Sound. It was nominated in four other categories, losing two to *Coming Home*: De Niro was nominated for Best Actor in a Leading Role but lost to *Coming Home*'s Jon Voigt, and Washburn lost Best Screenplay to the writers of *Coming Home*. In addition, Cimino won a Golden Globe for best direction. It would be his last major award. Cimino's career never recovered from the spectacular expense and box-office failure of his next film, *Heaven's Gate* (1980).

Film historian Dave Thomson called *The Deer Hunter* "one of the great American films," a story of tragic male pride and "one of the few American films that work like a novel. It is unsettling, yet it is mysterious" (Thomson 2008, 209). In the decades since its release, *The Deer Hunter* has become one of the few Vietnam War films to be widely acclaimed as a masterpiece, yet its reputation relies on its artistry, not its history.

HISTORICAL BACKGROUND

The 2.5 million enlisted men who served in the Vietnam War were drawn from the largest generation in U.S. history, the 27 million men who came of draft age during the war. However, the troops in Vietnam "represented a distinct and relatively small subset" of the baby boom and were "not representative of the generation as a whole," according to a historian of the war. Eighty percent of the enlisted men were working class or poor, a distinct change from World War II in which virtually the entire nation shouldered arms against the enemy, and "most young men from prosperous families were able to avoid the draft, and very few volunteered" (Appy 1993, 6). A Los Angeles attorney specializing in draft-related cases said at the time, "Any kid with money can absolutely stay out of the Army with 100 percent certainty" (Ward 2017, 160). The ability to attend college provided millions of middle-class youth with a precarious but real and entirely legal possibility of dodging the draft.

From one perspective, ground combat was a role best assigned to men from industrial or farm labor backgrounds, environments where physical danger and "dirty work" were accepted as facts of life. During the Vietnam War years, an average of 14,000 American workers died each year from industrial accidents, a casualty rate equaled in Vietnam in only one year, 1968 (Levison 1975, 77). The supply of men from blue-collar backgrounds was large. Heavy industry powered the U.S. economy through this period; the idea that a college degree was a necessary ticket to employment did not become universal until the early 1980s as deindustrialization took hold.

The possibility of military service loomed in the future for every young man since President Harry S. Truman reinstituted conscription in 1947. Upon turning 18, all men were required to register with the Selective Service. Even at that time, a small minority of Americans objected. On Abraham Lincoln's birthday (February 12) in 1947, nearly 500 men burned their draft cards in protest, but the gesture had no ripple effect. The Cold War had begun, fear of the Soviet Union was pervasive, and the Korean War (1950–1953) was met with private grumbling but little public objection. Sentiment shifted slightly by May 2, 1964, when over 1,000 men assembled outside the United Nations to protest "American imperialism" and chanted "We won't go" to an overseas war. Twelve of them ceremoniously burned their draft cards, a crime under federal law. In 1964, 1.7 million men born in 1946, the year the baby boom began, reached the age of 18 and were subject to the draft. According to Clark Dougan and Samuel Lipsman, "The vast majority of them, of course, never gave it a second thought." Most Americans regarded registering for the draft as a "civic duty." In 1964, the draft claimed 6,000–7,000 each month from youth ineligible for deferments based on college attendance, health status, and other factors. Two-thirds of Selective Service registrants expected to reach the age of 26, the highest year of eligibility for the draft, without being called up (Dougan and Lipsman 1984, 72).

The situation changed in 1965 after Lyndon B. Johnson sent combat troops into action in Vietnam. In May of that year, the Selective Service, through its 4,080 local draft boards, sent induction notices to 15,100 men. By December, that number grew to over 40,000, sparking a growing protest movement. Penalties for violating conscription laws included fines of up to $10,000 and prison sentences of five years. The Federal Bureau of Investigation monitored and photographed antidraft protestors, who were sometimes assaulted by counterdemonstrators (Dougan and Lipsman 1984, 72–75).

The anxiety faced by college students seeking to avoid the draft became one of the legends of the 1960s. Local draft boards possessed some discretion for deciding whether students "were making satisfactory progress to a degree." Most boards were lenient. However, the rules became stricter in 1966 when the Selective Service implemented the College Qualification Test. Under what became known as the "Vietnam exam," undergraduates needed to score at least 70 out of 150 points to remain exempt from the draft. Graduate students needed to score 80. "At that point, things changed," said Timothy K. Wright, a Harvard student at that time, describing the lottery system that determined the likelihood of being inducted into the army. "Everybody had a number and if you had a low number—even if you were in college—you had to show up" (Hatt 2016).

Some inductees purposefully flunked the physical examination at the induction center, which became a popular way to avoid the draft. Stories circulated of inductees exaggerating sports injuries, jabbing pins into their arms to simulate heroin use, raising blood pressure by drinking massive amounts of coffee before the exam, or overeating for months to exceed the weight limit. Despite the successful efforts by millions of college students to avoid the draft, the dark cloud of anxiety never lifted. Many feared that if the war continued on its present course in 1968, deferments would be tightened or abolished altogether (Dougan and Lipsman 1984, 76–77). Some 40,000 Americans fled to Canada to avoid the draft. Most stayed after the war, "making up the largest, best-educated group this country ever received," according to a Canadian government report (Valiante 2015).

The Vietnam War looked considerably different outside university campuses. Illustrating the gap between college and blue-collar youth are comments collected in Boston's working-class Dorchester neighborhood, where teenage friends continued to enlist as late as 1968. "We all ended up going into the service about the same time—the whole crowd," recalled Dan Shaw, who joined the Marine Corps. "In working-class neighborhoods like his, military service after high school was as commonplace among young men as college was for the youth of upper-middle-class suburbs—not welcomed by everyone but rarely questioned or avoided" (Appy 1993, 11–12).

The disparity in casualty rates between working-class neighborhoods and affluent suburbs was striking. Young men from Dorchester were four times more likely to die in Vietnam than their generational peers from wealthy Massachusetts towns. Those statistics were not confined to the East Coast.

In Illinois, youths from neighborhoods with median family incomes of under $5,000 ($36,000 in 2018 dollars) were four times more likely to die than those from districts where median family incomes were over $15,000 ($109,000 in 2018) (Appy 1993, 12).

Because of the high number of men drafted or enlisted, the war's impact landed especially hard on small towns and blue-collar suburbs. Towns with populations of under 1,000, which included only a dozen or so youths of draft age, suffered terrible casualties per capita. In the 1960s, only 2 percent of Americans lived in such towns, yet 8 percent of those who died in Vietnam came from places such as Clayton, Kansas (pop. 127), Alma, West Virginia (pop. 296), and Almond, Wisconsin (pop. 440) (Appy 1993, 14). Mike Clodfelter of Plainville, Kansas, enlisted in the army in 1964 and wrote a memoir of his Vietnam deployment. He recalled that from his hometown, "all but two of a dozen high school buddies would eventually serve in Vietnam and all were of working class families, while I knew of not a single middle class son of the town's businessmen, lawyers, doctors, or ranchers from my high school graduating class who experienced the Armageddon of our generation" (Clodfelter 1976, 109). Similarly, as of 1969, the 400 soldiers from Long Island killed in Vietnam were "overwhelmingly white, working-class men" (Useem 1973, 83).

During the Vietnam War, the U.S. military achieved a higher degree of racial integration than it had ever enjoyed. As a writer for *Ebony* magazine put it in a 1968 article, "The Negro has found in his nation's most totalitarian society—the military—the greatest degree of functional democracy that this nation has granted to black people" (Jefferson 1968). Years later, a historian of the war commented on the irony: "Precisely when the enlisted ranks were becoming increasingly integrated by race, they were becoming ever more segregated by class" (Appy 1993, 22). Given their lower educational attainments, working-class draftees and volunteers, regardless of ethnic heritage, were not usually steered toward officer training or specialized roles but consigned to ground combat. Eighty percent of the men who went to Vietnam possessed a high school education or less (Appy 1993, 25).

The social imbalances within the U.S. Army only increased in 1966 with the implementation of Project 100,000. The scheme, devised by Defense Secretary Robert McNamara, lowered army admission standards by accepting men who would have failed the qualifying examinations previously in place. Billing it as a program to assist the nation's "subterranean poor," McNamara claimed it was an opportunity for that segment of the population "to return to civilian life with skills and aptitudes which for them and their families will reduce the downward spiral of decay" (Helmer 1974, 9). While conceived as part of Johnson's Great Society as well as a way of increasing manpower for the war, the result was "to send many poor, terribly confused, and woefully uneducated boys to risk death in Vietnam" (Appy 1993, 32). The army did not want those draftees and derided them as "McNamara's Morons." An infantryman recalled that there were "kids in our platoon that should have been in special ed," lacking even the ability to read (Ward 2017, 164).

Throughout the war, uncertainty hung over the process of who might or might not be called by the draft. Congress and the Department of Defense continually tinkered with Selective Service regulations. Before 1967, married men were exempt from the draft, and in 1965–1966, the marriage rate rose 10 percent among 20- and 21-year-old men. By 1967, a married man had to have at least one child to be exempt, resulting in many births (Ward 2017, 160). Also in 1967, the government ended deferments for students in graduate school, although those already enrolled were usually allowed to continue working toward their degree. As a result, the proportion of college graduates serving in Vietnam rose from 6 percent in 1966 to 10 percent in 1970 (Appy 1993, 36).

The Pentagon requested the mobilization of Army Reserves and the National Guard for duty in Vietnam, but Johnson hesitated for fear of turning the families and friends of those middle-class weekend soldiers against the war. Only 15,000 were sent to the conflict. Joining the Army Reserves or the National Guard became an acceptable and relatively safe way of fulfilling the obligation for military service. In many states, an "old boy" network of "socially and economically prominent" citizens aided the ability to join the National Guard. African Americans were almost invisible in the National Guard (Baskir 1978, 48–52). Many men unable to enlist in the Army Reserves or the National Guard joined one of "the safer services—the Coast Guard, Navy, and Air Force" (Ward 2017, 160).

As the fighting in Vietnam continued, support for the war fell among the working class while opposition to the antiwar movement grew more strident. On May 8, 1970, hundreds of construction workers wearing yellow hard hats and carrying American flags broke up an antiwar rally in Manhattan. The workers then marched to City Hall and forced authorities to raise the flag that had been lowered to half-staff in honor of the students killed four days earlier during a protest at Kent State University by National Guardsmen.

At other rallies, the "hard hats," as the media dubbed them, carried signs reading "Support Our Boys in Vietnam." The men doing much of the fighting on the ground often were literally their boys. A firefighter who lost his son in Vietnam remarked that the sons of the elite "don't end up in the swamps over there" but are deferred, "get sent to safe places," or "get out with all those letters they have from their doctors." He went on to criticize the "peace crowd," not because he believed in the cause for which the war was being fought, but because "they don't really love this country." He grew bitter as he spoke of antiwar activists. "My son didn't die so they can look filthy and talk filthy and insult everything we believe in" (Coles 1971, 131–134). Class resentment hardened the generation gap.

DEPICTION AND CULTURAL CONTEXT

Although *The Deer Hunter*'s producer, Michael Deeley, shared the assumption of many viewers that the movie's protagonists were drafted, the idea isn't borne out by the screenplay. Cimino and Washburn left unexplained the reasons behind the departure of Mike, Nick, and Steve. They display no dissatisfaction or apprehension at the prospect of fighting in Vietnam. A factory coworker casually remarks, "Take care of yourselves," as if they were simply taking a long trip. One of their close companions, the tavern owner and gifted musician John, insists, "I'd be going with you guys if it wasn't for my knee, you know it." The casual attitude of some young men about to depart for Vietnam was not entirely unknown at this stage of the war. Army Private Jon Neeley, drafted along with several of his friends, recalled that they were "curious" about Vietnam, "basically pretty patriotic," and "figured this was our duty." He added, "I guess I just accepted it and figured, hey, let's go give it a shot—make the best of it" (J.R. Ebert 1993, 22).

The Deer Hunter opens in 1967, based on the prevalence of one of that year's hit songs, Frankie Valli's "Can't Take My Eyes Off of You," heard on the jukebox of John's bar and performed by the band at Steven and Angela's (Rutanya Alda) wedding reception. Assuming that the protagonists are the age of the actors who played them, Mike and Nick would have been 35 and Steve 29 years old. They were all comfortably past the age of conscription and "too old to have enlisted in Vietnam," according to film historian Dave Thomson, who lists the discrepancy as one reason some critics dismissed the film as unrealistic (Thomson 2008, 209). Given the army's increasing need for manpower, could a desperate recruiting officer have accepted them as volunteers? At least they were healthy enough to pass the physical, unlike John and their ill-looking friend, Stan. Even if it was conceivable that the army would have taken them, men past the early 20s seldom volunteered. Mike, Nick, and Steve were established in their jobs, and Steve was about to be married just days before leaving for boot camp. As historian Christian Appy recounted, volunteers for Vietnam were usually 19 or 20 years old, just out of high school and still footloose (Appy 2015, 134).

However, the actors carry themselves with such youthful bravado that it becomes possible to overlook their ages. Deeley and Cimino were casting for box-office recognition in De Niro's case and gritty believability all around; there was a scarcity of teenage actors in 1978 with sufficient gravitas and recognition to fit the parts as written.

"*The Deer Hunter* is one of the few films about the Vietnam War that even tries to explore the backgrounds of working-class characters" (Appy 1993, 81). Critics unfamiliar with that milieu were often puzzled by the protagonists' acceptance of the war. The *New York Times*'s Vincent Canby found it "terrifying" that not "once does anyone question the war or his participation in it" (Canby 1978). Commentators with a greater understanding of the protagonists and their worldview were less surprised. According to Appy, the generation that went to Vietnam "grew up enchanted by military culture," spending countless hours in yards and fields reenacting their fathers' war and "watching World War II movies on TV into the early morning hours, idealizing aggressive macho stars like John Wayne, and harboring boyhood fantasies of military heroism" (Appy 2015, 124).

Until the hard fighting of the January 1968 Tet Offensive shattered illusions, the mainstream media's coverage of the war reinforced the idea that Vietnam would be a field of glory for American manhood. The editorial illustrated on the cover of *Time* magazine's October 22, 1965, issue, under the banner "The Turning Point in Viet Nam," celebrated the "remarkable turnabout in the war" caused by "wave upon wave of combat-booted Americans—lean, laconic and looking for a fight." Cimino's stated intention was to explore the world of those men in light of the widespread antiwar sentiment after Tet. "During the years of controversy over the war, the people who fought the war . . . were disparaged and isolated by the press," he said. "But they were common people who had an uncommon amount of courage." He added, "My film has nothing to do with whether the war should or should not have been" (Quoted in Kent 1978).

Although actually filmed at eight different cities and towns in the United States, *The Deer Hunter* afforded a big-canvas depiction of Clairton, Pennsylvania, 10 miles south of Pittsburgh. Life in Clairton consumes much of the film's three hours and provides a backdrop more heavily detailed than the inner lives of its characters or the scenes set in Vietnam. Cimino added points of interest by choosing a place typical of the era's smaller factory towns yet unique for its ethnic and religious heritage. The men and women of *The Deer Hunter* descended from Russian immigrants who arrived in steel country by the early 20th century and maintained adherence to Eastern Orthodoxy, a minority Christian faith in the United States. The extensive wedding scene, filmed in Cleveland's Saint Theodosius Orthodox Cathedral, provides a visual and aural pageantry distinct from the practices of most Americans. However, as was usual even with immigrant groups that retained their identity, memories of the homeland inevitably became fused with a fervent embrace of American patriotism.

The wedding reception is held at an American Legion hall filled with Stars and Stripes and hung with a large banner reading: "Serving God and Country Proudly." Amplifying that sentiment, the bandleader lauds Mike, Nick, and Steve for "going to Vietnam to proudly serve their country." But like an omen, an uninvited guest appears at the hall, a Green Beret who sits by himself at the bar and sullenly studies his drink. Mike is excited by the sight of the elite soldier in his distinct uniform, greets him animatedly, and offers to buy him a drink. "What's it like over there?" he asks the Green Beret eagerly, anticipating stories of adventure from Vietnam. Mute as death, the soldier offers no answer.

The reasons for the dour response were readily apparent to the audience that embraced *The Deer Hunter* in the 1970s, but Mike and his friends were oblivious to the implication that Vietnam would be no easy ride.

The confidence shown by the three friends was steeped in the macho exhilaration of football as well as the quieter sport of hunting, which was seen since frontier days as "an antidote to recurring fear: the softening of the American man" (Barcott 2018). When tested in Vietnam, only Mike would benefit from their apprenticeship in manhood on the gridiron and in deer hunting.

The Deer Hunter shifts out of Clairton and plunges directly into a combat zone in Vietnam with a village ablaze in napalm, U.S. helicopters buzzing overhead, and a North Vietnamese soldier hurling a grenade into a shelter where a mother and her child had taken refuge. Mike kills the soldier with a blast from his flamethrower. In the confused fighting that follows, the Vietcong take Mike, Nick, and Steve as prisoners.

Although staged in Thailand, Deeley asserted that the Vietnam scenes were otherwise "shot in real circumstances, with real rats and mosquitoes, as the three principals were tied up in bamboo cages that had been erected along the River Kwai." Thais played the Vietcong. The local man who played the Vietcong commander had "a particular dislike of Americans" and relished the hard blows he administered to his prisoners in the headquarters hut. "The reaction on Chris' face was for real," Deeley recalled. Nick's pain upon being struck was not acting. The production used equipment authentic to the Vietnam War, but because the equipment and personnel came from the Royal Thai Army, Deeley noted, "One day they simply didn't turn up for work" because of problems on the Cambodian border (Deeley 2009, 175–176).

In the Russian roulette scene, the Vietcong torture their captives by forcing them to play a deadly game of chance. It contains *The Deer Hunter*'s most viscerally disturbing images and was the film's most memorable and controversial segment. Russian roulette was apparently unknown in Southeast Asia and no one could locate verifiable reports of the game being played by the Vietnamese. Deeley admitted, "For a while in press meetings, Cimino darkly hinted at evidence of this horrific practice, but in truth we never had a jot of proof," (Deeley 2009, 198). Because some interpreted the scene as depicting the inherent barbarism of the Vietnamese people, ethicist Peter Marin was not alone in accusing Cimino of "a xenophobia and racism as extravagant as anything to be found on the screen since our World War II films about the Japanese" (Marin 1995, 90).

But whether or not the Vietcong actually forced POWs to play Russian roulette, the captivity of Mike, Nick, and Steve reflects the brutality of the Vietnamese communists toward their American prisoners. It was a valid allegory, given the many horrifying stories of Vietcong atrocities told by GIs. In the ground war, the communists took few prisoners and usually killed any

Americans who fell into their hands. Specialist Jack P. Smith of the Seventh Cavalry Regiment recalled hearing North Vietnamese troops in the dark, killing wounded Americans outside the U.S. defensive perimeter. "They'd yell for their buddies and babble awhile, then turn the poor devil over and listen to him while they stuck a barrel in his face and squeezed" (Quoted in Summers 1984). According to Jon Neeley, "It seemed they just wanted to see how far they could go with dismemberment, humiliation, [anything] to make the American look bad" (Quoted in J. R. Ebert 1993, 290). Most U.S. POWs were not enlisted men but officers, pilots, and airmen shot down over North Vietnam. Only around 250 Americans captured on the ground in Southeast Asia by the Vietcong or Laotian communists were kept alive as POWs. They were "hauled long distances between VC hideouts in deteriorating condition" but suffered "fewer episodes of planned, programmatic torture" than the POWs held in North Vietnamese prisons. As shown in the film, Americans held by the Vietcong were kept in bamboo cages. One POW who tried to escape was reportedly beheaded by his captors. A few men did succeed in escaping, but their accounts "could not be fully corroborated and contained inconsistencies that may have stemmed in part from malaria-induced hallucinations" (Rochester 1999, 6–8). An unusual situation was recounted by Dan Pitzer, a Green Beret held captive by the Vietcong from 1963 through 1967. After two African American soldiers were also captured, the Vietcong decided to release them in neutral Cambodia as a gesture of "solidarity" with the civil rights movement in the United States. Since one of the black soldiers was seriously ill, Pitzer, a medic, accompanied them to provide care. Pitzer was greeted in Phnom Penh by antiwar activist Tom Hayden. "We got into some hot and heavy arguments," Pitzer said, adding that Hayden might not have realized that the affair was a propaganda stunt, not a goodwill gesture (Pitzer 1985, 159–163). In *The Deer Hunter*, Mike, alone among his friends, has the presence of mind to execute a daring flight from captivity.

Ironically, given the attention the Russian roulette scene drew to *The Deer Hunter*, Cimino initially wanted to discard it from the original screenplay as written by Garfinkle and Redeker. He soon realized, as Deeley recalled, that he "was not going to be able to do without the motif of Russian roulette, which in its terrible sense of jeopardy seemed not only a tremendous dramatic engine but also a kind of metaphor for a nation's involvement in war" (Deeley 2009, 164, 166). However, Cimino denied that playing roulette symbolized America's suicidal engagement in Vietnam.

Mike returns to Clairton in or shortly after 1972, based on the song heard on the jukebox in a bar, Waylon Jennings's "Good Hearted Woman." He wears a Green Beret and three rows of ribbons on his chest, although his promotion to the Special Forces was unlikely given his background. Steve is also back in the area, but no one will tell Mike where he is. Mike persists and locates him in a Veterans Administration hospital, a spotless and well-run facility in contrast to the brutally realistic depiction of a VA hospital in the film *Coming Home* and at odds with reports from the period of filth and disorder at VA facilities for Vietnam veterans. Some of the accusations made against the understaffed facilities were shocking, including the account by a quadriplegic veteran who was manhandled by aids, a veteran allowed to lie "in my own human waste" for hours before a nurse emptied his urine bag and, without washing her hands, thrust a thermometer into the patient's mouth. When he complained, she replied, "What difference does it make? It's *your* urine" (Nicosia 2001, 333). The bingo game conducted by volunteers from Shriners International (a nonprofit organization) is the most realistic detail. "I'm going to stay here. It's great. It's like a resort," Steve tells Mike. Something inside Steve had snapped, and he never recovered from his harrowing experience as a prisoner of the Vietcong.

The Deer Hunter descends into melodrama when Mike arrives in Saigon in search of Nick as the city is about to fall to communist forces. Panic and confusion are in the streets as Vietnamese loyal to South Vietnam's disintegrating government or with ties to U.S. forces desperately try to find a way out. The staged scenes in Thailand are interspersed with television footage taken during the American evacuation of Saigon in April 1975.

Reality is strained during Mike's pursuit and discovery of Nick, who by then had long ago given up on life. An American civilian arriving in Saigon in the last days before it fell would not have been a welcome sight, even if he had managed to find a flight to Tan Son Nhut before the airport was closed due to North Vietnamese shelling. The U.S. embassy was focused on evacuating not only every American in South Vietnam but also hundreds of unmarried Vietnamese women whose children had been fathered by GIs and thousands of other refugees with some connection to the United States who besieged the compound. Ken Moorefield, special assistant to the ambassador, recalled that he "saw many people in shock" at the embassy, where only a few Foreign Service officers "took the initiative to operate and do what could be done." By April 28, 1975, bombs fell near the building where embassy staff tried to sort through the claims of civilians seeking evacuation. "The lights fell out, crashed on our desk. The Vietnamese were yelling and screaming. And the American officers just kept working" (Moorefield 1985, 232–234). In the end, even fixed-wing military planes were unable to take off and land in Saigon. Helicopters from U.S. Navy ships carried out the embassy evacuation, Operation Frequent Wind.

More effective and truer to life are scenes in Clairton as Mike tries, emotionally and psychologically, to come home after the things he experienced in Vietnam. He is even uncertain over whether to attend the welcome home arranged by his friends, prepared to greet him with a cake festooned with little American flags and a hearty "Three cheers for the Red, White and Blue!" Mike is suffering from a relatively mild form of what was then termed "post-Vietnam syndrome," a raft of conditions later wrapped under the more general heading of post-traumatic stress disorder. Among those milder symptoms Mike experiences are "guilt feelings for those killed and maimed" and "preoccupation with the fate of friends still overseas." A psychiatrist from the period identified the question asked by many veterans: "How do we turn off the guilt?" (Shatan 1972).

CONCLUSION

The Deer Hunter is less a film about the Vietnam War than a story using the war as an exploration of human character under duress and the tragedy of living after life's illusions have been shattered. "It was about how individuals respond to pressure," Deeley wrote, "different men reacting quite differently, steel workers in extraordinary circumstances" (Deeley 2009, 198). It was also "a film predominantly about fate and the ineluctability of desire," a point driven home by the reckless chances taken on the road by the guys before leaving Clairton (Bliss 1985, 169). The game of pursuit they played with a semitrailer is no less dangerous than Russian roulette. Their car, a late 1950s model with tail fins, embodied the boundless optimism of American industry in the decade before Vietnam, the 1950s. Many objects and moments shown in *The Deer Hunter* are similarly invested with meaning. The opening scene in Clairton showing the friends working with molten steel at the plant is visually linked to the fiery napalm in the opening scene in Vietnam.

Cimino described *The Deer Hunter*'s characters as exemplifying "a working class who are viewed as both the war's heroes and its victims" and hoped the film had helped "the late 1970s audience to feel somewhat relieved of its uneasiness and distress over the war" (Quart 1990, 167).

In the film's moving and emotionally ambiguous conclusion, Mike, John, Stan, and Linda gather at the bar and sing "God Bless America" in voices too sad to be celebratory. None of the characters know what they should feel. Marin could have been describing the scene when he wrote: "What paralyzed us was not simply the guilt we felt about Vietnam, but our inability to confront and comprehend that guilt: our refusal to face squarely what had happened and why" (Marin 1995, 86).

FURTHER READING

Appy, Christian G. 1993. *Working-Class War: American Combat Soldiers and Vietnam*. Chapel Hill, NC: University of North Carolina Press.

Appy, Christian G. 2015. *American Reckoning: The Vietnam War and Our National Identity*. New York: Viking.

Bach, Steven. 1985. *Final Cut: Art, Money, and Ego in the Making of Heaven's Gate, the Film That Sank United Artists*. New York: Newmarket Press.

Barcott, Bruce. "Wily Bucks and Ferocious Bears: A History of American Hunting, From Blue-Collar Pastime to Macho Sport." *New York Times*, June 24, 2018.

Baskir, Lawrence M., and William A. Strauss. 1978. *Chance and Circumstance: The Draft, the War, and the Vietnam Generation*. New York: Alfred A. Knopf.

Biskind, Peter. "The Vietnam Oscars." *Vanity Fair*, March 2008.

Bliss, Michael. 1985. *Martin Scorsese and Michael Cimino*. Metuchen, NJ: Scarecrow Press.

Canby, Vincent. "The Deer Hunter." *New York Times*, December 15, 1978.

Clodfelter, Michael. 1976. *Pawns of Dishonor*. Boston: Branden Press.

Coles, Robert. 1971. *The Middle Americans*. Boston: Little, Brown and Co.

Cook, Fred J. "Hard-Hats: The Rampaging Patriots." *The Nation*, June 15, 1970.

Deeley, Michael, with Matthew Field. 2009. *Blade Runners, Deer Hunters and Blowing the Bloody Doors Off: My Life in Cult Movies*. New York: Pegasus Books.

Dougan, Clark, and Samuel Lipsman. 1984. *A Nation Divided: The Vietnam Experience*. Boston: Boston Publishing Company.

Ebert, James R. 1993. *A Life in a Year: The American Infantryman in Vietnam, 1965–1972*. Novato, CA: Presidio Press.

Ebert, Roger. "The Deer Hunter." *Chicago Sun-Times*, March 9, 1979.

Griffin, Nancy. "Last Typhoon Cimino Is Back." *New York Observer*, February 10, 2002.

Harmetz, Aljean. "Oscar-Winning 'Deer Hunter' Is Under Attack as a 'Racist' Film." *New York Times*, April 26, 1979.

Hatt, Laura E. "LBJ Wants Your GPA: The Vietnam Exam." *Harvard Crimson*, May 23, 2016.

Helmer, John. 1974. *Bringing the War Home: The American Soldier in Vietnam and After*. New York: Free Press.

Jefferson, Thomas A. "Negroes in the Nam." *Ebony*, August 1968.

Kael, Pauline. "The Deer Hunter: The God-Bless-America Symphony." *New Yorker*, December 18, 1978.

Kent, Lucia. "Ready for Vietnam? A Talk with Michael Cimino." *New York Times*, December 10, 1978.

Levison, Andrew. 1975. *Working-Class Majority*. New York: Penguin Books.

Marin, Peter. 1995. *Freedom & Its Discontents: Reflections on Four Decades of American Moral Experience*. South Royalton, VT: Steerforth Press.

Moorefield, Ken. 1985. "The Fall of Saigon." In *To Bear Any Burden: The Vietnam War and Its Aftermath in the Words of Americans and Southeast Asians*, edited by Al Santoli. New York: E. P. Dutton.

Nicosia, Gerald. 2001. *Home to War: A History of the Vietnam Veterans Movement*. New York: Crown Publishers.

Pitzer, Dan. 1985. "The Release." In *To Bear Any Burden: The Vietnam War and Its Aftermath in the Words of Americans and Southeast Asians*, edited by Al Santoli. New York: E. P. Dutton.

Quart, Leonard. 1990. "*The Deer Hunter*: The Superman in Vietnam." In *From Hanoi to Hollywood: The Vietnam War in American Film*, edited by Linda Dittmar and Gene Michaud. New Brunswick, NJ: Rutgers University Press.

Rochester, Stuart. 1999. *Honor Bound: American Prisoners of War in Southeast Asia, 1961–1973*. Annapolis, MD: Naval Institute Press.

Shatan, Chaim F. "Post-Vietnam Syndrome." *New York Times*, May 6 1972.

Siskel, Gene. "The Deer Hunter." *Chicago Tribune*, March 9, 1979.

Summers, Harry G., Jr. "The Battle of the Ia Drang Valley." *American Heritage*, February–March 1984.

Thomson, Dave. 2008. *"Have You Seen . . .?": A Personal Introduction to 1,000 Films*. New York: Alfred A. Knopf.

Useem, Michael. 1973. *Conscription, Protest, and Social Conflict*. New York: Wiley.

Valiante, Giuseppe. "U.S. Vietnam War Draft Dodgers Left their Mark on Canada." *Canadian Press*, April 16, 2015.

Vallely, Jean. "Michael Cimino's Battle to Make a Great Movie." *Esquire*, January 9, 1979.

Ward, Geoffrey C., and Ken Burns. 2017. *The Vietnam War: An Intimate History*. New York: Alfred A. Knopf.

Chapter 5

Apocalypse Now (1979)

Although the first draft of the screenplay for *Apocalypse Now* was completed in 1969, in the midst of the Vietnam War, filming did not begin until 1976. Faced with many obstacles, the movie was not released until 1979. Even then, it was unfinished, and several alternate versions surfaced over the following three decades. Directed by Francis Ford Coppola (1939–), who revised the screenplay from John Milius's original draft, it stars a legend of post–World War II Hollywood, Marlon Brando (1924–2004), and furthered the careers of Martin Sheen (1940–), Robert Duvall (1931–), and Laurence Fishburne (1961–). *Apocalypse Now* concerns a covert mission to locate and kill a rogue American Special Forces officer, encamped with tribal militia on the Vietnam-Cambodia border. Although it reflects on no specific incident from the Vietnam War, the hallucinatory nightmare it depicted has left the public with many of the war's most enduring images. *Apocalypse Now* is considered a milestone in film history, as much for its artistry as for its technically and emotionally difficult production, which ran years over schedule and millions of dollars over budget.

The first sound heard in the movie is the chop-chop-chop of spinning rotor blades, and that helicopter noise recurs through much of *Apocalypse Now*. However, aside from a few memorable scenes, that crucial airborne aspect of the Vietnam War—the helicopters that U.S. generals thought would win the day—is secondary to the plot. Like *The Odyssey*, *Apocalypse Now* is a perilous journey on water past hostile tribes. Like Odysseus, the protagonist of *Apocalypse Now*, Captain Willard (played by Sheen), has been through a long war and wonders about what awaits should he ever come home. His journey has no certain end.

Coppola had no intention of filming the sort of straightforward Vietnam War story focused on the reaction of ordinary GIs under fire that soon became common plot points in Hollywood movies. Coppola was a man of "expansive ambitions" in a period when American film reached a golden age of artistry. Standing on the box-office record-setting success of *The Godfather* (1972), Coppola was looking for another great American saga. With Vietnam he found a tragedy big enough to suit his ambitions (Schumacher, 1999, 175). The war afforded an opportunity to contemplate how the eternal issues of power, morality, and responsibility played out in 20th-century America. He was less interested in commenting on Vietnam than on the larger questions of "war and the human soul" (Murray, 1975).

That *Apocalypse Now* made no clear statement for or against the war also resulted from the contrasting perspectives of the authors of its screenplay, Coppola and Milius. Coppola held to the liberal view that the war was wrong. Milius's only regret was that the war was wrongly executed.

The seed of *Apocalypse Now* was planted in 1968, while the war raged on with no end in sight. Milius, a film student at the University of Southern California, began collecting Vietnam War stories from returning GIs, including a tale of soldiers surfing on the Mekong River after a bloody firefight. "I wanted to go to Vietnam but I had asthma," Milius said. He coined the title for *Apocalypse Now* by inverting the counterculture ideal of "Nirvana Now" he saw on buttons worn by hippies and discussed turning his screenplay into a film with a fellow classmate, George Lucas (Gallagher 1982).

Lucas planned to shoot *Apocalypse Now* in 16mm *cinema vérité* style, mixed with footage taken from network news and cast with off-duty soldiers to enhance the documentary realism, before his career changed direction with the success of his film *American Graffiti* (1973). By 1974, Coppola's American Zoetrope Studio obtained rights to Milius's screenplay. Coppola still wanted Lucas to direct, but Lucas was already making plans for his own epic, *Star Wars*. Coppola was in a hurry. He wanted to release *Apocalypse Now* in time for America's Bicentennial (1976). He missed his deadline by three years (Schumacher 1999, 184–185).

Both Milius and Coppola had Joseph Conrad's *Heart of Darkness* in mind for the film. Conrad's journey through the Congo Free State, the scene of unspeakable horror by exploitative colonists and the subject of a worldwide human rights outcry, inspired his 1906 novella. The story's protagonist, Marlow, is sent up the winding Congo River to a remote outpost in search of an overseer called Kurtz whose behavior startled even the most ruthless Congo colonizers. Marlow's orders were to retrieve Kurtz. "There were rumors that a very important station was in jeopardy, and its chief, Mr. Kurtz, was ill," Marlow recounted. Marlow is repelled by Kurtz's evil, yet cannot deny his eloquence and the hypnotic force of his personality (Conrad 1942, 43).

THE BROWN WATER NAVY

The Vietnam War is chiefly remembered as a land and air war, but the U.S. Navy also played a vital role. The first navy personnel arrived in Vietnam with the Military Aid Assistance Group in 1950. By the end of the Vietnam War, some 1,842,000 sailors had served in Southeast Asia.

The navy performed many functions. It patrolled South Vietnam's coast to prevent infiltration from the North; its aviators participated in raids on North Vietnam and provided helicopter support for troops in the South; its advisers trained and supported the South Vietnamese navy; its medical corps played an important role in treating casualties; its landing craft dispatched marines in amphibious assaults; and its warships pounded the coast of Vietnam with their big guns.

However, the navy's signal contribution to the war took place in the Mekong River Delta, where patrol boats plied the channels and the Mobile Riverine Force combined squadrons of shallow-draft vessels with a U.S. Army infantry brigade. The "brown water navy," as it was nicknamed, recalled the U.S. Navy's campaign to wrest control over the Mississippi River and other inland waterways during the Civil War. The slow-moving armored monitors, the gunboats that led the assault squadrons on the Mekong, were not unlike Civil War ironclads and, similarly, engaged enemy forces at close range. The Riverine Force was also equipped with a variety of landing craft, floating barracks, minesweepers, mortar barges, and auxiliary craft.

Milius kept the name Kurtz but changed Marlow to Willard in his screenplay. While describing his draft of the screenplay, Milius noted, "It deals with the nature of war" and "man's inherent bestiality . . . It said, 'Here you're going to see it all: you're going to see the exhilaration of it all, you're going to see the horror of it all; you're going right into the war with no holds barred'" (Thompson 1976).

Milius wrote in the manner of German novelist Ernst Jünger, a frontline commando in World War I whose spirit animates many scenes in the completed film. Jünger's memoir, *Storm of Steel* (1920), is a remarkably dry-eyed account of almost unimaginable horror without analyzing the justice of the war or assessing the waste of life, the futility of a lost cause, or the role of chance in survival. Like Kurtz and Willard, Jünger fought without hatred until "sorrow, regret, pursued me deep into my dreams." Jünger's war was "a gory carnival" (Jünger 2016, 95, 241).

The sensibility Milius brought to the screenplay was closer to Jünger's immersion in the adrenaline rush of war than to Coppola. The director said, "My contributions were to make it more like *Heart of Darkness*" (Schumacher 1999, 194). In Milius's early drafts, Willard changed sides and joined with Colonel Kurtz, the rogue commander of a remote outpost, and defended his compound against an attack by U.S. helicopter gunships. In the finished film, Willard, burdened with regret, kills Kurtz, who already seemed to await the angel of death. Echoing Conrad, Kurtz's last words were, "The horror, the horror."

Mapping out the screenplay from literary and real-life sources proved relatively easy when compared with getting it filmed. Despite his previous success at the box office, Coppola had a hard time finding financial backers for *Apocalypse Now*. Investors wondered whether American audiences were ready for so graphic a depiction of a war they would rather forget and worried about the attitude of audiences elsewhere in the world where the war had been a flashpoint for anti-American sentiment. The U.S. Army refused to assist the production; the Pentagon and Department of Defense were not amused by the screenplay's black humor and condemned the notion that the army would murder a rogue officer such as Kurtz rather than bring him home for medical care (Schumacher 1999, 194–195).

Casting the picture also proved troublesome, especially since Coppola was hoping that star power might convince investors to gamble on his film. The director approached the leading lights from the new generation of actors to play Captain Willard, but Steve McQueen, James Caan, Robert Redford, Al Pacino, and Jack Nicholson turned him down (Coppola 1979, 11–13).

However, the actor who had inspired them all, Marlon Brando, eventually became intrigued by the role of Colonel Kurtz. He was America's premier method actor, trained in the psychology of experiencing rather than representing the lives of characters, and he galvanized a generation with his naturalistic acting in *A Streetcar Named Desire*. Moody and increasingly difficult to direct, Brando saw his career decline through the 1960s, but it was revitalized by his unforgettable performance as Don Corleone in Coppola's *The Godfather*. Although he was a wild card, Brando was at least a bankable name.

Coppola and his crew were shocked by Brando's appearance. "Marlon is very overweight," Eleanor Coppola, who accompanied her husband during filming, confided to her diary. "Francis and he are struggling with how to change the character in the script. Brando wants to camouflage his weight and Francis wants to play him as a man eating all the time and overindulging" (Coppola 1979, 126). Brando seems to have won the argument. His 20 minutes of screen time suffuse *Apocalypse Now* with a particular grade of darkness. The low lighting and concealment that characterize his scenes may have resulted from Brando's desire to conceal his obesity but added an aura of mystery to the story. "You spent a week there talking to me about the film, clarifying it in your own mind but also listening attentively to what I said," he later told Coppola. "Besides restructuring the plot, I wrote Kurtz's speeches, including a monologue at his death. It was the closest I've ever come to getting lost in a part and one of the best scenes I've ever played" (Quoted in Mizruchi 2014, 267, 271).

For Willard, Coppola settled on Harvey Keitel, an ex-marine turned method actor who played tough, streetwise roles. However, Keitel quit after a few weeks. Replacing him was Martin Sheen, not a marquee name in those years but affordable for a director already concerned with cost overruns and available to begin work. For supporting cast, Coppola recruited a pair of actors who had worked with him on *The Conversation* (1974), Frederic Forrest and Harrison Ford. Robert Duvall, previously seen in *The Godfather*, signed on for what proved to be one of the film's most memorable roles, the air cavalry's Lieutenant Colonel Kilgore.

Coppola's next problem was finding a suitable location, a stand-in for Vietnam, whose communist regime remained hostile to the United States. With its tropical landscape, Queensland, Australia, was under consideration as a friendly environment for filming, but the Australian government refused to supply Coppola with helicopters and other military hardware, much less the troops he wanted as extras. He eventually found a willing patron in Philippines President Ferdinand Marcos. Excited by the prospect of drawing American dollars into his country, the dictator rented Coppola his military's Huey Cobra helicopter gunships and M-16 assault rifles, the same weapons used by the United States in Vietnam. Fearing that Muslim rebels from the Moro National Liberation Front, fighting a guerilla war against the Philippine government, might seize the armaments and even kidnap Coppola for ransom, Marcos provided security as well as cheap labor. Coppola used actual Vietnamese extras when possible, recruiting several hundred of them from a refugee camp near Manila (Coppola 1979, 29).

Problems dogged *Apocalypse Now* throughout the shooting schedule. Keeping the squadron of helicopters on hand proved difficult as the real-life Philippines pilots were sometimes called away to fight a real guerrilla war unfolding elsewhere in the Philippines. Coppola's wife, Eleanor, whose diary of the production was later published as *Notes*, recorded the confusion. "It is hard to know what is going on," she wrote. "There is no news of the war in the government-controlled press" (Coppola 1979, 26). However, the local media were unable to conceal the effects of Typhoon Olga that tore across Luzon in May 1976, killing hundreds of Filipinos, leaving thousands homeless, and destroying Coppola's sets, which had to be rebuilt nearby.

The mud, the muck, and Coppola's uncertainty over the movie's direction permeated the production as *Apocalypse Now* took on a life of its own. "The way we made it was very much like the way Americans were in Vietnam," Coppola said. "We were in the jungle. There were too many of us. We had access to too much money, too much equipment; and little by little we went insane" (Quoted in Levine 1979).

The long and often disastrous shoot, which became a battle against nature and a war among the cast and crew, charged a heavy toll on Coppola, jeopardizing his marriage and, perhaps, his sanity. In her published journal, Eleanor recalled asking her husband "what his inner voices were telling him to do. He said they tell him to do nothing, don't push, don't act, just wait." She continued, "The more he works on the ending, the more it seems to elude him as if it is there, just out of view, mocking him" (Coppola 1979, 254). The director was not the only victim of the insanity. After Sheen suffered a heart attack and a nervous breakdown, Coppola used the actor's brother, Joe, as a stand-in for some scenes. Sheen recovered and returned to the set.

By the time principal filming concluded on May 31, 1977, *Apocalypse Now* required 238 days to shoot at a cost of $27 million. Coppola went home to California with over a million feet of footage that had to be edited into a coherent film. "He said it was all there," his wife recalled, comparing his process to Michelangelo's method of carving away the surface of a stone block to reveal a statue. "He said all he had to do was cut away the part that wasn't *Apocalypse Now* and there the film would be" (Coppola 1979, 173).

The difficulty Coppola had in making *Apocalypse Now* was already legendary before the final scenes were shot. "The picture was attacked, long before it opened, as a model of Hollywood excess and vanity," wrote film historian Dave Thomson (Thomson 2008, 44). Even as United Artists prepared to release the film, Coppola remained baffled by the immensity of what he had undertaken. At an invitation-only May 11, 1979, screening at Mann's Bruin Theater near UCLA, audience members, largely Hollywood stars and studio employees, were given a questionnaire inviting them "to help me finish the film" (Schumacher 1999, 249, 251). His grandiose remarks in the months before the general public saw the film did not mask his confusion. At a press conference at the Cannes Film Festival, where *Apocalypse Now* won the Palme d'Or along with German director Volker Schlöndorff's *The Tin Drum*, Coppola famously declared that his film was "not about Vietnam—it *is* Vietnam. It's what it was really like" (Levine 1979). The sense of confusion permeating the film mirrored the uncertain direction of the war and the experience of many combatants.

Apocalypse Now was already generating controversy from the versions screened for exclusive audiences before its release to the public. The film was confusing and disenchanting for some commentators. Rona Barrett, America's most prominent Hollywood gossip columnist in the 1970s, called it "a disappointing failure" on ABC's *Good Morning America* (Schumacher 1999, 250). Writing in the *Chicago Tribune*, Gene Siskel pronounced the first two hours as "mostly stunning" but the conclusion "not easy to comprehend." Comparing it with *Coming Home* and *The Deer Hunter*, he found it "a much more subtle film, which appeared to hold the audience's attention until the ending, when many people seemed confused" (Siskel 1979a).

Apocalypse Now drew attention from an unusual avenue in the weeks before its public release with the publication of Eleanor Coppola's journal, *Notes*. Public interest may have been stoked by her account of her husband's infidelity as well as his overall emotional instability during the production, but as the *New York Times* wrote, *Notes* "made me want to see his movie" (Lehmann-Haupt 1979). Curiosity was high but so was anxiety in the movie industry in the months after the movie's August 1979 debut and its gradual rollout to theaters across the country. As late as October, Siskel could still write: "The guess here is that the general public is not interested in another Vietnam film" (Siskel 1979b).

Other critics expressed concerns that echoed the remarks Siskel published earlier in the year. The early scenes were generally considered riveting, but the ending eluded preconceptions of what a war movie should show. The *New York Times*'s Vincent Canby dismissed *Apocalypse Now*'s conclusion. "When we arrive at the heart of darkness," he chided, "we find not the embodiment of evil, of civilization junked, but an eccentric actor who has been given lines that are unthinkable but not, unfortunately, unspeakable" (Canby 1979). Soon enough, those lines he dismissed would become among the most memorable ever spoken in a Hollywood movie. If critics were mostly puzzled, the public proved willing to follow Willard on his ride into darkness. *Apocalypse Now* soon grossed over $78 million domestically and experienced similar success in many overseas markets (Cowie 2014, 132). It received eight Oscar nominations, winning two for sound and cinematography.

Roger Ebert was among the few writers who immediately understood the enduring significance of *Apocalypse Now*. He called it a "masterpiece" and predicted, "Years and years from now, when Coppola's budget and his problems have long been forgotten, 'Apocalypse' will still stand, I think, as a grand and grave and insanely inspired gesture of filmmaking—of moments that are operatic in their style and scope, and of other moments so silent we can almost hear the director thinking to himself" (R. Ebert 1979).

Like the Vietnam War, *Apocalypse Now* roamed restlessly across the imagination of the American public as well as its director. Interest only grew with the release of Eleanor Coppola's documentary, *Hearts of Darkness: A Filmmaker's Apocalypse* (1991). During *Apocalypse Now*'s production in the Philippines, Coppola asked his wife, a photographer but not a filmmaker, to make a documentary of the project for the United Artists publicity department. The footage sat in storage for years until the Showtime cable channel offered to fund it as a full-length film. "I was surprised when I was invited into the editing room, and saw that the editors were using *Notes* as the foundation for the documentary," she recalled. "I tried to make sure that the material didn't get out of balance, one way or another." Her husband had final approval. "There was stuff in the final cut that he was uncomfortable about—stuff that he thought made him look too nuts—but in the end he didn't want to tell those sincere filmmakers that they couldn't make the film the way they wanted to, because he had always fought against people telling him what *he* could do" (Schumacher 1999, 443–444).

Hearts of Darkness was a reminder of Coppola's struggle to make sense of the enormous body of footage he shot in the jungles of the Philippines. It included bits from a deleted segment that soon became known as the "French Plantation Scene." *Hearts of Darkness* whetted curiosity over what

Coppola omitted when editing the original release of *Apocalypse Now* to a manageable two and a half hours, and stirred the fretful director into rethinking the decisions he made in 1979. The new version of *Apocalypse Now*, released under the title *Apocalypse Now Redux* (2001), included 49 minutes of material omitted from earlier versions. New music was composed for some scenes, and several actors were called back to rerecord dialogue.

Like its predecessor, *Apocalypse Now Redux* debuted at Cannes. It provoked arguments among critics and devotees over whether the additional scenes added or subtracted from the film's impact. Most fans concurred with Ebert's assessment. "Longer or shorter, redux or not, *Apocalypse Now* is one of the central events of my life as a filmgoer" (R. Ebert 2001). He might have added, longer or not, it remains the vision most Americans and filmgoers around the world have of the Vietnam War.

HISTORICAL BACKGROUND

With the inauguration of Richard Nixon in 1969, the year in which *Apocalypse Now* is set, the Vietnam War entered a new and uncertain phase. Nixon won the presidency on a platform that promised a crackdown on protesters but also an end to the war that had generated the unrest. He spoke guardedly of a "secret plan" to end the war. At his inaugural address, Nixon never mentioned Vietnam by name, but his reference was clear. "We are caught in war, wanting peace," he said. But evidence of that war marred his inaugural parade down Pennsylvania Avenue when militants—chanting pro-Vietcong slogans, waving Vietcong banners, and burning American flags—assaulted the presidential motorcade with rocks and beer cans (Kilpatrick 1969).

With Harvard academic Henry Kissinger (1923–) as his national security adviser, Nixon proceeded with his plan with such secrecy that the Joint Chiefs of Staff learned of his initiatives only through White House memos stolen for them by a navy yeoman. The secretary of state, William Rogers (1913–2001), and the State Department were similarly kept in the dark. The troops on the ground and their commanders were left to guess America's next moves. Nixon had concluded that the war was unwinnable. "But we can't say that, of course," he told his advisers. "In fact we seem to have to say the opposite, just to keep some bargaining leverage" (Ward 2017, 364).

Despite their personal differences, Nixon and Kissinger acted almost as one in foreign policy and saw the world with a larger strategic imagination than most of their predecessors. They agreed that increasing the commitment of conventional forces would result in casualties and disruption unacceptable to the American public. Kissinger wrote, "We lost sight of one of the cardinal maxims of guerilla war; the guerilla wins if he does not lose. The conventional army loses if it does not win" (Kissinger 1969).

The use of nuclear weapons against North Vietnam, proposed by Senator Barry Goldwater (R-AZ; 1909–1998), presented unacceptable risks of a global conflagration involving communist China and the Soviet Union. Kissinger was aware of Chinese leader Mao Zedong's (1893–1976) thoughts on the subject. "The atom bomb is a paper tiger which the U.S. reactionaries use to scare people," Mao declared. "It looks terrible, but in fact it isn't. Of course, the atom bomb is a weapon of mass slaughter but the outcome of a war is decided by the people" (Mao 1967, 140). China had its own nuclear arsenal and, more so than the Soviet Union, its leaders appeared willing to endure mass slaughter.

Nixon and Kissinger were willing to discount South Vietnam as a lost cause if, in the short run, American prestige could be maintained. They called their scheme "Vietnamization," which meant the steady handoff of responsibility for the war to the South Vietnamese military, lavishly equipped and trained, accompanied by the steady withdrawal of U.S. forces. Less important than whether South Vietnam could defend itself unaided against North Vietnam and the Vietcong for more than a few years was giving America the appearance of having achieved "peace with honor." The South could fall. "What is involved now is confidence in American promises," Kissinger wrote. "However fashionable it is to ridicule the terms 'credibility' or 'prestige,' they are not empty phrases; other nations can gear their actions to ours only if they can rely on our steadiness" (Kissinger 2003, 21).

Their Machiavellian plan advanced along several fronts. To cool down the antiwar movement at home, Nixon announced that he was moving toward ending the draft and instituting an all-volunteer army. Worried about being abandoned, the South Vietnamese government needed to be reassured with money and arms. To pressure North Vietnam to negotiate a peace accord that would give the United States cover for a complete withdrawal of combat forces, Nixon was willing to ratchet up the air war, unleashing a secret bombing campaign in neutral Cambodia and punishing air strikes against the North.

The new commander of U.S. forces in Vietnam, General Creighton Abrams Jr., was unhappy with his directives from Washington. "He knew then that he was doomed to a rear guard action," Kissinger wrote, "that the purpose of his command would increasingly become logistic redeployment, not success in battle" (Kissinger 1979, 272–273). But while emphasizing the empty promise of "pacification" of the South Vietnamese countryside by herding civilians into supposedly secure "strategic hamlets," Abrams continued to order major ground engagements against North Vietnamese units whenever they could be found in the jungles of South Vietnam.

In May 1969, U.S. marines, South Vietnamese troops, and the 187th Infantry Regiment of the 101st Airborne Division were ferried by helicopter into the A Shau Valley, a 28-mile chasm of jungle and marsh pointing like a dagger from the Ho Chi Minh Trail across the Laotian border toward the key South Vietnamese cities of Hue and Da Nang. The valley was heavily defended by a crack North Vietnamese regiment. In a letter to his parents, Sergeant Stephen E. Fredrick of the 187th Infantry wrote that his unit was "catching hell." He worked day and night at Firebase Helen, the army's forward position, to keep the assault supplied. He was glad he was not on the front line. "My old platoon went in first and they got the first three choppers in the combat assault shot right out of the sky by small arms, automatic weapons, and rocket grenades." Addressing the home front, he added: "The people back there take it for granted that it will soon be over because the damn government puts out these kind of rumors. All the while our finest young men, the forgotten ones, die over here in the spring of their life" (Quoted in J. R. Ebert 1993, 329).

The most storied American ground battle of 1969 occurred in the A Shau Valley and later became the topic of a popular film by British director John Irvin, *Hamburger Hill* (1987). The North Vietnamese were dug into a peak the Vietnamese called Dong Ap Bia ("Mountain of the Crouching Beast"), labeled Hill 937 on U.S. Army maps but dubbed "Hamburger Hill" by GIs who complained that they were treated like meat run through a grinder by their officers. Lieutenant Colonel Weldon F. Honeycutt, commander of the 187th, ordered 10 charges up Hill 937, each one thwarted by the determined enemy. South Vietnamese troops finally took the hill after it was pounded by 201,000 artillery rounds, 1 million pounds of bombs, and 152,000 pounds of napalm. However, they were pulled back to allow the 187th to reap the publicity. By this time, the North Vietnamese bunkers were empty; their forces had slipped down the forested mountainside and back into Laos (Ward 2017, 391–393).

In his letter home, Frederick commented on news reports of the engagement. "Whatever they say, don't believe it because we have been getting our a—kicked," he wrote. "We have lost over 300 men killed and wounded in the last five days. I have had to take the bodies of a lot of my friends off the choppers in the last few days" (Quoted in J. R. Ebert 1993, 330). If his dispirited attitude was not universal, it was widespread among U.S. troops in the period mirrored by *Apocalypse Now*. The cause no longer mattered, and victory seemed unattainable.

DEPICTION AND CULTURAL CONTEXT

The jungle is the first thing seen in *Apocalypse Now*. Soon enough, the deep green strands of foliage are filtered through the smoky yellow haze of grenades before erupting in fireballs of napalm. Helicopters buzz wasp-like in the foreground. In *Apocalypse Now*, the jungle is more than a backdrop and becomes integral to the story, a mute character recalling "the high stillness of the primeval forest" described by Conrad in *Heart of Darkness*

(Conrad 1942, 43). The jungle was the dominant landscape confronting GIs outside Vietnam's crowded cities. "If you know her you can live in her real good, if you don't, she'll take you in an hour. Under," one GI remarked about the jungle (Herr 1978, 10). The quote came from Michael Herr's eyewitness account of the war, *Dispatches* (1978). Coppola admired the book's gritty poetry and hired Herr to write Willard's voiceover narration, which reveals the protagonist's thoughts about the war and his mission.

With its opiated Oriental modes and singer Jim Morrison's weary declaration "of all elaborate plans—the end," The Doors' "The End," heard over the opening scene, amplifies the mood of the film's protagonist, Willard. Although the lyrical references to a "desperate land" and a "wilderness of pain" where "all the children are insane" seem apt, according to the director's sound designer, Walter Murch, Coppola also wanted "the film soundtrack to partake of the psychedelic haze in which the war had been fought." He not only wanted to represent the rock music listened to by the troops in Vietnam, but to achieve the "far-out juxtaposition of imagery and sound; for the soundtrack not to be just a literal imitation of what you saw on the screen but at times to depart from it" (Boorman 1996, 159–160). The enigmatically doom-laden Doors' song summarizes how Coppola felt upon completing the film and, more important, how many Americans thought about the war's conclusion.

In the film's opening scene, Willard is unshaven and staring at the ceiling of his Saigon hotel room, where the whirling fan echoes the chop-chop of helicopters in his mind. He is tormented, suffering from combat fatigue, as the military iteration of post-traumatic stress disorder was then called. "Every time I think I'm going to wake up back in the jungle," he says. And yet, a warrior spirit still twitches within. "All I could think of was getting back into the jungle. Every minute I stay in this room I get weaker. Charlie squats in the bush getting stronger," he adds, referring to the enemy, dubbed Charlie by U.S. troops. While steeling his strength by performing Tai Chi, Willard goes berserk, smashing a mirror with his hand, trailing blood across the bedsheets, wiping his face red, and letting out a silent howl.

Willard feels guilt for what he has seen and done. He has a divided soul, not unlike the movie's attitude toward the war—or the conflicted attitudes of Americans who felt their country should have won but were burdened by the knowledge of waste and carnage, missed opportunities, and, perhaps, the realization that victory was always in doubt. "I wanted a mission, and for my sins they gave me one," he says. "It was a real choice mission. Now that it's over," he recalls, "I never want another." Willard is helicoptered to an army intelligence headquarters housed in a prefabricated building, an accurate depiction of U.S. bases that recreated middle-class American life with easy chairs, a couch, and a crowded dining room with a china cabinet. Waiting for him are Lieutenant General Corman (G. D. Spradlin), Colonel Lucas (Harrison Ford), and a CIA agent (Jerry Ziesmer) who watches and listens. The subject of Willard's mission is Colonel Walter E. Kurtz, a Special Forces operations officer.

Lucas plays a mysterious tape "monitored in Cambodia" of Kurtz engaging in what clearheaded officers can only interpret as psychobabble. "I watched a snail crawl along the edge of a straight razor," drawls a weary voice instantly recognizable as Brando's. "That's my dream, that's my nightmare, crawling, slipping along the edge of a straight razor." Kurtz goes on to speak of incineration, "pig after pig, cow after cow, village after village . . . and they call me an assassin," he concludes in tones of recrimination. The general explains that Kurtz was "one of the most outstanding officers this country ever produced." In guarded language inspired by Conrad, Kurtz's "methods" had become unsound. As in *Heart of Darkness*, an unsound operation, in this case the U.S. intervention in Vietnam, had decided that one of its own had crossed the boundary into the impermissible. The general stands for the older generation of officers who commanded operations from their headquarters in Saigon. Like Generals Westmoreland and Abrams, one imagines Corman as a capable officer in World War II and Korea who got lost in Vietnam.

Kurtz's specific methods and misdeeds are never fully enumerated at headquarters. Lucas will say only that the colonel's indigenous followers, the Montagnards, "worship him like a god," a familiar conceit concerning white adventurers taken from Conrad and Rudyard Kipling. The general adds that Kurtz "took matters into his own hands" and that "things get confused out there . . . with these natives." He goes on to reflect the thought at the heart of Coppola's vision for *Apocalypse Now*: "There's conflict in every human heart between the rational and the irrational, between good and evil, and good does not always triumph."

Willard's mission, Lucas explains, is to infiltrate Kurtz's compound and "terminate the colonel's command." The CIA agent finally speaks, spelling out the order more clearly. "Terminate with extreme prejudice," he says. Willard can reach Kurtz only by sailing up the Mekong River through dangerous, enemy-occupied jungle.

The Vietnamese call the Mekong Cuu Long Giang, the River of the Nine Dragons, but in the delta country that fans out from the South China Sea until touching Cambodia, nine cannot begin to enumerate the number of water routes and channels. The Mekong Delta consists of thousands of miles of waterways, including majestic island-studded rivers and meandering streams flowing through lush jungles, straight-edged canals, and irrigation ditches for the patchwork of rice paddies that has been called Vietnam's breadbasket. The water is the region's lifeline; traveling by sampan or junk is easier than trekking through the jungle or slogging across the soft ground of rice paddies and marshes.

The delta begins only 30 miles south of Saigon. During the war, the cobweb of water was called the IV Corps Tactical Zone, a region larger than the Netherlands with nearly 6 million inhabitants, many adhering to religious sects peculiar to the delta. The war devastated the land and its people. As a 1968 *National Geographic* story reported, "Most of the bridges had been blown up by the Viet Cong. The countryside showed defoliated trees here and there; and everywhere craters—small from artillery, larger from the B-52s." The delta had become increasingly unsafe outside large towns, and even district seats were vulnerable to snipers. U.S. and South Vietnamese patrol boats imposed a dusk-to-dawn curfew on the waters, enforced with the aid of Starlight Scopes, an early night vision device (P. T. White 1968).

Willard is assigned to one of the U.S. Navy vessels from the River Patrol Force operating on the Mekong, a 31-foot craft known as a PBR (Patrol Boat, River) with a fiberglass hull capable of running in shallow water and armed with rotating .50-caliber machine guns. He does not disclose the nature of his mission to the boat's skipper, Chief Petty Officer Phillips (Albert Hall), or engage in much conversation with the youthful crew, described by him as "rock and rollers with one foot in the grave." Like the military units that figured in dozens of World War II movies, the crew represents an American microcosm, but unlike their predecessors, the diverse Americans aboard the patrol boat have no common cause to fight for, no defense of country or liberty for which to risk death. The machinist, a New Orleans cook everyone called Chef (Frederic Forrest), is "wrapped up too tight" for Vietnam. Gunner's Mate Lance Johnson (Sam Bottoms) is a California surfer. The other gunner's mate, known as Clean (Laurence Fishburne), came from a ghetto in the South Bronx. Serious as death and just as indifferent to human foibles, Phillips seldom bothers to impose military discipline on his disorderly crew.

Willard broods amid the peculiar sounds of the Vietnam War. The distant rolling thunder comes from the unseen B-52s dropping tons of bombs beyond the horizon, probably an allusion to the massive air raids on communist sanctuaries in Cambodia. Clean's transistor radio is tuned to the Armed Forces station broadcasting from Saigon with a format adapted from Top-40 AM radio. "Good morning, Vietnam!" the cheery GI DJ announces. He relays a request from the city's mayor "to keep Saigon beautiful" before spinning "a blast from the past," the Rolling Stones' "(I Can't Get No) Satisfaction," an ironic choice on Coppola's part given the setting.

As the PBR goes up river, with Lance surfing behind and the churning wake carelessly ruining laundry day for Vietnamese women on the shore, Willard reads the dossier on the man he was ordered to kill. Like all Green Beret officers, Kurtz underwent paratrooper training and rigorous psychological testing before receiving top-secret clearance (Moore 1965, 15–16). Even in the context of the elite Green Berets, the résumé is impressive. Kurtz had joined the Airborne at the unusually old age of 38; from there he transferred to the Special Forces in Vietnam, where he wrote a report on the situation that so displeased the Joint Chiefs of Staff and President Lyndon B. Johnson that it was stamped secret and filed away.

The contrast between Kurtz's West Point-Harvard credentials and the rambling monologue "monitored in Cambodia" puzzles Willard. "I heard that voice on the tape, and it really put a hook in me," he says. Willard's voiceover monologues emulate the hardboiled detective cadence of film noir. Whether by plan or accident, *Apocalypse Now* became a sophisticated mélange of Hollywood genres—of war movies, film noir, and Westerns.

The Western motifs arrive with the First Cavalry Division regiment detailed to escort Willard's PBR through Vietcong-held territory. The cavalry are depicted with only slight artistic license. In *Dispatches*, Herr wrote that they wore "the most comforting insignia in all of Vietnam, the yellow-and-black shoulder patches of the Cav," and when they landed, "you were with the pro's now, the elite" (Herr 1978, 155–156). As Willard accurately notes, the cavalry rode helicopters in Vietnam, not horses, but the unit's commander, Lieutenant Colonel Bill Kilgore (played by Duvall), is determined to maintain regimental traditions. He wears a black felt broad-brimmed hat with crossed cavalry sabers, and his men sport the yellow kerchiefs associated with America's horse soldiers. A bugler blows "Charge!" as Kilgore's helicopters rise to meet the enemy. In the evening, Kilgore's troopers enjoy barbecue as he serenades them on a guitar around the campfire like a singing cowboy from an old Hollywood picture.

The battle scenes involving Kilgore pass out of the Hollywood narrative tradition and into surrealism. In the first engagement, Kilgore's forces are mopping up a village infiltrated by the Vietcong; a flustered Roman Catholic chaplain conducts mass for the GIs as fires burn around them. Coppola is seen behind a camera, playing a television director frantically waving at Willard. "Just look like you're fighting!" he shouts in a wry commentary on the distance between reality and its representation. In Vietnam, an actual event might be staged; in Hollywood, there are no actual events, but the staging of reality threatens to become more powerful than the real thing.

A voice intones through a loudspeaker, "We are here to help you" in English, a language unfamiliar to villagers who are being driven, screaming and crying, into American vehicles. The situation alludes to a vast project implemented by the South Vietnamese government but directed and funded by the United States. The Strategic Hamlets Program relocated many thousands of rural Vietnamese into supposedly economically sustainable villages protected by government troops and local militias. The objective was to pacify the countryside by depriving the Vietcong of people they could terrorize, govern, or recruit.

The scene in *Apocalypse Now* is an anachronism; by 1969 the Strategic Hamlets Program had been shut down as a failure. The Vietcong had little difficulty in infiltrating the supposed safe zones. The forced relocation of peasants only spurred resentment against the Saigon regime; many slipped out of the hamlets and tried to reestablish their old lives or joined a growing underclass of displaced people in South Vietnam's big cities. The Strategic

Hamlets Program became a propaganda boon for the communists, evidence of Saigon's disregard for its own citizens. Although off by several years, *Apocalypse Now* accurately depicts the way villagers were often removed by gunpoint as their homes were burned to prevent their return (Karnow 1997, 335–336).

Kilgore's second battle is *Apocalypse Now*'s most memorable scene, the air cavalry assault on a Vietcong-governed village. With Richard Wagner's "Flight of the Valkyries" blaring from loudspeakers, Kilgore's gunships swoop down on a peaceful setting. The Vietcong militia scrambling to defend the town is no match for the concerted fire engulfing them, albeit they manage to shoot down one helicopter as the grass huts of their village explode into fireballs. Kilgore makes no distinction between combatants and civilians, but then the distinction is hard to maintain after a young girl, acting as if trying to escape the Vietcong's clutches, tosses a hand grenade into a helicopter.

The scene remains breathtaking decades later, achieved—several years before the advent of computer animation—by real machines in flight piloted by human hands. Vietnam veteran Dick White, a helicopter pilot during the war, oversaw the scene. "With my helicopters, the boats and the high morale of the well-trained extras we had, there were three or four countries in the world we could have taken easily," he bragged (Orth 1977). In the aftermath, as fighter bombers obliterate unseen enemies in the jungle with their payloads, Kilgore utters, "I love the smell of napalm in the morning." Willard eyes him with dismay, as if to say, "Could he be any less crazy than Kurtz?"

There were many such villages. After the 1968 Tet Offensive, the United States estimated that just 4,500 of South Vietnam's 12,500 hamlets were secure; "nearly 3 million South Vietnamese were no longer even nominally loyal to Saigon" (Ward 2017, 292). More often than the cavalry, it was the marines or army infantry who moved into such villages on foot. Sergeant Jack Freitag recalled his Marine Corps platoon entering a village displaying a large Vietcong star at its entrance. The marines "blew up everything we could see that was booby-trapped. And every step of the way we had to," he said. In this particular incident, the marines did not enjoy Kilgore's element of surprise. The entire village, including women, children, chickens, and dogs, had escaped through a tunnel system, leaving behind only booby traps (J. R. Ebert 1993, 303–304).

After continuing the slow journey upriver, the PBR stops to refuel at an advance base, lit up like an amusement park at night with the sound of rock music wafting in the air. Illustrating the lavish U.S. expenditure on the war, the base is stocked with enough provisions to supply a small city. The illicit pleasure of Panama Red, a brand of high-grade marijuana, can easily be found in the shadows. A helicopter lands with a party of *Playboy* playmates. Scantily clad in cowgirl outfits, they dance and gyrate to the tune of a song popularized by Creedence Clearwater Revival, "Suzy Q," in a stadium surrounded by oversize phallic shells painted with unit emblems. Some of the women are also humping M-16s, suggesting that sex is war conducted by other means. The stadium bleachers are filled with whooping and hollering GIs letting their fantasies run wild until, like bulls panting against their cage door, they break through the thin line of military police and charge onto the stage. The playmates scramble for the safety of the helicopter and exit the way they came as pandemonium continues down below. John Kerry, a Vietnam veteran who survived to become a U.S. senator and secretary of state, recalled a similar scene. "The visions of Ann Margret and Miss America and all the other titillating personalities who would have made us feel so at home hung around us for a while until we saw three Chinook helicopters take off from the field and presumed that our dreams had gone with them" (Quoted in Brinkley 2004, x).

The entertainment provided to troops, depicted in *Apocalypse Now*, was provided by the United Services Organization (USO) during the war. Established as the United States was about to enter World War II, the United Services Organization provided servicemen—and men were the primary intended audience—with entertainment through 1945, and again when the Korean conflict began in 1950. Even before the United States officially committed combat troops to Vietnam, the USO opened a center in Saigon in 1963. USO clubs soon proliferated throughout Vietnam and Thailand, where U.S. bomber squadrons were stationed, and were staffed by miniskirt-clad female American volunteers.

The USO's role in Vietnam is chiefly remembered for sponsoring "camp shows" featuring well-known entertainers such as Bob Hope, Redd Foxx, and Anita Bryant who performed at large U.S. bases (Westheider 2007, x). Along with comic one-liners and monologues, the camp shows trafficked in more salacious entertainment. Accompanying Hope was 1960s sex symbol and movie star Raquel Welch, tasked with arousing the audience with provocative dancing. "Sending girls like me to Vietnam to entertain the troops is like teasing a caged lion with raw meat," she said (Ward 2017, 327). Marine Sergeant Ron Kovic recalled that his buddies' response to Hope's show "came out of fear and loneliness—convicts in a prison would have done the same thing." He added that Hope "used women in the shows to get a rise out of us—it seemed like he was always leaving with the women and we were always staying with the war. The *Apocalypse Now* scenes with the *Playboy* bunnies typified what it was really like in those troop shows—the terrible frustration and anguish" (White 1980). After the war, Kovic wrote a best-selling account of his experiences that was transformed into a popular movie, *Born on the Fourth of July*.

Willard contrasts the U.S. soldiers with "Charlie," who fights relentlessly without the benefit of recreation or the hope of vacation. "He had only two ways home—death or victory," he says. As the PBR pushes farther upriver,

Willard resumes reading Kurtz's dossier. He learns that the colonel assassinated several South Vietnamese officers, suspecting them of being double agents. Afterward, "enemy activity dropped to nothing" in his sector. The screenplay reflects the reality that South Vietnam's security forces were infiltrated to an alarming degree by Vietcong sympathizers. In 1970, the CIA estimated that as many as 30,000 communist agents had infiltrated South Vietnam's forces (Ward 2017, 419). It also alludes to the Phoenix Program, a secretive CIA-South Vietnamese operation in which paramilitary teams "routinely carried out torture, murders and assassinations, accusations that American officials denied" (Miller 2017). Kurtz apparently exceeded his authority. "He kept going and he kept winning his way," Willard says. "The VC knew his name by now, and they were scared of him," Willard adds, approvingly.

Willard eventually reveals his destination to the PBR's commander. They will cross the border into Vietnam's ostensibly neutral neighbor. "We're not supposed to be in Cambodia," Willard says, telling Phillips something the skipper already knows. By 1969, Cambodia's wily chief of state, Prince Norodom Sihanouk (1922–2012), maintained his country's precarious neutrality by turning a blind eye to North Vietnamese bases on his frontier while secretly permitting U.S. air raids on those bases. The exchange between Willard and Phillips reflects the reality of U.S. secret operations across the Cambodian border years before Nixon ordered a full-scale invasion in May 1970, in a failed bid to uproot the North Vietnamese from the country.

While under way on the Mekong, Willard reads a photocopy of the last letter Kurtz sent to his young son back in the United States. "My situation here has become a difficult one," Kurtz admitted. His superiors have accused him of murder for killing the South Vietnamese double agents. But as Kurtz explained in his letter, what is called ruthless in war is only another name for clarity. He cast himself as a Nietzschean superman, imbued with an ancient warrior aristocratic ethos, not the meekness and restraint of Judeo-Christian values. "I am beyond their timid, lying morality," he concluded.

With Willard absorbed in somber reflections on Kurtz's war, the PBR crew lark around drinking beer and smoking pot. They are in no condition to conduct a "routine check" on a passing sampan and disregard Willard's instructions to let the boat pass. The small wooden craft is filled with barrels of rice, vegetables, and fish; chickens and pigs cackle and grunt from their cages. Chef boards the sampan, and Phillips barks orders to keep searching for contraband. Chef grows angry and agitated as he overturns the barrels and strews their contents across the deck. The Vietnamese and the Americans lack a common language and are unable to communicate. When one Vietnamese moves abruptly, Clean opens fire with his machine gun, mowing down the civilians and nearly hitting Chef. A badly wounded woman in the sampan barely survives the barrage. Phillips is prepared to follow standard operating procedure and take her to the nearest medical station, but Willard will not have his mission diverted again. He dispatches the woman with a single shocking gunshot. "I told you not to stop. Let's go," he says. The only survivor from the sampan is a white puppy.

The scene is indicative of the high anxiety faced by American forces in a war where the enemy could be nowhere and anywhere. Army Private Tim O'Brien of the Americal Division recalled enduring many similar situations as an infantryman on patrol. "We didn't know why we were in a village, what we were supposed to accomplish. So we'd kick around jugs of rice and search houses and frisk people, not knowing what we were looking for. And somebody might die" (Quoted in Ward 2017, 431).

The war's most notorious massacre of civilians by U.S. troops, at My Lai, occurred in 1968 but did not become public knowledge until American news reporters broke the story in November 1969. The circumstances of the My Lai Massacre did not result from a spontaneous outburst of anxiety but was premeditated mass murder with the victims numbering in the hundreds. Like the story told in *Apocalypse Now*, secrecy shrouded My Lai and many U.S. operations in Vietnam. The My Lai Massacre was deliberately covered up by the U.S. command in Saigon, which released false reports of a "day-long battle" in the village against the Vietcong. Despite the involvement of a chain of command that included a captain as perpetrator and generals in the cover-up, the highest-ranking officer charged in connection with the massacre was Lieutenant William Calley, a platoon commander (Greiner 2009, x).

Reality becomes surreal once again as the PBR reaches the last American outpost on the river, Do Long Bridge. The damaged structure is strung with lights like a carnival attraction. Each night the Vietcong blow it up and each day the U.S. forces rebuild. Herr's remark in *Dispatches* typified situations faced by Americans in many sectors of Vietnam: "We had the days and he had the nights" (Herr 1978, 14). The PBR arrives at night in the midst of a fire-fight pitting beleaguered American forces against an unseen enemy. Lane had "dropped acid," but the scene he wanders through is as much an etching of hell as a bad LSD trip. Soldiers swim up to the boat in the Stygian river, pleading like the damned for a chance to go home. Desperate men dug in behind sandbags fire into the darkness. A breakdown in command and control has occurred. Wreckage is strewn everywhere. Lurid fires burn. After retrieving a satchel of mail addressed to them, Willard and his companions push on.

The river brings them only more calamity as the men sort through the mailbag. Willard reads a message from headquarters revealing that a Captain Colby had been sent on the same mission to kill Kurtz months earlier but joined with the renegade colonel. The crew glances at a newspaper from home with headlines telling of the arrest of Charles Manson for ordering a bizarre series of murders; the Manson Family will come to seem a twisted analogue to Kurtz's followers. Clean listens to a cassette tape from his mother, a spoken-word letter urging him to stay clear of bullets. Her voice tells him, "We love you very much," as an ambush along the river takes his life. Phillips had treated Clean with avuncular concern throughout. His face fills with horror. When they are ambushed again, this time by tribesmen showering the PBR with arrows and spears, Phillips is felled. In an incongruously tender scene, Lance buries his skipper at sea, as it were, cradling Phillips before releasing him into the flowing water, watching his face slowly recede into the river.

One of the film's strangest scenes was cut from *Apocalypse Now*'s theatrical release but later restored for *Apocalypse Now Redux*. The "French Plantation Scene" begins on the river in dense fog; visible is the outline of the shore with a ruined shed on river's edge. Willard and the crew land with guns drawn but are soon surrounded by a company of armed French and Vietnamese men and women, materializing like specters from the mist. They are the extended family and employees of a rubber plantation owner and are still flying a tattered French tricolor. The French assist in a full military burial for Clean, complete with "Taps." And then, dressed formally for dinner, they gather with Willard and his companions in their elegant plantation house for wine and dinner. Serving them are Vietnamese waiters in white jackets. Chef pronounces the food superb.

The conversation around the dinner table includes a contentious history of Vietnam from a French perspective. The head of the household, Hubert de Marais, shows Willard a roster of intruders they have killed in defense of their property—Vietcong, North Vietnamese, South Vietnamese, and, yes, Americans. "Perhaps it was a mistake," he shrugs. The example of French defeat in World War II, Indochina, and Algeria only steels his determination to stay on. He blames the United States. "The Vietcong were invented by the Americans," he insists. The particle of truth in his statement reflects on the support Ho Chi Minh received during and immediately after World War II by U.S. intelligence (Ward 2017, 15–16). He also blames indecisive politicians in Paris, defeatist civilians, and leftist protestors, paralleling conservative sentiments in the United States about Vietnam. By the end of the meal, he pronounces himself eager for Willard and the crew "to go on with your war."

The scene cuts back without explanation to the PBR in the fog. The incongruity of the French Plantation episode is striking. Were the French still shipping rubber downriver for sale in Saigon? How were they able to maintain their luxurious if heavily armed way of life, cut off and in the midst of a raging war? One can read the scene as Willard's daydream—or a ghost story inserted into an already eclectic production. Film critic Roger Ebert wrote, "It helps me to understand it when Coppola explains that he sees the French like ghosts; I questioned how they had survived in their little enclave, and accept his feeling that their spirits survive as a cautionary specter for the Americans" (R. Ebert 2001).

Kurtz's domain resembles the innermost circle of hell, ringed by crosses with bodies strung up from the crossbars. The riverbanks are lined with skulls and votive candles, turning carnage into a perverse sacrificial rite. Greeting the PBR are ranks of canoes filled with Montagnards, faces painted and torsos naked, waiting silently as Willard draws near. A Philippines jungle tribe called the Ifugaos lived on Coppola's set and stood in for the Montagnards. They were paid in food (Schumacher 1999, 219).

Their canoes part to allow Willard to proceed to the embankment, a set of steps leading to a structure resembling the ruins of Angkor Wat. Not unlike the Manson Family's marker, "HELTER SKELTER," left at the scene of their murders, "OUR MOTTO APOCALYPSE NOW" is scrawled across a wall.

The literary roots of *Apocalypse Now* were only one pillar on which the story stood. The other was its link to the reality of war in remote jungles of Indochina in places that often fell within no certain boundaries. One cannot help but think of Colonel Kurtz when reading the account from the First Vietnam War (1945–1954) by French correspondent Lucien Bodard. Recalling the backwater conflict that raged between the French and the Vietnamese communists, Bodard wrote of French officers in remote posts who turned "naked men with silver collars into passable soldiers with bush hats, belts and submachine guns" but "would refuse to put the Meo and Man highlanders into the regulation boots, for barefoot they were the finest marchers in the world" (Bodard 1967, 23).

In America, where thousands of their refugees eventually settled, the Meo are better known as the Hmong. From 1965 through 1975, the Hmong, dwelling in the hill country of Vietnam and Laos, fought a "Secret War" against Vietnamese and Laotian communists with the aid of the CIA. "They were better than anyone else around," said Bill Lair, the CIA agent who led the agency's paramilitary operations in Laos. "They could move a lot faster than the enemy" (Lloyd-George 2011).

Like the Hmong, the Montagnards were an ethnic minority, hill people despised by their more numerous and civilized neighbors in Vietnam. The U.S. Special Forces, the Green Berets to which Kurtz belonged, established bases among the Montagnards, and the CIA helped organize them and other hill tribes into Civilian Irregular Defense Groups. They were admired by their American handlers for their warrior prowess in the difficult terrain beneath the darkness of the jungle canopy (Brennan 2015). In *Dispatches*, Herr described real-life counterparts to Kurtz, albeit they were CIA agents, not U.S. Army, and operated a few years earlier than the 1969 time frame of *Apocalypse Now*. While covering the war, Herr came across "spooks" who "forced their passion on the locals, who they'd imitate, squatting in black pajamas." Among them, "one man who 'owned' Long An Province, a Duke of Nha Trang" and others who "ran their operations until the wind changed and their operations got run back on them" (Herr 1978, 50).

Among the natives is a hyperactively animated American wrapped in cameras and bandannas. The wild-eyed man (played by Dennis Hopper) identifies himself as a photojournalist. "I've covered the war since '64," he says.

He would have been one of an army of war correspondents who descended on Vietnam during the 1960s, many of them covering the conflict for heartland newspapers, radio, and television as well as the national networks and print media. Many correspondents were content to file their reports from the relative safety of Saigon, but Hopper's photojournalist would have been among the press-card-carrying adventurers who tagged along with troops in combat and ventured into the country's remote provinces. Describing himself and his colleagues, Herr wrote, "We were all a little crazy to have gone there in the first place" (Herr 1978, 188).

Hopper brilliantly improvised much of his scattershot monologue. He says that Kurtz "enlarged my mind" and calls him "a poet-warrior in the classic sense." Echoing Manson's followers, he adds, "These are all his children as far as you can see. We're all his children." The character was drawn from Kurtz's always smiling, mad Russian companion in *Heart of Darkness*, and the *Apocalypse Now* screenplay preserves a key line from Conrad's text. "You don't talk to Kurtz, you listen to him," the photographer insists (Schumacher 1999, 221; Conrad 1942, 61).

As in *Heart of Darkness*, the steps leading to Kurtz's house are adorned with severed heads. "You can't judge the colonel like an ordinary man," Hopper's madman continues. Many of Kurtz's heavily armed followers, Captain Colby and a few Americans sprinkled among them, are glassy-eyed and lurch about like zombies. The tribespeople appear as described in *Dispatches*: "The Montagnards in all of their tribal components make up the most primitive and mysterious portion of the Vietnamese population . . . Often living in nakedness and brooding silence in their villages" (Herr 1978, 93). Lance never comes down from his acid trip and wanders among the natives like a flower child at Woodstock.

Willard is eventually taken captive by the Montagnards and brought to Kurtz's lair, a place of "malaria, nightmares." Kurtz is concealed inside a recess in the wall of the ruined temple where he dwells. A joss stick burns, and candles give a furtive light; the low murmur of Kurtz's voice is heard before he is seen.

As Kurtz, Brando played off of the persona he had long ago crafted. The colonel's hard whisper recalled his previous role for Coppola as Don Corleone in *The Godfather*. Truman Capote's description of Brando could apply to Kurtz's recitations in *Apocalypse Now*. "The voice went on, as though speaking to hear itself, an affect Brando's speech often has, for, like many persons who are intensely self-absorbed, he is something of a monologist" (Capote 1957).

As Willard approaches Kurtz, the camera inches closer to reveal a large man dressed Vietnamese style, in black pajamas, reclined on an Oriental daybed. Kurtz pulls himself up, face still concealed in shadow. The small talk that ensues is unsettling. Kurtz asks where Willard is from, and hearing Ohio, he recounts a childhood journey down the Ohio River and a flower plantation along the riverbank. "You'd think that heaven fell on the Earth," he murmurs. Willard's face is tense in the flickering firelight; Kurtz's shaven head glows in the dark.

Kurtz knows full well why Willard has come despite the captain's evasive answers. In one of *Apocalypse Now*'s many memorable lines, he derides Willard and the generals he represents as "an errand boy sent by grocery clerks to collect a bill." He has Willard imprisoned in a bamboo cage, much as Americans visualized the captivity of U.S. prisoners of war by the North Vietnamese. Willard lapses into shock when Kurtz casually tosses Chef's severed head into his cell.

The Montagnards carry Willard back into Kurtz's sanctum, where he recovers his wits. He is left unguarded, as if Kurtz has decided that his own death has become preferable to continuing his gloomy life and that Willard might as well be death's agent. Willard listens as Kurtz recites T. S. Eliot's "The Hollow Men," a poem that, like the closing scenes of *Apocalypse Now*, is fragmentary in form as it evokes a journey across the rubble of modern life. Willard glances across the colonel's handful of books. He finds Johann Wolfgang von Goethe, the Bible, Jessie L. Weston's *From Ritual to Religion*, an exploration of the Arthurian legends and the Holy Grail, and James George Frazer's *The Golden Bough*, an influential account of the evolution and anthropology of religion and magic. They are books the well-read Brando might have kept in his own library.

Kurtz relates an incident from earlier in his tour of duty with the Special Forces. As part of the U.S. campaign to win the hearts and minds of the Vietnamese, his unit inoculated the children of a village. As soon as he left, the Vietcong returned and cut off the arms of those children. "I remember I cried, I wept like a grandmother," he says. "And then I realized that they were stronger than we." He describes them as "men who fought with their hearts. They had the strength, the strength to do that." The incident inspired him to call upon the "primordial passion to kill without feeling, without passion, without judgment."

The incident may be fictitious but adheres to American reports of the "calculatedly barbaric" actions of the Vietcong, intent on terrorizing civilians not inclined to support their cause. The *New York Times* reported that guerrillas "gouged out a chunk of a village official's calf and ate it before killing him" and that "pieces of skin were flayed from the thighs of women to force them to divulge their husband's whereabouts" (Tuohy 1965).

Willard listens without a word and resolves to carry out his mission. Kurtz appears to wait for the end. In his dying moments, he quotes his predecessor in *Heart of Darkness*, borrowing Conrad's line, "The horror, the horror." Coppola's dramatic conclusion was pulled together from several other elements. The director observed a ceremony of the Ifugaos, whose hypnotic chanting climaxed with the sacrifice of a water buffalo. He decided to cut between that ceremony, with its ritual sacrifice by machete, and Willard's sacrificial murder of Kurtz with a knife. Coppola's old friend and classmate Dennis Jakob is credited with investing *Apocalypse Now* with Arthurian elements and introducing Coppola to *The Golden Bough* and its archetype of the death and resurrection of gods and kings. According to Frazer, "The man-god must be killed as soon as he shews [sic] symptoms that his powers are beginning to fail, and his soul must be transferred to a vigorous successor before it has been seriously impaired by the threatened decay" (Frazer 1959, 224–225).

The Montagnards readily accept Willard as their new god-king, showing him obeisance as he passes through their ranks after killing Kurtz. Taking Lance by the hand like a child, he returns to the PBR and silently pulls away from its mooring. The boat's radio suddenly blasts a message from headquarters, trying to contact Willard. He shuts it off. We hear Kurtz's ghostly whisper, "The horror, the horror." The screen fades to black.

CONCLUSION

Apocalypse Now ends inconclusively. Willard's mission is accomplished, but to what greater end is left to the viewer's imagination. The conclusion mirrored the way many Americans felt about a war that had been costly in human as well as material terms but had achieved nothing beyond death and destruction. Not unlike Willard, many GIs returned from the conflict lacking the sense of victory or accomplishment that buoyed veterans of the nation's other foreign wars. Distinct from many movies that followed, *Apocalypse Now* was less concerned with depicting specific historical incidents than with conveying the larger sense of history by suggesting the emotional and ethical context of a divisive war.

FURTHER READING

Bodard, Lucien. 1967. *The Quicksand War: Prelude to Vietnam*. London: Faber and Faber.

Boorman, John, and Walter Donohue. 1996. *Projections 6*. London: Faber and Faber.

Brennan, Elliot. "The Forgotten People of Vietnam's War." China Policy Institute, April 16, 2015.

Brinkley, Douglas. 2004. *Tour of Duty: John Kerry and the Vietnam War*. New York: Harper Collins.

Canby, Vincent. "The Heart of 'Apocalypse' Is Extremely Misty." *New York Times*, August 15, 1979.

Capote, Truman. "The Duke in His Domain." *New Yorker*, November 9, 1957.

Conrad, Joseph. 1941. *A Conrad Argosy*. New York: Doubleday.

Coppola, Eleanor. 1979. *Notes*. New York: Simon and Schuster.

Cowie, Peter. 2014. *Coppola*. Milwaukee: Applause Theatre & Cinema Books.

Ebert, James R. 1993. *A Life in a Year: The American Infantryman in Vietnam 1965–1972*. Novato, CA: Presidio.

Ebert, Roger. "Apocalypse Now." *Chicago Sun-Times*, June 1, 1979.

Ebert, Roger. "Apocalypse Now/Redux." *Chicago Sun-Times*, August 10, 2001.

Frazer, James George. 1959. *The New Golden Bough: A New Abridgment of the Classic Work*. New York: Criterion.

Gallagher, John. "John Milius." *Films in Review*, June–July 1982.

Greiner, Bernd. 2009. *War Without Fronts: The USA in Vietnam*. New Haven, CT: Yale University Press.

Herr, Michael. 1978. *Dispatches*. New York: Alfred A. Knopf.

Jünger, Ernst. 2016. *Storm of Steel*. New York: Penguin.

Karnow, Stanley. 1997. *Vietnam: A History*. New York: Penguin.

Kilpatrick, Carroll, and Don Oberdorfer. "Richard M. Nixon Becomes President with 'Sacred Commitment' to Peace." *Washington Post*, January 21, 1969.

Kissinger, Henry. "The Vietnam Negotiations." *Foreign Affairs*, January 1969.

Kissinger, Henry. 1979. *White House Years*. Boston: Little, Brown.

Kissinger, Henry. 2003. *Ending the Vietnam War: A History of America's Involvement and Extrication from the Vietnam War*. New York: Simon & Schuster.

Lehmann-Haupt, Christopher. "Books of the Times." *New York Times*, August 7, 1979.

Levine, G. Roy. "Francis Ford Coppola Discusses *Apocalypse Now*." *Millimeter*, October 1979.

Lloyd-George, William. "The CIA's Secret War." *The Diplomat*, February 25, 2011.

Mao Tse-Tung. 1967. *Quotations from Chairman Mao Tse-Tung*. Peking: Foreign Language Press.

Miller, Edward. "Behind the Phoenix Program." *New York Times*, December 29, 2017.

Mizruchi, Susan L. 2014. *Brando's Smile: His Life, Thought, and Work*. New York: W. W. Norton.

Moore, Robin. 1965. *The Green Berets*. New York: Crown.

Murray, William. "The Playboy Interview: Francis Ford Coppola." *Playboy*, July 1975.

Orth, Maureen. "Watching the Apocalypse." *Newsweek*, June 13, 1977.

Schumacher, Michael. 1999. *Francis Ford Coppola; A Filmmaker's Life*. New York: Crown.

Siskel, Gene. "Coppola's 'Apocalypse' Excellent, Yet Confusing." *Chicago Tribune*, May 14, 1979.

Siskel, Gene. "Coppola's Sales Tactics Fuel his 'Apocalypse' Launching." *Chicago Tribune*, October 14, 1979.

Thompson, Richard. "Stoked." *Film Commentary*, July–August 1976.

Thomson, Dave. 2008. *Have You Seen . . .? A Personal Introduction to 1,000 Films*. New York: Alfred A. Knopf.

Tuohy, William. "A Big 'Dirty Little War." *New York Times Magazine*, November 28, 1965.

Ward, Geoffrey C., and Ken Burns. 2017. *The Vietnam War: An Intimate History*. New York: Alfred A. Knopf.

White, Peter T. "The Mekong River of Terror and Hope." *National Geographic*, December 1968.

Chapter 6

Platoon (1986)

Distributed by Orion Pictures, *Platoon* arrived in December 1986, in advance of a spate of Vietnam War movies including *Hamburger Hill* (1987), *Hanoi Hilton* (1987), *Full Metal Jacket* (1987), and *Garden of Stone* (1987). While all of those films were already in production, the attention *Platoon* received, having been screened in New York and Los Angeles in time for Oscar consideration, and being featured on the cover of the January 26, 1986, *Time* magazine, generated interest among moviegoers and support in the movie industry for the sudden torrent of films that looked back on Vietnam.

Platoon was distinguished for being written and directed by a former combat serviceman, Oliver Stone (1946–). A Yale University dropout from an affluent background, Stone was unhappy with the plans his family had made for him and, as he said, "knew there was a world waiting to be discovered." He went to Saigon for six months in 1965 where he taught English (Ciment 1987). After an interval of travel, he enlisted in the U.S. Army and asked to be assigned to Vietnam. He arrived with the 25th Infantry Division and served a one-year deployment in various capacities from 1967 to 1968. By all accounts, he was a good soldier, and he came home with a Bronze Star for bravery and a Purple Heart with one Oak Leaf Cluster for twice being wounded.

He also returned with feelings of guilt. Like *Platoon*'s protagonist, Chris Taylor, who represents Stone, he upbraided himself for participating in "morally repulsive things." As film historian Patrick McGilligan (1951–) put it, Stone did not intend for *Platoon* to be "a grand universal statement about men in war," as was *The Deer Hunter* or *Apocalypse Now*, but the writer/director attempted "to exorcise his own ghost from Vietnam" (McGilligan 1987).

Platoon focuses on Stone's real-life unit, Bravo Company, Third Battalion, 25th Infantry Division. As he descends onto the tarmac from the transport plane, Taylor's first sights of Vietnam are body bags of the men the new arrivals have replaced. Bravo Company is sent to the Cambodian border and engages in dangerous "night ambushes" in the jungle. Taylor becomes aware of divided attitudes within Bravo between soldiers who followed the hardline Sergeant Barnes and those aligned with the more compassionate Sergeant Elias. After losing men to booby traps, the company raids a village suspected of communist sympathy, discovers a cache of weapons and supplies, and summarily punishes the inhabitants. Barnes advocates taking the harshest measures against Vietnamese civilians while Elias urges a more nuanced approach. The question of "illegal killings" of civilians soon hovers over the unit. The moral issue over obeying the rules of war or reverting to barbarism results in conflict and violence as the men take sides. Bravo Company's opponents include not only guerillas but also well-trained and well-equipped "Main Force" Vietcong units as well as North Vietnamese army regiments infiltrating into South Vietnam from across the Cambodian border. In the climactic battle scene, Bravo endures the full force of a well-planned communist attack. Drug use is prevalent in Bravo Company; racial tensions occasionally flare. Taylor, as Stone's mouthpiece, expresses his opinions in voiceovers that echo the letters he writes to his grandmother back home.

Determined to turn his experience in Vietnam into a coming-of-age story, Stone prepared a first draft of *Platoon* as early as 1974. However, Stone was a newcomer in Hollywood in the 1970s, and the opportunity to make a personal film on a controversial subject had to wait until he earned initial success as a screenwriter and director. The movie industry remained wary of Vietnam, at least before the success of *Coming Home*, *The Deer Hunter*, and *Apocalypse Now*, and it took several years before studios even considered the project. According to Stone, production studios considered his screenplay as "too grim" (Cooper 1988).

While addressing the Vietnam War from different perspectives from the filmmakers who preceded him, Stone also wrote a screenplay based on the memoir of wounded Vietnam veteran Ron Kovic, *Born on the Fourth of July*, whose story had already inspired *Coming Home*. "I worked with a series of directors on it" as the 1970s ended, Stone recalled. Al Pacino committed to playing the lead role. "We rehearsed it: Al played it. I saw all the roles played. It was really happening. And then the money fell out at the last possible second and the film collapsed" (Cooper 1988). Stone eventually made *Born on the Fourth of July* (1989) with Tom Cruise in the lead role.

Stone said he gave up on Vietnam as a subject until *The Deer Hunter*'s director, Michael Cimino, with whom he wrote the screenplay for *Year of the Dragon* (1985), convinced him to take *Platoon* off the shelf. "He said that Vietnam was coming around and that [Stanley] Kubrick would bring a

PRINCE NORODOM SIHANOUK (1922–2012)

Although Lyndon B. Johnson never met Prince Norodom Sihanouk, he expressed grudging admiration for the Cambodian leader. The U.S. president recognized Sihanouk as a skillful politician, a consummate dealmaker, and a deal breaker.

Sihanouk was at the center of Cambodian politics throughout his life. As a member of Cambodia's royal family, he became king in 1943 at a time when Japan occupied the French protectorate of Cambodia. He negotiated his country's independence from France in 1953, abdicated two years later, but established a one-party regime with himself as prime minister and later as head of state.

During this time, he navigated a perilous course between communist China, North Vietnam, and the United States, suppressing the Cambodian Communist Party (Khmer Rouge) while allowing North Vietnamese and Vietcong troops to use his country as a base of operations against South Vietnam. In 1970, a pro-U.S. military coup overthrew Sihanouk, and he fled to Beijing, where he organized a government in exile. When the Khmer Rouge seized Cambodia in 1975, he returned as head of state but was eventually kept under house arrest. When communist Vietnam invaded Cambodia in 1979 and drove the Khmer Rouge into the jungle, he escaped and headed an anti-Vietnamese resistance that held on to Cambodia's seat in the United Nations.

In 1990, the non–Khmer Rouge factions came together to form a coalition government with Sihanouk as president. Three years later, the monarchy was restored, and he resumed his original role as king. In 2004, he abdicated a second time, passing the throne to his son.

Whether as king, prime minister, head of state or president, Sihanouk demonstrated remarkable resilience as he piloted his country through a series of disasters.

lot of attention to the issue" with his plan to direct the film that became *Full Metal Jacket*. Cimino planned to produce *Platoon*, but not unlike the fate of the original project for *Born of the Fourth of July*, the promised financial support fell through (McGilligan 1987).

Stone finally found financial backing for *Platoon*. The British production company that worked with him on his previous movie, *Salvador*, Hemdale Film Corporation, invested $6 million, giving Stone a modest but feasible budget. He shot the film in 54 days in the Philippines with a cast of emerging actors. Charlie Sheen (1965–), the 19-year-old son of Martin Sheen, who played the protagonist of *Apocalypse Now*, starred as Taylor; Tom Berenger (1949–), who gained notice for his role in *The Big Chill* (1983), played Sergeant Barnes; Willem Dafoe (1955–), a thespian near the beginning of his film career, played Sergeant Elias.

As had been the case with previous Vietnam War movies, the U.S. military refused to cooperate. Instead, the Philippine army assisted in the making of *Platoon*, renting helicopters, fighter bombers, infantry weapons, and a military base for rehearsals to the production, as well as providing army units to play the role of North Vietnamese troops (Riordan 1995, 188). Stone's own wartime experience guided his direction, yet he hired retired U.S. Marines Captain Dale Dye (1944–) and other ex-marines "to train my actors by pushing them to the limit," Stone recalled. "They didn't let them sleep; they made them walk in the jungle," subjecting them to enough hardship to leave them "irritated, worried, frightened. I wanted them to look like us," he said, referring to the real soldiers of Bravo Company (Ciment 1987). Dye's basic training involved 10-mile marches shouldering 50-pound backpacks, sleeping in foxholes, and practicing with real weapons. Sheen recalled, "It was a hundred percent military. We were told if we disobeyed an order, we'd be off the film" (Riordan 1995, 192).

The film's apparent realism and its dramatic action scenes, as well as its introspection, gained *Platoon* a wide audience. It eventually earned $250 million in box-office receipts. Predictably, it drew some fire from both ends of the political spectrum. From the left came cries that the movie was "unreflective about the moral nature of war itself, a Vietnam movie undisturbed by the voices of dissent that heated this country in 1967–68" (Kramer 1987). The *New Republic* shot from the right in a March 1987 editorial, complaining of *Platoon*'s "appeasement, isolationism, defeatism" and blaming its "attitude" for the atmosphere in which the Ronald Reagan administration was forced to conduct Central American military interventions in secrecy through a series of events leading to the Iran Contra scandal. Answering such criticism, Stone replied, "*Platoon* isn't about politics or the government's fault; it's about boys in the jungle" (McGilligan 1987).

However, for the most part, *Platoon* received approval from across the spectrum of opinion. *Washington Post* conservative columnist Charles Krauthammer (1950–2018) compared the film to the recently dedicated Vietnam War Memorial in Washington, DC, for "the same seeming freedom from politics" (Krauthammer 1987). Liberal historian David Halberstam (1934–2007), who covered the Vietnam War for the *New York Times*, saw *Platoon* in a special screening for veterans. "One could feel the cumulative tension of men watching a terrible but important part of their lives flash in front of them again," he wrote. "It was a special kind of quiet in the theater, a tense, almost fearful quiet, as if they had been transported back to the worst moments of their lives." He added, "Rarely have I seen an audience so completely transported into the world of the cinematic image in front of them" (Toplin 2000, 111).

Film critics were largely positive. The *New York Times*'s Vincent Canby called *Platoon* "possibly the best work of any kind about Vietnam since Michael Herr's book *Dispatches*" and described it as "a dramatization of mental, physical and moral chaos" (Canby 1986). For David Denby (1943–), writing in *New York* magazine, "*Platoon* is the kind of Vietnam picture that many of us have longed for." He praised it for telling a "young soldier's story without copping out on the ineradicable bitterness and confusion of the Vietnam War" (Denby 1986). The *Chicago Sun-Times*'s Roger Ebert called *Platoon* "the best film of 1986" (R. Ebert 1986). However, some critics, such as Pauline Kael in the *New Yorker*, expressed mixed opinions. She praised *Platoon*'s screenplay for capturing "the soldier's frustration" and "revenge fever" but criticized Stone for "jacking up the melodrama to an impossible pitch" in the depiction of Elias's death (Kael 1987).

At the 1987 Academy Awards, *Platoon* received eight nominations and won Oscars for Best Picture, Best Director, Best Sound Mixing, and Best Film Editing. It earned several other top honors from the Golden Globes and the Directors Guild of America. *Platoon* has endured as one of the most respected Vietnam War films for the pinpoint accuracy of its historical depictions. British film historian Dave Thomson praised Stone for turning "complex ideas and problems into crowd-pleasing movies" and *Platoon* for deserving "its reputation as the proper American admission of pain over Vietnam" (Thomson 2010, 933).

HISTORICAL BACKGROUND

Support units from the 25th Infantry Division, nicknamed "Tropic Lightning" for its lightning flash insignia, were sent to South Vietnam as part of the U.S. advisory mission as early as 1963. The division's combat brigades began to arrive at the end of 1965. From that time through the 25th's departure in the spring of 1971, the division was deployed across the 40 to 60 miles that separated Saigon from the Cambodian border. It was dangerous territory, and the 25th's casualties, including some 5,000 killed, were among the highest suffered by the U.S. Army during the Vietnam War. At times the number of casualties exceeded the number of newly arrived recruits. Glen Olstad, an armored personnel carrier mechanic, was given a five-day infantry course and thrust into battle. Olstad objected, insisting that he was trained as a mechanic. The sergeant responded, "You *were* a mechanic." When Olstad threatened to write his congressman on the grounds that such a reassignment violated regulations, the sergeant told him: "When your congressman stands in front of my desk and says 'no,' then you won't [become an infantryman]—until then, you will!" (Quoted in J. R. Ebert 1993, 100–101). The division included an authorized strength of 17,000, but "in practice, combat units were invariably under strength." Along with foot soldiers, the division included mechanized infantry riding in armored personnel carriers, artillery battalions, and a squadron of tanks (Bergerud 1993, 4–5).

The 25th's Area of Operations (AO) encompassed four provinces, Tay Ninh, Hau Nghia, Binh Long, and Binh Duong, containing largely flat ground save for a magnificent outcrop of stone, Nui Ba Den (Black Virgin Mountain), where the United States established an observation post despite a network of tunnels burrowed into the mountain by communist troops.

Two rivers and many canals traversed the AO, which consisted of jungle, rice paddies, and still-active rubber plantations. The paved road, Highway 1, linked Saigon to Cambodia, and the 25th guarded convoys and bridges along the route. During the dry season, temperatures climbed to 110 degrees during daylight.

The AO brushed against the suburbs of Saigon on the east and ostensibly neutral Cambodia on the west. There, the Vietcong and the North Vietnamese army had established themselves with the connivance of Cambodia's wily chief of state, Prince Norodom Sihanouk. Although he disliked all Vietnamese, Sihanouk recognized "the power of Hanoi" and "believed that he had no alternative to reaching an ambiguous *modus vivendi* with the communists." In 1965, he secretly allowed the Vietcong and North Vietnamese army to establish "sanctuaries" on his side of the Cambodia-Vietnam border. In 1966, Chinese Prime Minister Zhou Enlai personally asked Sihanouk to allow aid to reach the Vietnamese by sea. With a certain reluctance but a willingness to profit from the deal, Sihanouk allowed additional supplies to reach the Cambodian border from the port of Sihanoukville. Chinese and Soviet Bloc merchant ships unloaded supplies that were trucked to the border, by the Cambodian army and a Chinese import-export company, along a highway that had been built with U.S. aid (Shawcross 1979, 64).

Sihanouk's decision to gamble on a tacit alliance with North Vietnam and the Vietcong had a decisive impact on the war. From 1959, North Vietnam supplied rebels in the country's south through the Ho Chi Minh Trail, a network of narrow roads and river crossings that passed southward inside the Laotian border. As the war heated up, North Vietnam sent its army units down the trail to support the Vietcong. Branching out from the Laotian border, the "Sihanouk Trail" extended the communist supply lines through Cambodia into South Vietnam. The trail straddled "villages in exile" settled by procommunist South Vietnamese who fled their country, along with supply dumps, field hospitals, base camps, and recreation centers for communist forces. The U.S. military refrained from overt attacks by land or air on communist positions in Cambodia during the war's early years in the hope of drawing Sihanouk to the American side. However, U.S. Special Forces conducted covert sabotage and espionage missions and recruited mercenaries from among the hill-dwelling Montagnard tribes who engaged in operations against communist forces. Eventually, Richard Nixon launched secret bombing raids on targets inside Cambodia. Sihanouk looked the other way, and North Vietnam kept silent in light of its often-repeated claim that it had no troops in neutral Cambodia (Shawcross 1979, 64).

The mission of the 25th Infantry Division before and during the period represented in *Platoon* was to hold key strongpoints, interdict North Vietnamese infiltration, and engage communist forces wherever they could be found within the AO. The 25th was headquartered in Cu Chi, 14 miles west of Saigon, described as "a small American city transplanted to the middle of

Vietnam" with a movie theater, a sauna, swimming pools, air-conditioned quarters, and officers and enlisted men's clubs. It was a regular stop for USO tours. Cu Chi was planted in countryside firmly held by the Vietcong, who in the base's early days had no trouble surfacing from underground tunnels and attacking from within the camp (Bergerud 1993, 28–35). Cu Chi was subject to frequent mortar attacks through the war, yet life there was relatively comfortable, and the base absorbed a large number of headquarters and support troops who saw no combat in the bush. "I didn't even really know that there was actual combat going on," recalled Dan Krehbiel, a veteran of the 25th (J. R. Ebert 1993, 97).

Beyond Cu Chi, the 25th established several other camps and firebases, essentially artillery positions designed to support infantry in the field. Those smaller bases were usually protected by barbed wire and earthen berms. One of the 25th's ongoing missions was to set up "perimeters," temporary positions often intended as bait for the enemy. American strategy called for luring the Vietcong and North Vietnamese into the open where artillery and airpower could inflict heavy casualties. The 25th participated in Operation Junction City (1967), a joint U.S.-South Vietnamese campaign to locate and destroy the mythic Central Office of South Vietnam (COSV), the Vietcong's "mini-Pentagon" said to be concealed in the jungles near the Cambodian border. Although Junction City resulted in casualties and the capture of enemy armaments, it never located COSV because it never existed in the form imagined by the U.S. military. In reality, a cadre of commanders formed COSV, which moved swiftly on foot from one place to another.

As implied in *Platoon*, the division's combat infantry spent much of its time in a succession of patrols "because of the necessity to find an enemy hidden in jungle or among civilians" (Bergerud 1993, 46–47). The 25th rarely encountered the North Vietnamese army until late 1967, around the time of Stone's arrival, but numerous lightning assaults by Vietcong guerillas and better-trained "Main Force" units targeted the division's positions. Superior American firepower inevitably carried the day, yet the enemy's capacity to absorb casualties seemed boundless. When the Tet Offensive began on January 31, 1968, the 25th stood its ground. Elements of the 25th defended the crucial Tan Son Nhut Air Base west of Saigon and took part in the vicious fighting that cleared Vietcong and North Vietnamese units from South Vietnam's beleaguered capital.

In May 1970, elements of the 25th took part in Nixon's "incursion" into Cambodia, intended as a swift assault to destroy communist sanctuaries across the border. "Damage done to the North Vietnamese Army and the Viet Cong was not as great as had been hoped," wrote a chronicler sympathetic to the aims of the incursion. The assault captured large quantities of supplies intended for communist forces operating in South Vietnam but could not reverse the course of the war (Nolan 1990, 439). Even before the incursion, token elements of the 25th had moved back to the division's home base in Hawaii as part of Nixon's Vietnamization plan. However, the 25th did not leave Cu Chi until December 15, 1970, and one of the division's combat contingents, the Second Brigade, remained in Vietnam until April 1971 (Bergerud 1993, 269–270).

DEPICTION AND CULTURAL CONTEXT

Among the major movies on the Vietnam War, *Platoon* stood apart as a lightly fictionalized memoir of its writer-director. In some cases, Stone even retained the names of his fellow soldiers. Stone carefully adopted several of *Platoon*'s combat or patrol scenes from his own experiences, altering or condensing the scenes only to better fit the dramatic arc of the story. The accounts of his fellow soldiers generally square with both the screenplay and Stone's recollections.

Like Taylor, the character representing Stone in the film, Stone arrived in Vietnam on a transport plane and was sent straightaway to a position near the Cambodian border. Stone and his alter ego were unusual among the men of the 25th. Unlike them, Stone was not part of the working class but a son of affluence; he was neither a draftee nor did he enlist to escape a social or economic dead end. Instead, as if emulating a character out of Ernest Hemmingway, he joined to test his manhood. "I wanted to see what I was made of. Would I be a coward? How would I react?" Stone explained. Verifying the essence of Stone's account of himself through Taylor, Crutcher Peterson, who served in Stone's platoon, said, "He was never a regular GI Joe. He was pretty green, a loner and moody, always writing things." Another veteran of the 25th, Ben Fitzgerald, recalled the reaction of the troops upon learning that Stone had volunteered. "Yeah, we all thought that was a little strange" (Riordan 1995, 40, 45, 56).

Taylor-Stone was a fish out of his element who gradually won respect for his ability to adapt to the role of a combat infantryman facing the continual danger of death. "The vets treated the new guys like meat, so you were expendable," Stone recalled. "Nobody was motivated, except to get out. Survival was the key. It wasn't very romantic" (Riordan 1995, 43). More seasoned soldiers often treated new arrivals ambivalently at first because they recognized new troops as replacements for friends lost to the war. However, as Sergeant Willie Williams put it, "My heart was open to a lot of the younger guys that came over, and I could sense the fear in them. I really felt for them." Other veterans of the 25th echoed Stone's tone of desperation. According to Glen Olstad, "There were times that you didn't know why you were still alive or hadn't been seriously wounded. I would say most of my tour I did not exactly expect to come home. Someplace, sometime, I expected I'd make the wrong move" (J. R. Ebert 1993, 129, 217–218).

There may have been a gap in morale between the 25th's original contingents and the draftees who arrived by the time of Stone's deployment. Robert Connor recalled that the "replacements came in with a different attitude. They were more belligerent and didn't care as much." Connor felt that they "didn't have enough time to train and become soldiers. They lacked the desire, dedication, and obedience." Captain Carl Quickmire served in the 25th in 1966 and returned in 1969 for a second tour. He found it was "an entirely different unit this time." He was struck by "the lack of career NCOs [noncommissioned officers], the men we called 'hard-core NCOs,' and the prevalence of the 'instant Jack' or instant NCOs" (Bergerud 1993, 95–96). They were, perhaps, men like Elias, given a field promotion to sergeant because of their aptitude for leading men but not their dedication to the army's ethos.

One such "instant NCO," Robert Conner, recalled the challenges he faced in leading a platoon. "You know, that's a lot of responsibility to put on a kid," he said. "Imagine an eighteen-year-old kid reading the map coordinates, saying, 'You go out here at dusk, go out 300 meters, and set up an ambush patrol'" (J. R. Ebert 1993, 97).

Platoon skipped over the "jungle warfare school" newly arrived infantrymen of the 25th received at Cu Chi. "The name is a lot more impressive than the school itself," Dan Vandenberg recalled. He compared it to "a walk through Disneyland" and added, "After that week, the brass could say they gave us a week of jungle training. At least, it was a good way to get acclimated to the climate" (Bergerud 1993, 18).

The movie's screenplay accurately reflects the seemingly unending round of patrols engaged by the companies (consisting of 160 men), platoons (40 men), and squads (10 men) of the 25th. The depiction of attacks by red ants and other insects and vermin was a daily concern. Sergeant Major Kenneth Stumpf complained that the red ants "stung like crazy" (Bergerud 1993, 18). "We usually slept with a towel over our faces," recalled Jerry Liucci, "or the mosquitoes would carry you away. The cocktail sauce they gave us for food wasn't edible but was great for leeches—you just squirt it on them, and they would drop off you." Whether from insects or anxiety over an enemy attack, sleep was difficult in the field. According to Colonel Ferguson, "Few of us enjoyed more than two hours of sleep in a day. This left us physically exhausted much of the time" (Bergerud 1993, 19, 111).

Little wonder Taylor falls asleep while on night patrol, allowing enemy forces to advance unseen beyond the perimeter and attack his squad by surprise. Stone said the incident happened just as *Platoon* depicted. "I let my people down. Then I awoke and the Viet Cong were there. These guys just appeared" (Riordan 1995, 44). As in the film, single squads usually conducted night patrols under a sergeant with a machine-gun crew, a medic, a forward observer, and five riflemen. They established a perimeter of Claymore mines that could be detonated to kill intruders. The exact siting of the perimeter was crucial because the intention was to call down mortar fire to destroy the enemy assault. By contrast, daytime patrols, also shown in the movie, were company size (Bergerud 1993, 107–108).

According to Captain Quickmire, "It essentially amounted to going out and beating the jungle every day and every night looking for the enemy." He recalled the names given to those missions: "search and destroy," "cordon and search," "sweep and search," "anvil and hammer." "Despite all the highfalutin' gadgets, intelligence for the most part was extremely poor" (Bergerud 1993, 106).

Major General Ellis Williamson (1918–2007), commander of the 25th from 1968 through 1969, conceded as much. "The Army at the time was designed and equipped for the European battlefield," he said. "Its target acquisition and intelligence sensors were conceived, designed, and produced with that in mind. The enemy in Vietnam, however, was different. He was foot mobile, operated from jungle sanctuaries, and was more often than not a 'night creature'" (Bergerud 1993, 100).

If the enemy was acclimated to the nighttime landscape, for the men of the 25th, darkness posed yet another danger. "There were many times, you were out on patrol and literally couldn't see your hand in front of your face," said Vandenberg. "The booby traps and natural obstacles were invisible. On the other hand, Charlie just thrived on night time. He could move through the dark and never make a sound. He knew exactly where he was going; he was good. It was always such a relief when you saw the sun come up." When attacked at night, as in *Platoon*, Vandenberg's men fired back blindly (Bergerud 1993, 109).

Morale among GIs slumped from the feeling that they fought an invisible enemy over unattainable objectives. "When you are fighting a war like Vietnam, you have no idea if you're doing anything useful militarily or not," said Larry Fontana, an officer in the 25th. "You know you killed and wounded more of them than you, and that is it. Nothing would have made me happier than to never have gotten into a fight. Only the crazies hoped to get into a fight while on patrol. Luckily, we had few crazies." A chronicler of the 25th added, "There was a notable lack of desire to grab the flag and charge a machine-gun nest. The men killed because they had to" to protect themselves and their unit (Bergerud 1993, 134).

Stone took care to include many telling details and maintain accuracy. Infantrymen who wanted to shirk patrols really did spray mosquito repellent on the soles of their feet to cause swelling. *Platoon*'s military adviser, Dale Dye, drilled the cast in proper army lingo. "I'd tell them things like, 'Never say, "over and out" because it's Hollywood, and it drives me nuts,'" he said (Riordan 1993, 1995, 50). *Platoon*'s dialogue echoes the voices of Vietnam servicemen, who called the country "the Nam" and fresh replacement soldiers "newbies." "The film is also littered with obscenities, as Stone refused to pull any verbal punches" (Toplin 2000, 77).

Platoon also frankly depicted drug use during the war. As Stone recalled, the marijuana smokers formed a group distinct from "the lifers, the juicers," meaning the heavy-drinking professional servicemen. Soldiers smoked pot in camp but not in the field because "it slowed the senses and quite often, your senses were the only thing that kept you alive" (Riordan 1995, 46). According to Captain Morgan Sincock of the 25th, "There was no heroin in the Army in 1968. Apparently that came later. There was marijuana." He added, "I never saw it used in our unit in the field. Again, it seemed to be an aspect of base camp life" (Bergerud 1993, 284).

In *Platoon*, Taylor's patrol found the mutilated body of one of their men outside a village of thatched huts or "hootches" as the GIs called them. The soldiers react in fear and anger, shooting a Vietnamese who tries to flee, killing a pig, rounding up the villagers for questioning, and dragging them out of their huts into the open. They drop grenades into holes that could be Vietcong hiding places or the entrances to bunkers. They uncover Czech machine guns, a weapon supplied by the Eastern Bloc to North Vietnam. The troops force one villager to dance by shooting at his feet. One soldier beats a civilian to death. Only one member of the company speaks enough Vietnamese to communicate with the frightened villagers. They tell him they have no choice because they are afraid of the communists. The troops set huts on fire and force the remaining villagers to evacuate, presumably to a strategic hamlet ostensibly controlled by the South Vietnamese government.

Stone said that he drew the scene from actual events. "We burned the villages. We did a lot of damage. Not on the My Lai scale, but we did it on a steady basis. It was random." He referred to the My Lai Massacre (March 16, 1968), a notorious incident in which a company from the 23rd Infantry Division killed hundreds of civilians from a village in central South Vietnam. Stone includes himself among the perpetrators depicted in *Platoon*. "I lost it and began firing at this old man's feet. I hated this guy. I told him to get out of the hole. He wouldn't get out and he wouldn't stop smiling. I made him dance. I just wanted to scare him to the verge of dying." Stone also understood the precarious position of the villagers. "I could see they were getting pressure from the other side. They were just into survival, like we were" (Riordan 1995, 58, 59).

He added that the attempted rape of a village girl by several of his fellow soldiers happened as shown. In the film, the would-be rapists treated Taylor's intervention with scorn, but as if retreating in the face of a witness, they withdrew before assaulting the girl. As Stone recalled, "Something in me snapped and I went over and broke it up. They weren't too happy about it, but when I saw them and saw how afraid she was, I had to do something about it, so I made them let her go" (Riordan 1995, 59–60). Bunny, played by Kevin Dillon (1965–), "really killed that woman. He battered her. He smashed her head with the stock of a '16 [M16], burned her hootch down, but it was in an isolated part of the village. Nobody saw it. It was just like a really quiet thing" (Cooper 1988).

The sequence of events Stone described was not unlikely given other accounts by veterans. Few U.S. Army units had more continual contact with Vietnamese villagers than the 25th, and the army "did almost nothing to prepare soldiers for the 'culture shock'—and the term is a good one here—that almost all of them encountered when coming to Vietnam," according to the division's chronicler. Dan Vandenberg admitted: "We didn't even think they were people," explaining his anger over villagers who lent no support or encouragement to U.S. forces. But he admitted, "If they'd have tipped us off, Charlie would have come that night and slit their throats" (Bergerud 1993, 221).

Sergeant Thomas Giltner, a platoon leader in the 25th, emphasized: "You could never tell who was the enemy and who was not. Therefore, you treated everyone with suspicion and distrust." He described the villagers as "pathetic farmers" who "wanted to be left to follow their ancestral ways" but "usually operated as local militia for the VC for purposes, at minimum, of intelligence gathering, observation of U.S. activities, ambushes, raids, and so on." He assumed that most villagers were "either VC agents or sympathizers or somehow under their influence" (Bergerud 1993, 222–223).

Veterans of the 25th also recalled brutality inflicted on the villagers from South Vietnamese and Vietcong forces. "You saw a lot of things and did a lot of things you didn't want to see or do because you had to. We didn't burn any villages," said the 25th's C. W. Bowan, but he admitted to burning individual hootches if the occupants were suspected of supporting the Vietcong. His unit turned suspects over to the South Vietnamese, and he described waterboarding and beatings at their hands. He also remembered the savagery of the communists. "They'd go in and take out a whole village," he said. "They'd do that to set an example for the hamlets around the area" (Bergerud 1993, 227).

Charles Albridge, a forward observer for the 25th, spoke for many of his comrades. "I don't doubt that My Lai happened: I just don't believe it happened with an extreme amount of regularity." He explained that civilians were inevitably killed as U.S. troops returned fire from villages. "I never personally saw civilians lined up and shot. We removed them from villages and moved them to camps." However, villages suspected of supporting the Vietcong were destroyed. "That was a standing order" (Bergerud 1993, 233–234).

Out of the moral quandary of how to fight a war where the enemy could be anyone came the dramatic axis of *Platoon*, the struggle between two sergeants with opposing views, Barnes and Elias. Barnes represents the utility of killing without hesitation to ensure the survival of yourself and your unit. Elias argues for a more deliberative assessment of each situation and an awareness of humanity in the war zone. Stone claimed that both men were real people and that he used their real names, although in reality they did not serve together or know each other. Even the sickle-shaped scar on Barnes's face was taken from life (Riordan 1995, 53–54). "Barnes had this cold stare that used to really terrify me," Stone said. "He was an incredible soldier. He'd been wounded six or seven times, yet he always survived" (Riordan 1995, 57). Stone described Elias as "a rock star in the body of a soldier. Real danger turned him on," yet he was a man of compassion. "Everybody seemed to love him except for the lifers and the juicers." Stone conceded that in the field, "It's easier to survive in the Barnes mode. The machine. You are part of a machine and the machine works." Curious about the veracity of the role he played, Berenger asked a platoon sergeant who had served in Vietnam "if he was as mean as I was in the film. He said, 'At times. Otherwise, your men will die'" (Riordan 1995, 202–203).

Platoon shows the killing of officers or NCOs by their own men, including Taylor shooting Barnes, whom he blames for the death of Elias, on the battlefield. In Vietnam those killings were called "fragging," from the fragmentation grenades that were often used. Stone never admitted to taking part in fragging but said that it occurred "six to ten times more than the official count. The officer corps—not just the officers but especially the top sergeants—were pretty much hated, most of them" (Riordan 1995, 471). By some accounts, as many as 900 fragging incidents occurred during the war. As a military officer admitted at the time, "The morale, discipline, and battleworthiness of the U.S. Armed Forces are, with a few salient exceptions, lower and worse than at any time in this century and possibly in the history of the United States" (Heinl 1971).

In *Platoon*, Lieutenant Wolfe, played by Mark Moses (1958–), is depicted as ineffectual and unable to keep his sergeants in line. As in any war, the competence of officers in Vietnam varied greatly. Enlisted men from the 25th recalled lieutenants who "really didn't know what was going on" or were so "gung-ho" that they ignored the reality on the ground. At least one lieutenant was court-martialed after exposing his men to friendly fire (Bergerud 1993, 143–144). Friendly-fire incidents as seen in *Platoon* were not uncommon, especially when artillery fire or air strikes were directed to the wrong coordinates.

While the men of the 25th spent much of their deployment on patrol, they also, as *Platoon* showed, engaged in pitched battles with the enemy. "Geography and some very wise leadership at Cu Chi spared the 25th Division many of the vicious Hamburger Hill–type battles that other divisions faced" (Bergerud 1993, 52). By the end of 1967 and into 1968, Vietcong Main Force and North Vietnamese regiments finally launched concerted attacks against the 25th. "You know, films like *Rambo* make it look real easy," Stone said, "but I remember the NVAs [North Vietnamese army soldiers] as being terrific fighters" (Riordan 1995, 206). Few who met them in combat disagreed. "Division veterans are quick to recognize the incredible bravery shown by the men trying to kill them" (Bergerud 1993, 152).

Platoon's climactic battle scene is based on a January 1, 1968, North Vietnamese attack on Firebase Burt near the Cambodian border. Eyewitnesses verify the film's account, including Captain Robert Hemphill, Bravo Company's commanding officer. A private in Bravo, Larry Robinson, recalled hand-to-hand combat as communist troops broke through the American perimeter. "There was a good description in the movie of what was happening," he said. "We were pinned down on all sides, isolated and scared to death. Then Oliver was sent down with another guy, Mike Blotchet, to try to get some of the guys out." He praised Stone for having "a lot of guts. His odds of dying were pretty good and it meant a lot to us for him to be able to bring some of the guys back alive." American losses in that battle were 25 dead and 175 wounded. The North Vietnamese lost 500 men. Captain Hemphill confirms that their bodies were bulldozed into a mass grave as shown in *Platoon* (Riordan 1995, 49, 50).

CONCLUSION

Platoon set the standard for realism against which all subsequent Vietnam War films were judged. While not affording a complete picture of events in the 25th Infantry Division's AO, *Platoon* accurately depicts the experiences of many combat troops in the 25th during the time of Stone's deployment. "Those guys are us," said veteran John Wheeler (Corliss 1987). Willem Dafoe, too young to have served in Vietnam, gained a new respect for the men who fought. "*Platoon* presses the question, 'Is there any morality in war?'" he said. "What kind of guy do you want leading you in war, Barnes or Elias? What's decent if you're dead?" (Riordan 1995, 209).

FURTHER READING

Bergerud, Eric M. 1993. *Red Thunder, Tropic Lightning: The World of a Combat Division in Vietnam*. Boulder, CO: Westview Press.

Canby, Vincent. "The Vietnam War in Stone's Platoon." *New York Times*, December 19, 1986.

Ciment, Michel. "Interview with Oliver Stone." *Positif*, April 1987.

Cooper, Mark. "Playboy Interview: Oliver Stone." *Playboy*, February 1988.

Corliss, Richard. "Platoon." *Time*, March 8, 1987.

Denby, David. "Bringing the War Back Home." *New York*, December 15, 1986.

Ebert, James R. 1993. *A Life in a Year: The American Infantryman in Vietnam, 1965–1972*. Novato, CA: Presidio Press.

Ebert, Roger. "Platoon." *Chicago Sun-Times*, December 30, 1986.

Heinl, Robert D., Jr. "The Collapse of the Armed Forces." *Armed Forces Journal*, June 7, 1971.

Kael, Pauline. "Platoon." *New Yorker*, January 12, 1987.

Kramer, Sydelle. 1987. "Platoon." *Cineaste* 15:3.

Krauthammer, Charles. "Platoon Chic." *Washington Post*, February 20, 1987.

McGilligan, Patrick. "Point Man." *Film Comment*, January/February 1987.

Nolan, Keith William. 1990. *Into Cambodia: Spring Campaign, Summer Offensive, 1970*. Novato, CA: Presidio Press.

Riordan, James. 1995. *Stone: The Controversies, Excesses, and Exploits of a Radical Filmmaker*. New York. Hyperion.

Shawcross, William. 1979. *Sideshow: Kissinger, Nixon and the Destruction of Cambodia*. New York: Washington Square Books.

Thomson, Dave. 2010. *The New Biographical Dictionary of Film*. New York: Alfred A. Knopf.

Toplin, Robert Brent, editor. 2000. *Oliver Stone's USA: Film, History, and Controversy*. Lawrence, KS: University of Kansas Press.

Chapter 7

Full Metal Jacket (1987)

Warner Brothers released *Full Metal Jacket* on June 26, 1987. By this time, Vietnam War movies were an accepted feature of the popular culture landscape, but *Full Metal Jacket* achieved distinction from its director and producer, Stanley Kubrick (1928–1999). Kubrick was one of the world's most respected filmmakers, with achievements that included *Dr. Strangelove: Or How I Learned to Stop Worrying and Love the Bomb* (1964), *2001: A Spacey Odyssey* (1968), and *The Shining* (1980). His first film to reach widespread acclaim, *Paths of Glory* (1957), was determinedly antiwar. However, *Full Metal Jacket* made no particular statement about the Vietnam War, even if it allowed some of its characters to voice their opinions. *Full Metal Jacket*'s theme is the dehumanization of military training and how that instruction played out in combat. The film showed the war's brutality but was not concerned with morality or strategy.

Kubrick became intrigued with the subject of Vietnam in 1980 when he was introduced to Michael Herr (1940–2016). A war correspondent whose book *Dispatches* (1978) offered a gritty and sardonic memoir of his Vietnam experience, Herr wrote the voiceover narration for the protagonist of *Apocalypse Now* (1979), played by Martin Sheen (1940–). Herr recalls Kubrick saying "he'd liked my book about Vietnam" but "didn't want to make a movie of it" and asked him to recommend "a good Vietnam story" (Herr 2000, 6–7). In 1983, Kubrick found that story when he finally read the Vietnam War novel *The Short-Timers* (1979) by Gustav Hasford (1947–1993). *Newsweek* called the novel "extremely ugly" but "the best work of fiction about the Vietnam War" (Clemons 1979).

Hasford, who served in the U.S. Marine Corps as a "combat correspondent" in Vietnam, penning propaganda for military publications, claimed his novel was not autobiographical. However, the experiences of his protagonist,

---

VIETCONG

On December 20, 1960, in a remote jungle village near the Cambodian border, the communist regime of North Vietnam organized a gathering ostensibly representing South Vietnamese dissident groups. The movement established on that day, the National Liberation Front, popularly known as the Vietcong, was dedicated to overthrowing South Vietnam's corrupt regime headed by President Ngo Dinh Diem and driving out his American backers. Despite efforts to make the Vietcong appear as a genuine coalition, it was dominated at all times by North Vietnam. Many of the Vietcong's formative members were sent from North Vietnam to organize cadres in the war against South Vietnam and its Western allies.

The Vietcong stepped up the Hanoi-supported insurrection against South Vietnam that had already been under way since Vietnam's division under the Geneva Accords (1954). Calling their guerilla army the Liberation Armed Forces of South Vietnam, the Vietcong was supplied with arms shipments sent along jungle trails from North Vietnam and was eventually backed by units of the North Vietnamese army. The Vietcong effectively governed large areas of South Vietnam's countryside at various times but never established control of the country's cities until it overran South Vietnam with the aid of North Vietnamese forces in 1975.

The Vietcong's "Provisional Revolutionary Government of the Republic of South Vietnam" claimed it stood for an independent and nonaligned (or neutral) South Vietnam that might eventually unify with North Vietnam. The Revolutionary Government had a seat at the table in Paris, negotiating the Peace Accords (1973) that officially ended the Vietnam War. In 1975, after the fall of Saigon, the Revolutionary Government became the official government of South Vietnam, but it operated under control of the North. In1976, North and South Vietnam merged to form the present Socialist Republic of Vietnam, and the Vietcong were relegated to history.

Private James T. "Joker" Davis, corresponded to his own postings in the war. Hasford explained that in writing *The Short-Timers*, he aimed to debunk the image of the Vietnam veteran as "a cold-blooded psychotic," and he blamed the U.S. government for fostering that image in an effort to undermine the antiwar movement led by returning veterans. Like his protagonist, Hasford underwent basic training at the Marine Corps Recruit Depot at Parris Island, South Carolina. "Short-time" refers to his 385-day tour of duty in Vietnam. It was his first novel, and several publishers rejected it before Harper and Row accepted the manuscript (Howard 1999, 161–162).

Although credited as a cowriter, Hasford was kept in the dark about the development of *Full Metal Jacket*'s screenplay and complained about the completed film. In particular, the protagonist, Joker, was more callous and less sympathetic in his novel than in the film. "They made you go to Vietnam," Kubrick told Hasford, but "people are going to have to pay to see this movie" (Duncan 2003, 170).

Mirroring the structure of Hasford's novel, *Full Metal Jacket* has two distinct parts. Part one follows the basic training Joker, Cowboy, and their platoon endure at the hands of Sergeant Hartman. The drill instructor is brutal to all recruits but is especially hard on the mentally and physically challenged Gomer Pyle. Troubled by his conscience through much of the story, Joker tries to help Pyle but to no avail. Part one culminates in Pyle's mental breakdown; the deranged recruit kills Hartman and himself on the eve of deployment to Vietnam.

Part two leaps forward to Vietnam in January 1968, where Joker serves as a combat correspondent for the military newspaper *Stars and Stripes*. When communist forces launch the Tet Offensive, which threatens to overwhelm the U.S. and South Vietnamese forces, Joker and combat photographer Rafterman (played by Canadian actor Kevyn Major Howard) are dispatched by helicopter to cover the fighting in Hue. They fall in with a squad that includes Cowboy and Animal Mother, a character from *The Short-Timers* refashioned to resemble Sylvester Stallone's Rambo. Advancing into the city, the squad suffers casualties from booby traps and sniper fire. They eventually overcome the sniper, a young girl wounded in the exchange of fire. Animal Mother wants to leave her to die in agony, but Joker, confronted again by a moral dilemma, decides to put her out of misery with a gunshot. The film ends with the marines marching while singing "The Mickey Mouse Club March," a typically sardonic Kubrick touch.

Determined not to follow the example of director Michael Cimino, who cast actors decades older than their roles in his Vietnam film, *The Deer Hunter* (1978), Kubrick auditioned his largely unknown young cast members via videotape. According to Kubrick, "The average age of American Marines was only eighteen. This is not going to be one of those films where ages are adjusted to accommodate Hollywood stars" (Howard 1999, 163).

For the Marine infantry, Kubrick chose Matthew Modine (1959–) as Joker, Arliss Howard (1954–) as Cowboy, Vincent D'Onofrio (1959–) as Gomer Pyle, Adam Baldwin (1962–) as Animal Mother, and Dorian Harewood (1950–) as Eightball. For the Parris Island drill instructor, Kubrick chose R. Lee Ermey (1944–2018) as Gunnery Sergeant Hartman. In real life, Ermey served as a Marine Corps drill instructor before being sent to Vietnam. His experiences led to his role as the drill instructor, Sergeant Loyce, in *The Boys in Company* C (1978) and his involvement in *Apocalypse Now* as technical adviser and helicopter pilot.

Kubrick wrote the screenplay for *Full Metal Jacket* and worked with Herr and Hasford largely through long-distance phone calls or mail. Assuming that audiences would not understand the meaning of *The Short-Timers*, Kubrick changed the name of his film to the more martial sounding *Full Metal Jacket* after the lead bullets encased within copper that are standard issue in the U.S. military (Howard 1999, 163).

Unlike every Vietnam War movie director since John Wayne (*The Green Berets*), Kubrick opted not to shoot his film in a suitably tropical setting. Instead, the reclusive filmmaker recreated Vietnam and the United States within a 30-mile radius of his English country home. The exteriors of the Parris Island Recruiting Depot were filmed at the Royal Army base at Basingstoke, and the interiors were studio sets. For the Vietnamese jungle, Kubrick arranged 100,000 artificial tropical plants fronted by transplanted palm trees from Spain. For the battlefield at Hue, Kubrick discovered that the abandoned Beckton Gas Works in London's Docklands bore close architectural resemblance to portions of the Vietnamese city. Studying thousands of photographs taken at Hue during the 1960s, Kubrick reproduced everything from signage to billboards in exact detail. The Beckton Gas Works was already partially demolished, and Kubrick's crew carefully rearranged the rubble to simulate the ruins of Hue. "You couldn't build that if you spent $80 million and had five years to do it," Kubrick said. A Belgian army colonel, a Kubrick fan, supplied the director with American-made M47 tanks. The Royal Army provided Westland Wessex helicopters similar to the Sikorsky H-34 Choctaws used by the U.S. Marine Corps in Vietnam (Howard 1999, 164–165).

Kubrick spent only $17 million making *Full Metal Jacket*, which returned $30 million in ticket sales during the first five weeks of release (Duncan 2003, 179). It was profitable and much discussed but not quite a hit, ranking only 23rd among 1987's highest-grossing movies and overshadowed by Oliver Stone's *Platoon*, released a year earlier and setting a standard for battlefield psychological realism that Kubrick had no interest in emulating.

Full Metal Jacket drew thoughtful criticism, both positive and negative. The *New York Times*'s Vincent Canby compared the film to "a series of exploding boomerangs. Just when you think you can relax in safety, some crazed image or line or event will swing around to lodge in the brain and scramble the emotions" (Canby 1987). The *Christian Science Monitor* reflected on "the contradictory human urge toward destructiveness and healing which is one of Kubrick's chief subjects" (Sterritt 1987). However, many critics and viewers agreed with the *New Yorker*'s Pauline Kael, who praised part one's "sadistic, pounding compulsiveness" but derided part two as "dispersed, as if it had no story." She also complained that the film's characters had no discernible inner life (Kael 1987). Likewise, Roger Ebert wrote, "The opening passages of 'Full Metal Jacket' promise much more than the film finally is able to deliver," adding that it "never recovers" after Sergeant Hartman and Pyle are dispatched (Ebert 1987).

Full Metal Jacket received an Oscar nomination for Best Adapted Screenplay but did not win. However, recent years have seen its status rise, though with Kael's caveat that part two was disappointing after the high-adrenaline rush of part one. The *Washington Post* described the film's first half as "an object lesson in the way great art is open to multiple interpretations" and called it "a masterpiece" only because Ermey "brought to life one of film's most indelible creations" (Bunch 2018). Writing in the *New York Times*, Anthony Swofford recalled how Ermey's "persona saturated military culture" and described the boot camp sequence as "beautiful and profane" as well as "terrifying and thrilling to watch" (Swofford 2018). Swofford was a Marine Corps veteran who saw *Full Metal Jacket* as a teenager, and his memoir of the Persian Gulf War, *Jarhead* (2003), became a best seller and was adapted into a film. "'Full Metal Jacket' wasn't the only reason I joined the Marine Corps, but it was a major one," he recalled (Swofford 2018). In 2001, the American Film Institute ranked *Full Metal Jacket* 95th in its "100 Years . . . 100 Thrills," which listed the top 100 most exciting, action-packed, suspenseful, or frightening movies in American cinema.

HISTORICAL BACKGROUND

The U.S. military began 1968 with every confidence of victory. "It lies within our grasp—the enemy's hopes are bankrupt," General William Westmoreland, the commander of forces in Vietnam, told the National Press Club. However, Secretary of Defense Robert McNamara had his doubts, and a study by the Rand Corporation, a nonpartisan research institute whose advice was often sought by Washington, concluded that "the revolutionary war in South Vietnam is being fought and lost" by the Nguyen Van Thieu (president of South Vietnam from 1965–1975) regime. In early January, American intelligence warned Ellsworth Bunker (1894–1984), the U.S. ambassador in Saigon, that Thieu would probably be unable to prevail against the communists (Bowden 2017, 38).

Hoping to topple the South Vietnamese government and drive out the Americans, North Vietnam planned a major offensive to coincide with the greatest holiday on the Vietnamese calendar, the Lunar New Year, a time when hostilities normally ceased, called Tet. The Tet Offensive commenced at midnight on January 30, 1968, when 84,000 North Vietnamese and Vietcong soldiers attacked Saigon, Da Nang, and Hue, along with 36 of South Vietnam's 44 provincial capitals, 64 of 245 district seats, and nearly 100 other hamlets and bases. The Vietnamese traditionally celebrated Tet with fireworks, and in many places the opening rounds may have been mistaken for holiday festivities. By sunrise it was apparent that the war had entered a new phase.

The United States was unprepared for the assault. "My God, it's Pearl Harbor all over again," said General William A. Knowlton (1920–2008) of the Ninth Infantry Division. Westmoreland's adjutant, General Creighton W. Abrams Jr. (1914–1974), slept through the early hours of Tet. The party at the U.S. embassy celebrating what Bunker called "the light at the end of the tunnel" was cut short when sappers blew a hole into the embassy wall and Marine Corps guards rushed him away in an armored personnel carrier. "There was an intelligence failure," Bunker later admitted (Ward 2017, 267).

For the rest of his life, Westmoreland continued to deny against all evidence that Tet caught him by surprise (Westmoreland 1976, 380–390). Many days into the offensive, with communist forces still firmly in control of the old imperial capital of Hue, Westmoreland remained fooled by the North Vietnamese diversionary attacks at the besieged base of Khe Sanh, which he insisted was their main objective. "I am in constant contact with developments around Khe Sanh," he assured President Lyndon B. Johnson as the Tet Offensive raged across South Vietnam. "The enemy has major forces in the area which he has not yet committed. Expect enemy initiation of large scale offensive action at Khe Sanh in the near future" (Bowden 2017, 197). For their part, the North Vietnamese also labored under illusions. Radio Hanoi called upon the people of South Vietnam to "rise up and launch attacks against the hideouts of the Thieu-Ky clique," as they called the South Vietnamese government led by president Thieu and vice president Nguyen Cao Ky (1930–2011) (Bowden 2017, 120). The popular revolt never occurred.

A historian correctly called the communist plan of action "audacious in its conception and stunning in its implementation," (Oberdorfer 1971, ix) yet in most places, communist forces held out for only a few hours against counterattacks. Within days, U.S. and South Vietnamese forces recaptured Kon Tum, Buon Ma Thuot, Hon Thiet, Can Tho, and Ben Tre. Ben Tre, leveled by U.S. artillery and air strikes, gave rise to one of the war's most notorious quotes when an unnamed major told an Associated Press reporter, "It became necessary to destroy the town to save it" (Arnett 1968). The communists experienced their greatest tactical success at Hue, where U.S. and South Vietnamese forces needed more than a month to expel the Vietcong and North Vietnamese. However, the attacks inside Saigon were brazen and shocking both to the U.S. government and the media even though the South Vietnamese army and police eventually crushed the assault with minimal American assistance. The communist attacks on Chi Hoa Prison and South Vietnam's navy headquarters, Armored Command, and Artillery Command were repulsed. Commandos briefly seized Radio Saigon but were unable to broadcast prerecorded tapes proclaiming the city's "liberation." Other commandos wearing South Vietnamese uniforms penetrated the presidential palace but were cut down. Although they were able to hold none of the installations they attacked, the Vietcong gained control of many of the city's neighborhoods. It took the government 10 days to take back full control over Saigon.

For Americans watching the Tet Offensive on television, some of the most unsettling images were of the U.S. embassy, its walls pockmarked by bullets and the Great Seal over the entrance knocked down. Dramatic accounts were published from the scene. Colonel George Jacobson, an embassy official, defended himself with a .45-caliber pistol tossed to him through an open second-floor window by an MP. "In one of the strangest scenes of the

Vietnam War, helmeted American troops ran crouching across broad Thong Nhut Boulevard to assault the gate of their own embassy," the *New York Times* reported. The Vietcong held sections of the embassy grounds for several hours. "Seven American helicopters landed on the roof to discharge a platoon of American paratroopers who raced down the stairways to come to the aid of Marine guards fighting to keep the enemy out of the main chancery building" (Mohr 1968).

The most visceral and widely published image was taken by Associated Press photographer Eddie Adams (1933–2004) on the streets of Saigon. Adams snapped a picture of Vietcong agent Nguyen Van Lem at the moment of his death agony. The startling image showed the chief of South Vietnam's National Police, Brigadier General Nguyen Ngoc Loan (1930–1998), summarily executing Lem with a revolver shot to the head.

Lem had probably led one of the Vietcong execution squads that terrorized the city, going house to house in some districts murdering anyone associated with the South Vietnamese government, even army enlisted men and their families. In some cases neighborhood residents were forced out of their homes to serve as jurors in "people's courts." The juries usually found the accused not guilty and the Vietcong honored their verdicts by releasing the prisoners. Many other Saigon residents were not as fortunate. A taxi driver recounted that the Vietcong "decapitated three people and left their bodies and heads at a coffee shop" (Ward 2017, 273).

The United States resolutely claimed victory by the end of the Tet Offensive in September 1968. Westmoreland called it "a striking defeat for the enemy on anyone's terms" and blamed the "attitude on the part of the American reporters" for contributing "to the psychological victory the enemy achieved in the United States" (Westmoreland 1976, 395, 404). In some respects this was true. The Vietcong and North Vietnamese were unable to hold any of the points they seized and lost nearly 50,000 men killed, wounded, or captured. North Vietnam's generals, who had opposed the offensive from the start, grumbled that they had "suffered unimaginable losses," according to Vietnamese writer Huy Duc (1962–). No unit engaged in Tet emerged intact, and many were devastated. General Tran Van Tra (1918–1996) admitted, "We did not correctly evaluate the specific balance of forces between ourselves and the enemy." Tet's objectives, he declared, were "beyond our actual strength" and "an illusion based on our subjective desires" (Karnow 1991, 544). However, the United States was never able to capitalize on its battlefield successes. "We underestimated the willingness of those peasants to pay the price" for war, said correspondent-turned-historian David Halberstam (1934–2007). "We had absolute military superiority" but the communists had "absolute political superiority" (Sorley 2011, 96).

The United States suffered a political, not military, defeat in the Tet Offensive. Despite prevailing over the communists, the offensive called into doubt the American military's claim that victory was in sight, and images of U.S.

troops desperately fighting to hold the embassy in Saigon weakened public support for Johnson's handling of the war, although support for the war initially remained high despite Tet. America's most trusted newsman, Walter Cronkite (1916–2009), previously supported U.S. policy in Vietnam. "And then in 1968 came Tet," he later wrote. Cronkite flew to Vietnam when Tet began and, not content to report from the relative safety of secure zones in Saigon, he went to Hue with a column of marines in the midst of the fighting. Wearing a flak jacket and helmet, he interviewed the marines as they struggled to retake the city. He left Hue in a helicopter he shared with the body bags of a dozen dead marines (Cronkite 1996, 254).

Cronkite had known Creighton Abrams from their service in World War II and spent an evening with the general. Abrams was "remarkably candid" about the shock of Tet, but Cronkite was disappointed that the general and his staff discussed only ways to "kill more Vietnamese" and had "no consideration of the bigger job of pacifying and restoring the country" (Cronkite 1996, 256–257). Cronkite delivered his findings to the American public on February 27 in a television special called "Report from Vietnam." He declared his disappointment in "the optimism of the American leaders" and cast doubt on "the silver linings they find in the darkest clouds." He called for ending the war by "negotiations, not the dictation of peace terms."

A *New York Times* exposé in March revealed the increasingly rancorous debate within the Johnson administration over what to do with Vietnam in light of Tet. Westmoreland, still convinced that victory was achievable, demanded massive reinforcements. Other "high administration officials," quoted anonymously, declared Vietnam a "bottomless pit" and that "all we thought we had constructed was built on sand" (Smith 1968).

By then, public support for the war, as well as for Johnson, was declining and the U.S. Senate Foreign Relations Committee held hearings on the situation in Vietnam. On March 12, 1968, the New Hampshire Democratic primary delivered another shock to Johnson when Senator Eugene McCarthy (1916–2005), little known until then outside his home state of Minnesota, claimed 41.4 percent of the vote on an antiwar platform, nearly defeating Johnson in the state. Four days later, Senator Robert Kennedy (1925–1968), who had already questioned the war, announced his candidacy for president. Despite his inability to grasp the situation in Vietnam, Johnson was an astute realist in domestic politics and understood what was possible and what was not. On March 31, in a televised address to the nation, Johnson announced that he would neither seek nor accept his party's nomination for the presidency.

DEPICTION AND CULTURAL CONTEXT

The first half of *Full Metal Jacket* comprises the most memorable depiction of a Marine Corps boot camp ever committed to a feature film. Kubrick granted the actor playing the drill instructor, R. Lee Ermey, the rare privilege of improvising his own lines. As a real drill instructor earlier in life, Ermey was able to create his character with unique sympathy. It was not an outsider's view of the Marine Corps' regimen. His poetically hilarious stream of invective exceeded even the prototype for his character in Hasford's novel. Was Hartman an exaggeration? "Nobody can be that nasty," Ermey once said, but he added that a good drill instructor is an actor giving a performance (Kagan 2000, 217). Ermey's Hartman may have given the best performance by a drill instructor in fiction and in real life.

Enhancing the realism of the boot camp scenes, Kubrick filmed Hartman's brutal first encounter with the recruits without rehearsal or advance warning. The shock on the actors' faces was an authentic reaction (Duncan 2003, 217). Throughout *Full Metal Jacket*, Kubrick was determined to avoid the false sentimentality that had long plagued Hollywood war movies, especially in the form of soldiers in combat or hard conditions taking time to tenderly share their innermost feelings with one another. When one scene began to drift in that direction, Kubrick reversed course and said, mockingly, "Shouldn't there be some guy playing a *harmonica* in the back" (Herr 2000, 42).

Hartman's tactics are in service to the Marine Corps' time-tested objective to break down the personality of civilian recruits and reconstruct them as marines. If Hartman behaves like a demonic adversary, it is to test his recruits against the remorseless adversaries they may face in battle.

The process begins in the opening scene with the shaving of the recruits' heads as if to strip them down to their chassis before the drill instructor begins to run them through their paces. On first encounter, he renames them in a forceful reminder that they are no longer who they once were. A smart-aleck remark about John Wayne earns the protagonist the name Joker. An African American becomes Snowball, and a Texan is dubbed Cowboy. Hartman saves the worst for a chubby and vacant-looking recruit who under normal circumstances would not have made it past the physical and psychological examinations—but Vietnam was not a normal time for the military. Hartman named him Gomer Pyle after the utterly inept character from a 1960s television comedy about the Marine Corps, a program so out of touch with reality that the Vietnam War was left unmentioned. Hartman punches Joker in the solar plexus, letting him know who is boss, but his campaign of humiliation against Pyle seems sadistic. "Get on your knees and choke yourself," he orders Pyle. However, Hartman has his reasons. "I will motivate you, Private Pyle!" Dangerous hazing by drill instructors similar to what was shown in *Full Metal Jacket* continues into the present day despite recent attempts by Marine Corps leadership to curb the practice. For example, in 2016 a drill instructor was demoted for choking recruits (Schogol 2017).

The demanding routine of marching, rifle drill, making bunks to order, and maneuvering through challenging obstacle courses has been seen in other movies, including the earlier Vietnam War film *The Boys in Company* C (1978), but seldom has the rationale behind the unflinchingly hard training been expressed with Hartman's sharp clarity. "Marines are not allowed to die without permission!" he insists. Because Pyle's deficiencies threaten to become a disgrace to his "beloved Corps" and to leave the unit vulnerable when under attack, Hartman encourages the men to work on him as a group. They discipline Pyle brutally by beating him with a bar of soap wrapped in a towel. Even Joker, who has befriended Pyle, reluctantly takes part. The group mentality of the Marine Corps is accurately expressed.

However, *Full Metal Jacket* shows that while the Marine Corps demands absolute discipline under fire, and a heightened sense of group affinity, it does not want its men to be mindless cogs in the machinery of death. The individuals Hartman is building from the raw material he was sent need to be able to think on their feet and make decisions. For this reason, Joker is rewarded for his willingness to disagree with Hartman by being made squad leader. "The Marine Corps does not want robots," Joker says in a voiceover. "The Marine Corps wants killers. The Marine Corps wants indestructible men—men without fear."

If Sergeant Hartman was intended as an exaggeration of a real drill instructor in order to paint a more vivid picture of the Marine Corps' spirit, the fictional instructor became a model for the real Corps in the aftermath of the film's release. Anthony Swofford, who joined the Marines Corps in 1988, recalled that Hartman's "persona saturated military culture" and that the "boys who wanted to serve believed that intimidation and humiliation were essential to the formation of their warrior selves. And drill instructors were happy to oblige" (Swofford 2018).

Part two of *Full Metal Jacket* introduces Joker to Vietnam, and pointedly, the opening scene finds him drinking at a makeshift outdoor bar where he is propositioned by a prostitute and her handler, a South Vietnamese soldier. As one chronicler of the war wrote, "The only Vietnamese most soldiers encountered were scouts, translators, whores, workers hired to perform menial jobs on American bases, or those who peddled goods and services nearby—licit and illicit" (Bowden 2017, 14). Servicemen in the country were issued a manual, *A Pocket Guide to Vietnam*, which admonished them to "honor" the local customs and "treat women with politeness and respect," but the instructions had little effect. Vietnamese and other Asians were routinely referred to with the racist pejorative "gooks." Marine John Musgrave recalled, "I never thought of them as anything other than my future enemy," adding, "I didn't know anything about the Vietnamese, and I didn't care" (Ward 2017, 203–204). *Full Metal Jacket* reflects that incomprehension. The Vietnamese are there to be exploited or killed.

Because he had written for his high school newspaper, Joker, now a sergeant, is given a "soft job" as a combat correspondent with the Information Services Office, a bureau "with a mandate to be positive." He continues to be jovially sarcastic about the circumstances surrounding him, gently pushing at the limit of permissible speech in the Marine Corps, and is admonished that only two kinds of articles are acceptable—human interest pieces about Americans helping the Vietnamese and accounts of victory over the Vietcong—echoing the reality of a combat correspondent's job. As in the movie, they were occasionally called upon to pick up rifles and fight alongside their fellow marines. They were generally well liked by combat troops hoping to see their names or faces in the military newspaper *Stars and Stripes* or the Marine Corps' *Sea Tiger* (Bowden 2017, 200). Closely adhering to the depiction of Joker and the photographer Rafterman, two marine combat correspondents, Steve Berntson and Dale Dye, were sent with the marines into the Battle of Hue. Not unlike the peace symbol Joker wore into battle, Berntson stenciled the face of *Mad* magazine's satirical mascot, Alfred E. Neuman, onto the back of his flak jacket along with the slogan, "What, Me Worry?"

Full Metal Jacket realistically presents the experiences Joker might have had in the lead-up to the Battle of Hue. He informed his commanding officer of rumors that Tet might be the occasion for a communist offensive, but as was the case across South Vietnam, the higher-ups ignored the reports. The members of Joker's detachment are surprised when shells begin falling on their base at Da Nang but spring into action like well-trained marines and form a skirmish line that repels the assault. As might have been true in reality, Joker and Rafterman are helicoptered to Phu Bai and they march on foot toward Hue alongside truck convoys and Marine Corps tanks. On the outskirts of the city, they come across a shallow grave of civilian dead, their bodies covered in lime. In that scene, Kubrick gives a glimpse of the communist reign of terror in which as many as 5,000 supporters of the South Vietnamese regime were slaughtered and buried in mass graves outside the city (Herr 1978, 85). The Vietcong also rounded up all foreigners, except the French, and marched the victims "down the nearly empty streets, their arms behind their backs, to prisoner collection points" where they were killed (Oberdorfer 1971, 565–570).

The battle Joker was sent to cover was one of the most decisive in the Vietnam War. Hue had been Vietnam's imperial capital and was South Vietnam's third-largest city, with a population of 140,000. It was a place of symbolic and practical importance, the former seat of the nation's dynasty and a place where North Vietnamese leader Ho Chi Minh spent his childhood. It was a seaport at South Vietnam's narrow center, only a one-hour drive along the highway to the Laotian border. If the communists took Hue, they could easily cut South Vietnam in half.

The North Vietnamese and their Vietcong subordinates planned the assault on Hue with great care. It was the cornerstone of the Tet Offensive. For months, young Vietcong girls on bicycles moved freely through the city, mapping out military posts, police stations, and the single American base, the Military Assistance Command Vietnam (MACV) compound. They located the homes of South Vietnamese officials and foreign civilians. Some of the girls were given money to rent houses that became arms depots and staging points. A network of procommunist civilians prepared itself for the day of the attack (Bowden 2017, 9).

Four North Vietnamese army regiments moved southward into position, sheltering in the jungle and counting on the support of villagers who had grown to hate the South Vietnamese regime. Eight Vietcong Main Force battalions, complete with artillery, waited for the signal to advance. For the "liberation" of Hue, North Vietnamese and Vietcong troops were issued fresh uniforms before battle to impress civilians with their professionalism. They were also given 12 rules of conduct not unlike the *Pocket Guide to Vietnam* handed to GIs. Facing them were 1,000 South Vietnamese troops and a few hundred Americans in the MACV base, which had been "regarded as a rear compound, well out of harm's way." Until January 30, 1968, Hue had been barely touched by the war (Bowden 2017, 15, 41–42).

Ironies were plentiful. The headquarters for the communist attack was a bombproof bunker in the nearby village of La Chu built by the United States but abandoned when the "strategic hamlet" was lost to the Vietcong. The communists confidently expected the people of Hue to rise up, greet them as liberators, and take arms against South Vietnamese and U.S. troops. However, aside from the Vietcong cells already operating in the city, the locals did their best to keep their heads down and stay out of harm's way once the fighting began. Although there had been indications of enemy troop movements, the Americans in Hue were confident that the communists were unable to mount an attack on the scale of what they soon encountered (Bowden 2017, 50).

Hue was dominated by a walled complex called the Citadel. The two-square-mile compound was enclosed by a double set of thick walls rising 26 feet above a moat. Eleven narrow bridges led to guarded gates. The Citadel contained the walled imperial palace with gardens, a lake, and outbuildings. The headquarters of South Vietnam's First Division, the Tay Loc Airfield, and the homes of the city's more affluent residents were located inside the Citadel. The fight for the complex was a crucial component in the Battle of Hue. A special Vietcong commando platoon trained to scale the walls, rip down the South Vietnamese flag, and replace it with the banner of the National Liberation Front. A Vietcong photographer accompanied them to document the event (Bowden 2017, 53–54).

Although the Citadel occupied an important part of Hasford's novel, given the expense of erecting a facsimile, Kubrick chose to set *Full Metal Jacket*'s combat scenes in the New City, the modern parts of Hue built under French rule. Those outer districts included a Roman Catholic cathedral, a prison, Hue University, various government offices, and rows of shops and movie theaters. The communist attack was carried out expertly with most objectives easily taken. The only holdouts were the South Vietnamese garrison inside the Citadel and the MACV compound, both of them besieged but supported by U.S. helicopters and navy patrol boats directing fire at the enemy.

Unlike in *The Short-Timers*, *Full Metal Jacket* doesn't include the devastating U.S. and South Vietnamese air strikes that helped break the communist hold on the city. In the novel, Hasford described "history in shattered blocks of stone" and "black roses of smoke [that] bloom in the Citadel" (Hasford 1980, 97). Such depictions were beyond Kubrick's budget and technical resources. The director excluded the wider Battle of Hue from his field of vision, concentrating instead on the experiences of one squad as it advanced with difficulty into the city's streets.

That portion of the Battle of Hue already received eyewitness press coverage at the time when the outcome was uncertain. The *New York Times* reported that the enemy "weathered repeated attacks" by marines. "At nightfall," on day four of the battle, "the Marines held only two square blocks of the smoking city" (Roberts 1968). *Full Metal Jacket* vividly conveys the difficulty those marines faced as they pushed into a city reduced to rubble. If anything, it spares the audience the sight of the bloated bodies, mostly communist troops and civilians caught in crossfire, that covered many streets. It rained through much of the battle, a point overlooked by Kubrick, and according to Herr, "The rain did things to the corpses that were worse in their way than anything the sun could have done" (Herr 1978, 77).

While not explicit, *Full Metal Jacket* implies the initial confusion of the marines as they entered Hue. Their commanders had no idea of the extent of the communist assault and could not comprehend the possibility that an enemy they regarded as ragtag guerillas could occupy a major city. The marines who rushed into Hue from their base at Phu Bai, eight miles away, were told to "just take your flak jackets and some gear because we'll be back for dinner" (Bowden 2017, 179). Instead, the battle dragged on for over four weeks, fought building by building and street by street. As one eyewitness put it, "Older men have told me about the street fighting in Italy, France, and Germany. It is like that—maybe worse—in this city" (Webb 1968). The assault by the marines Joker falls in with, the "Lusthog Squad," is realistically depicted. One squad member expresses the grudging respect the North Vietnamese soldiers earned in the marines' eyes, saying, "We're going to miss not having anyone who's worth shooting" once they return home. Like the real marines advancing into Hue, the Lusthog Squad halts when fired upon and fans out, moving forward, ducking behind any available shelter, whether the burned-out hulk of a car or fragments of destroyed buildings, and resuming their forward run while returning fire.

The marines were untrained for urban warfare, and in the Corps' history, they had fought only once under those conditions, in Seoul, Korea, in 1950. According to the Marine Corps' sole manual on street fighting, *Combat in Built-Up Areas*, the tactic was to move through walls, not around them, by blasting forward, demolishing anything in their way. In *Full Metal Jacket*, the marines advance under that principal, leveling buildings with rocket-propelled grenades and heavy machine-gun fire.

Despite unpreparedness and faced with the disadvantage of attack against highly motivated and well-armed defenders, the marines performed as bravely in reality as on screen. As shown in *Full Metal Jacket*, sniper fire claimed many casualties, the toll rising because marines never left behind one of their own, whether dead or alive. The Lusthog Squad steps into a section of the New City that the North Vietnamese evacuated overnight but encounters booby traps and a lone sniper directing deadly fire their way. The movie's sniper, a civilian teenage girl, is emblematic of the many lone snipers who slowed the marines' advance. They were armed with AK-47s, which functioned well both as a sniper's rifle and an automatic assault weapon. A recent history of the Hue battle located one such girl who survived the war. She joined the Vietcong's Young Pioneers not from "the global clash of ideas that brought American soldiers to Vietnam" but because her family had suffered under the South Vietnamese regime and were committed to a Vietnam free of foreign control. She had been trained to shoot AK-47s, fire AB-40 rocket launchers, and hurl hand grenades (Bowden 2017, 5–8).

CONCLUSION

Full Metal Jacket does not present a full picture of the Battle of Hue but accurately addresses the battle from the slow-moving, low-to-the-ground perspective of marines fighting to take the city. The film only hints at the extent of the carnage. Seventy percent of Hue was destroyed during the fighting, and most of the residents were left homeless (Herr 1978, 83). Marine casualties totaled 142 killed and 1,100 wounded. Enemy deaths were estimated at 8,000 (Shulimson 1997, 213). *Full Metal Jacket* is unique for its resolute refusal to sentimentalize, sugarcoat, or allegorize the experience of men in combat. The film's reputation has grown in the years since its release, among film buffs for its technical achievements and among war movie buffs for its unforgettable depiction of marines in boot camp.

FURTHER READING

Arnett, Peter. "Major Describes Move." *New York Times*, February 8, 1968.

Bowden, Mark. 2017. *Hue 1968: A Turning Point of the American War in Vietnam.* New York: Atlantic Monthly Press.

Bunch, Sonny. "R. Lee Ermey Made 'Full Metal Jacket' a Movie that Marines and Antiwar Protestors Could Love." *Washington Post*, April 25, 2018.

Canby, Vincent. "Kubrick's 'Full Metal Jacket' on Viet Nam." *New York Times*, June 26, 1987.

Clemons, Walter. "Killing Ground." *Newsweek*, January 1, 1979.

Cronkite, Walter. 1996. *A Reporter's Life*. New York: Alfred A. Knopf.

Duncan, Paul. 2003. *Stanley Kubrick: The Complete Films*. Cologne, Germany: Taschen.

Ebert, Roger. "Full Metal Jacket." *Chicago Sun-Times*, June 26, 1987.

Hasford, Gustav. 1980. *The Short-Timers*. New York: Bantam Books.

Herr, Michael. 1978. *Dispatches*. New York: Alfred A. Knopf.

Herr, Michael. 2000. *Stanley Kubrick*. New York: Grove Press.

Howard, James. 1999. *Stanley Kubrick Companion*. London: B. T. Batsford.

Kael, Pauline. "Full Metal Jacket." *New Yorker*, July 13, 1987.

Kagan, Norman. 2000. *The Cinema of Stanley Kubrick*. 3rd ed. New York: Continuum.

Karnow, Stanley. 1991. *Vietnam: A History*. New York: Viking.

Mohr, Charles. "U.S. Aide in Embassy Villa Kills Guerilla with Pistol." *New York Times*, January 31, 1968.

Oberdorfer, Don. 1971. *Tet! The Story of a Battle and its Historic Aftermath*. New York: Doubleday.

Roberts, Gene. "Enemy Maintains Tight Grip on Hue." *New York Times*, February 3, 1968.

Schogol, Jeff. "Investigators Find Hazing at Marine Corps Recruit Depot in San Diego." *Marine Corps Times*, May 3, 2017.

Shulimson, Jack, Leonard A. Blaisol, Charles R. Smith, and David A. Dawson. 1997. *U.S. Marines in Vietnam: The Defining Year, 1968*. Washington, DC: History and Museums Division, Headquarters U.S. Marine Corps.

Smith, Hedrick, and Neil Sheehan. "Westmoreland Requests 206,000 More Men, Stirring Debate in Administration." *New York Times*, March 10, 1968.

Sorley, Lewis. 2011. *Westmoreland: The General Who Lost Vietnam*. Boston: Houghton Mifflin Harcourt.

Sterritt, David. "*Full Metal Jacket* Kubrick's View of Viet-Nam." *Christian Science Monitor*, June 26, 1987.

Swofford, Anthony "'Full Metal Jacket' Seduced My Generation and Sent Us to War." *New York Times*, April 18, 2018.

Ward, Geoffrey C., and Ken Burns. 2017. *The Vietnam War: An Intimate History*. New York: Alfred A. Knopf.

Webb, Alvin B., Jr. "Struggle for Hue Is Deadly." *Philadelphia Inquirer*, February 5, 1968.

Westmoreland, William C. 1976. *A Soldier Reports*. Garden City, NY: Doubleday.

Chapter 8

We Were Soldiers (2002)

Paramount Pictures released *We Were Soldiers* on March 1, 2002, following a glut of undistinguished war movies such as *Behind Enemy Lines*, *Hart's War*, and *Collateral Damage*, and the film was barely profitable in its first year of release. The movie was budgeted at $75 million, but the year-end domestic gross for *We Were Soldiers* was only $78,122,718, and it ranked 34th among 2002's top movies, according to the website Box Office Mojo. However, the film struck a positive chord among its audience for validating the courage and decency of American soldiers after a succession of movies that depicted the Vietnam War in a darker light. For many moviegoers, *We Were Soldiers* was a welcome tonic in the confused aftermath of the September 11, 2001, terrorist attacks, as America entered another war against shadowy enemies in distant places.

The source for *We Were Soldiers* was a nonfiction account of the Battle of Ia Drang (1965) by two of its participants, Lieutenant General Harold G. "Hal" Moore (1922–2017) and Joseph L. Galloway (1941–). At the time of the battle, Moore was a lieutenant colonel and commanded a battalion of the Seventh Cavalry Regiment while Galloway was a correspondent covering the war for the press syndicate United Press International (UPI). Not content to observe the war, Galloway was an active participant in combat who wore fatigues and carried a submachine gun. At Ia Drang, he rescued a wounded trooper under enemy fire and was later awarded a Bronze Star.

The film opens with an incident from an earlier phase in the Vietnam War in which a French unit is wiped out in an ambush led by a young communist officer, Nguyen Huu An (1926–1995), played by a Vietnamese-born actor, Duong Don (1957–2011). The next scenes establish Moore's character as a family man and leader of men; he is shown having a loving relationship with his wife, Julie, played by Madeleine Stowe (1958–). The origin of air cavalry is shown to be grounded, like that of the Green Berets, in the Kennedy administration's realization that the next war would be unconventional in nature. Moore's adjutant, Sergeant Major Basil Plumley, is a tough, no-nonsense drill instructor played with a touch of comedy by Sam Elliott (1944–). Other key cast members are introduced form Moore's First Battalion, Seventh Cavalry, including Major Bruce "Snake" Crandall, played by Greg Kinnear (1963–); Second Lieutenant Henry Herrick, played by Marc Blucas (1972–); Sergeant Ernie Savage, played by Ryan Hurst (1976–); and Second Lieutenant Jack Geoghegan, played by Chris Klein (1979–). After arriving in Vietnam, they are joined by Galloway, played by Canadian actor Barry Pepper (1970–).

Moore's unit is thrown into action upon arrival in Vietnam. Elements of his battalion are sent into the Ia Drang Valley to hunt for North Vietnamese army (NVA) troops engaged in an attack on a Green Berets outpost. Based on faulty intelligence, Moore expects to find only a few hundred North Vietnamese, but his small force of 400 troopers is confronted instead by a full North Vietnamese division numbering 4,000 men led from an elaborate underground complex of bunkers and tunnels by An, now a lieutenant colonel. Moore's soldiers capture a communist scout but are lured into the first in a series of ambushes and endure many assaults from the North Vietnamese infantry that has surrounded them. Casualties are heavy. Moore's unit can be reinforced and supplied only by helicopters arriving in landing zones under enemy fire. At one point, Moore is forced to establish a new landing zone in a place farther from gunfire by clearing trees and making a flat surface for the helicopters. Despite his ingenuity and the bravery of his men, defeat looks certain. Moore then sends the "Broken Arrow" signal to the U.S. headquarters in Saigon, the code word in cases when an American unit is about to be overrun. Massive air strikes are ordered, which destroy the North Vietnamese and cause Lieutenant Colonel An to evacuate.

Years later, Galloway revisited the battle in an account for *U.S. News & World Report*, breaking ground by interviewing North Vietnamese commanders for their perspective. The lengthy article earned the National Magazine Award and became the basis for his book. Coauthored with Moore and largely told in the officer's voice, *We Were Soldiers Once . . . And Young* was published by Random House (1992) and became a *New York Times* best seller. It was widely praised. The unsigned review in the library journal *Kirkus Reviews*, which called the book "an authoritative briefing whose band-of-brothers perspectives make it a genuinely affecting addition to the growing record of America's involvement in Vietnam," was typical (*Kirkus Reviews* 1992). However, other critics noticed a lack of depth or context. According to the *Los Angeles Times*, "The individual stories it tells are courageous and moving, the attention it draws to the valor and sacrifices of ordinary soldiers important and long overdue. But almost every important

GENERAL VO NGUYEN GIAP (1911–2013)

Vo Nguyen Giap was the Vietnamese commander credited with defeating three of the world's great powers, France, the United States, and communist China,. In addition, he was responsible for crushing South Vietnam and eliminating the military capacity of the Cambodian Khmer Rouge.

Although he founded the North Vietnamese army (Vietnamese People's Army), Giap had no formal military training. Giap was a history instructor in a French-language academy in colonial Vietnam who studied *The Art of War* by the ancient Chinese writer Sun Tzu and the campaigns of Napoleon. He was also fascinated by the exploits of a more contemporary figure, T. E. Lawrence. Known as "Lawrence of Arabia," the British officer led Arab tribesmen in a successful hit-and-run campaign against the militarily superior Turkish army during World War I.

Giap had a fine grasp of strategy as well as logistics. He transformed Ho Chi Minh's ragtag band of rebels into a formidable force complete with artillery, transport, and medical units. His leadership, along with the political determination of the Vietnamese Communist Party and a willingness to endure heavy casualties, is credited with pushing the French and the United States out of Vietnam. In the brief interim between the French withdrawal (1954) and the beginning of full-scale guerilla war against the pro-U.S. South Vietnamese regime (1959), Giap was also responsible for establishing North Vietnam's air force and navy.

After the fall of Saigon to his forces (1975), Giap oversaw the invasion of Cambodia that toppled the Khmer Rouge regime and beat back an assault against Vietnam by the Khmer Rouge's Chinese communist ally (1979). Giap was sometimes marginalized in the political leadership of North Vietnam for his criticism of the brutality of some of his country's policies. In retirement he became a critic of Vietnam's environmental policies. He was given a hero's funeral.

THE CAVALRY'S CONNECTION TO THE PAST

Throughout the film, many small but telling details are accurately addressed visually, not with unnecessary dialogue. For example, posted on a sign is the Seventh Cavalry's motto, "Gary Owen," a reference to the regimental marching tune sung a century earlier. George Armstrong Custer's Seventh Cavalry Regiment chose the song as its marching tune as the Seventh rode into battle against Native Americans on the western frontier. Throughout *We Were Soldiers*, the film draws comparison between Moore's encircled regiment and Custer's own demise in the Battle of Little Bighorn (1876). Like other air cavalry commanders in Vietnam, Moore stressed his regiment's continuity with the past even if helicopters had supplanted horses (Moore and Galloway 1992, 25).

question the reader might have about the deeper issues of this battle go unanswered and unasked" (Boyles 1992).

The Hollywood career of *We Were Soldiers*' writer and director, Randall Wallace (1949–), began when his screenplay based on the life of his ancestor, 13th-century Scottish leader William Wallace, attracted the attention of actor-director Mel Gibson (1956–). The resulting film, *Braveheart* (1995), was a hit and won Wallace an Oscar nomination for Best Screenplay. Having gained notice in Hollywood on the strength of his historical blockbuster, Wallace set out to adapt *We Were Soldiers Once . . . And Young*. It was a long process but had the full cooperation of the book's authors, and he even sought their counsel on casting Gibson as Lieutenant Colonel Moore. "Randy Wallace mentioned Mel back in 1996, and of course, I was enthusiastic," Moore said. "[When he finally] signed on I was delighted—he's the best actor in the world and a man of high morals" (Hollywood.com n.d.). Gibson already had an impressive track record playing soldiers from the past, starting with his breakout role in the Australian film *Gallipoli* (1981) and more recently as a commander from the American Revolution in *The Patriot* (2000), but he was nervous about playing a living person. After meeting Moore, though, Gibson was convinced he could fill the role. "Once I met him, he wasn't scary, he was just a regular guy. He's admirable," Gibson said in an interview for Hollywood.com. "I have a great deal of respect for him. He gave me access to his life and his feelings and his thoughts—he was very dignified and very generous and gracious" (Hollywood.com n.d.).

In an interview with Galloway's old employer, UPI, Gibson said he was determined to make *We Were Soldiers* different from previous Vietnam War movies. "It's less cynical," he said. "It was true to the experience of those guys over there." Gibson described the "great desire" of the book's authors "to bring closure and to tell that story, particularly on film, that they were not all a bunch of drug-taking, baby-killing, lieutenant fraggers" (Butler 2002). Although Gibson was not credited as a coproducer, the actor's Australian-American-based Icon Productions partly financed *We Were Soldiers*.

Wallace's challenge in writing the screenplay for *We Were Soldiers* was to condense an account that included dozens of real-life participants in the Battle of Ia Drang into a two-hour narrative focused on a manageable number of characters. With that in mind, Wallace wrote a letter to every American survivor of the battle to explain "why I wasn't necessarily going to portray what each individual had done." He added, "I needed the story to represent everyone, and in order to do that, I had to pick certain individuals who were part of this narrative that really got down to the promise of 'I will leave no man behind'" (Blackwelder 2002).

While the film is shot primarily from the American perspective, like the book, it respectfully accommodates the enemy. Moore and his counterpart, An, are often juxtaposed and shown barking orders into field telephones as they desperately try to manage a battle over which they were losing control. During the battle scenes, *We Were Soldiers* cuts away to the home front to show Julie's work with the wives of service members. The film ends with Moore's homecoming and his visit, years later, to the Vietnam Veterans Memorial in Washington, DC.

We Were Soldiers was filmed entirely in the United States. Wallace had the cooperation of the U.S. Army and the Georgia and California National Guard, although the production rented most of the military hardware from private sources. The air cavalry training sequence was filmed at Fort Benning, Georgia. The Vietnam scenes were shot on the grounds of Fort Hunter Liggett in Monterey County, California, and attempted to recreate the terrain of South Vietnam's Central Highlands. Stunt doubles and digital effects were employed, but the helicopters in flight and the explosions on the ground were real.

Critical reviews of the film were mixed. Writing in the *Chicago Sun-Times*, Roger Ebert praised Gibson and Elliott for depicting their characters "with quiet authority." He noted that in *We Were Soldiers*, "Americans do not automatically prevail in the style of traditional Hollywood war movies" and commended the director for cutting between Moore and An, showing both commanders as "smart and intuitive" (R. Ebert 2002). Likewise, in its review, *Entertainment Weekly* hailed the film for its fairness: "The writer-director bestows honor—generously, apolitically—not only on the dead and still living American veterans who fought in Ia Drang, but also on their families, on their Vietnamese adversaries, and on the families of their adversaries too" (Schwarzbaum 2002).

In his *New York Times* review, A. O. Scott found much to admire as well as to criticize. He lauded the film for the "hard, realistic focus" of its combat scenes but chastised the depiction of the home front for its "maudlin tableau of young soldiers and their pretty, worried wives" (Scott 2002). The *New Yorker*'s David Denby was harsher, condemning *We Were Soldiers* as "a piece of hero worship" devoted to Moore, adding, "Randall Wallace, who wrote and directed the movie, never quite deals with the war that he hopes to redeem" but "gets the scramble and near-panic of close combat, the desperate improvisations" (Denby 2002). Britain's *The Guardian* was harsher still, condemning the film as "Hollywood's latest, sanctimonious war picture" and Wallace for rejecting "hindsight or any sort of vision" (French 2002). *We Were Soldiers* received no major award considerations. In all, the film grossed $114,660,784 worldwide, a modest success compared with its budget.

HISTORICAL BACKGROUND

The clash between the United States and the People's Army of Vietnam, as the North Vietnamese army was officially called, was not inevitable. However, once the U.S. military committed to supporting South Vietnam in a combat role, the North Vietnamese prepared to test the mettle of their new enemy by drawing them into a fight. For North Vietnam, the Battle of Ia Drang was a test run in the widening war.

The People's Army had its origins in communist leader Ho Chi Minh's "war of liberation" against his country's French colonial masters. In 1945, Ho's small guerilla force grew formidable with American aid. In that year, a six-man team from the Office of Strategic Services (OSS), a forerunner to the Central Intelligence Agency (CIA), parachuted in the mountainous jungles to assist him in his campaign against the Japanese. Ho's movement, the Vietminh, were given thousands of American-made weapons, enabling them to march into Hanoi as World War II (1939–1945) ended and secure an arsenal from the surrendering Japanese. By the time they engaged the French in combat, the Vietminh possessed a well-organized and motivated army capable of small-scale conventional warfare but also of slipping into the "almost limitless sanctuary of bamboo-screened villages in the Vietnamese countryside" from which they could conduct guerilla raids and build a political infrastructure (McAlister 1970, 18–19).

By 1947, Ho's forces were already receiving support from the Chinese communists, even before Mao Zedong secured full control of his country's mainland. Apart from irregular guerrilla units and assassination squads, the Vietminh army expanded into 10 regiments with supply systems, training camps, and workshops for producing munitions concealed under the canopy of the jungle. Communist tactics in the war against the French and their Vietnamese allies were more or less identical to the means later employed in the war against the Americans and their allies. The Vietminh ruled much of the countryside at night and butchered anyone suspected of supporting France. "The only corpses that the French never found were those of the Vietminh. The enemy always carried away his dead and wounded," and the French were left to fabricate body counts based on "the grass covered with bloodstains" (Bodard 1967, 14, 16–17).

After achieving victory in China, Mao threw his full support behind the Vietminh in 1950, supplying them with Soviet and Chinese arms and sending advisers. The Vietminh army grew to 300,000 men supported by a militia of nearly 2 million. In 1954, they launched a full assault on the French fortress at Dien Bien Phu in northwestern Vietnam, assisted by artillery dug into the surrounding hills and camouflaged from the air. Dien Bien Phu's surrender on May 7, 1954, led to the French withdrawal from Vietnam and the country's partition into pro-Western South Vietnam, whose capital was Saigon, and communist North Vietnam, governed from Hanoi.

The army of the Democratic Republic of Vietnam, as North Vietnam called itself, was tasked with many responsibilities beyond securing the borders and suppressing rebellion by anticommunist citizens of the new state. The distinction between military units, civil engineers, and farm brigades was largely irrelevant as the People's Army dug wells and irrigation ditches and provided labor for the newly established state farms (Military History Institute 2002, 7, 32). At the time of Vietnam's partition, the People's Army stood at 340,000 men, mostly infantry but supported by artillery, antiaircraft, signals, and logistics units. Their weaponry drew from armories that originated in France, the United States, the Soviet Union, China, imperial Japan, and even czarist Russia. The ruling Communist Party's central committee proclaimed a Five Year Military Plan (1955–1959) to build the army into a fully modern force with standardized armaments supplied by the Soviet Bloc and the People's Republic of China, among them the formidable AK-47 assault rifle. Communist Party cadres were threaded throughout the military, encouraging troops "to strictly adhere to discipline and rules" and caring for their "material and spiritual needs." Upon achieving the Five Year Plan's goals, Ho implemented universal national military service in 1960, effectively establishing an entire nation in arms (Military History Institute 2002, 22–23, 34, 37).

Ho continued to dream of a unified communist Vietnam and, after forcefully consolidating control over the North, quietly encouraged rebellion in the South. The partition of Vietnam was scarcely completed before armed struggle by communists in the South against the South Vietnamese regime began. In the first years it was a losing battle. By 1957, South Vietnamese forces, armed by the United States, killed or imprisoned nearly 90 percent of communist cadres in the South. Ho responded cautiously, aware that after the bloody stalemate of Korea, neither the Soviet Union nor communist China was prepared to fully underwrite another major war (Ward 2017, 41).

North Vietnamese military intervention in the South occurred in steps against the backdrop of quiet power struggles pitting hardline communists led by the party's general secretary, Le Duan (1907–1986), against the more patient Ho. As early as 1959, the Communist Party's central committee adopted Resolution 15, which called for ending "the plight of the poor and miserable people in the South" and defeating "each wicked policy of the American imperialists and their puppets." To that end, hundreds of former South Vietnamese residents, communists who had moved north after their country's partition, returned home to reinforce the rebellion. Among their ranks were technicians, military instructors, and field commanders. The network of jungle paths known as the Ho Chi Minh Trail was expanded to better supply the insurgency. Resolution 15's effect was to accelerate a brutal civil war with no quarter given on either side (Ward 2017, 42–43).

Most Americans gave little thought to Vietnam, and the U.S. government remained certain that with the aid of American advisers and a massive infusion of arms, the South Vietnamese army would continue to suppress communist advances. However, *Time* magazine sounded an alarm in July 1959, warning that "communist infiltrators have stepped up their campaign of terrorism," assassinating South Vietnamese officials daily and, growing bolder, attacking a compound where U.S. advisers were quartered, killing two (*Reporting Vietnam Part One* 1998, 1–2). By this time, North Vietnam established transportation units to ferry supplies by truck or foot down the

Ho Chi Minh Trail. They were ordered to avoid clashes with the enemy and to "walk without leaving a trace, cook without smoke, and speak without making noise" (Military History Institute 2002, 53).

While the Vietnamese communists were happy to admit nationalists, Buddhists, and other dissidents into the struggle for South Vietnam and made a show of operating as if in coalition, in their own minds they had no doubt of who was in charge. On December 20, 1960, the National Liberation Front, popularly known as the Vietcong, was established to serve "as our revolutionary government administration," according to Hanoi's official history of the war. The Vietcong's Liberation Army of South Vietnam included Main Force regiments operating from remote jungle and mountain camps, fully armed by the North and augmented with tens of thousands of People's Army regulars, essentially on loan, some of them "regroupees" of procommunist refugees from the South. Hanoi considered Vietcong forces as "part of the People's Army of Vietnam, having been organized, developed, educated, and led by the party" (Military History Institute 2002, 67, 115). Except on a local level, where part-time Vietcong guerillas laid mines, planted booby traps, and sniped at their opponents with a motley array of cast-off guns, the line between Vietcong and North Vietnamese forces was increasingly a fiction maintained by Hanoi so that it could present itself as the nonaggressor in the civil war that engulfed the South. American troops on the ground were aware of a distinction between North Vietnamese regulars and Vietcong guerillas largely because the former wore uniforms and the latter were indistinguishable from civilians. For GIs, their attitude was similar to soldiers anywhere in the world fighting an invisible enemy. "I could respect the NVA [North Vietnamese army]. They put on the uniform and they came at you head on," said Marine Private Jeff Yushta. "But dealing with the Viet Cong was real hard because they didn't stand up and fight like men. It was real easy for me to dehumanize the Viet Cong" (J. R. Ebert 1993, 246).

Despite its growing engagement in the South, North Vietnam's army was largely confined to its borders until 1964, when entire North Vietnamese regiments began operating in the South. According to one explanation for the shift in tactics, Hanoi concluded "that the Viet Cong lacked the skill and experience to defeat the South Vietnamese Army in the sort of stand-up conventional battle that would be necessary to topple the South Vietnamese government" (Woodruff 2000, 12). A more widely held view sees the Vietcong on the rise against an unpopular South Vietnamese regime that failed to administer the country outside the cities and lost control over the countryside each night in a replay of the war against the French. Meeting in Hanoi in the final months of 1963, the Vietnamese Communist Party's central committee debated over how to proceed with the war. Le Duan won the argument against the more cautious Ho and implemented a plan that would push the North Vietnamese army into direct combat with the United States and South Vietnam. America was unaware of that meeting but would soon feel the results. For their part, the Vietnamese communists refused to publicly acknowledge any division among their leaders and blandly stated that the central committee "displayed a new level of maturity" in "its ability to organize and implement actions for the resistance war against the Americans to save the nation" (Military History Institute 2002, 125).

In the short run, Le Duan's aggressive strategy failed. He hoped to destroy the South Vietnamese regime "before the Americans could intervene on its behalf," but the growing role played by North Vietnamese regulars "had actually accelerated that intervention." By 1967, the war was a stalemate on the ground, and while punishing U.S. air raids did not shake the resolve of North Vietnamese citizens, it destroyed much of the country's infrastructure and set it back economically. Hanoi received contradictory advice from its patrons. The Soviet Union counseled a negotiated settlement with the United States while China urged it to press on to victory (Ward 2017, 206).

Le Duan took China's advice and mounted the Tet Offensive in January 1968, a military catastrophe for the North but a propaganda victory for calling American optimism into question. As Vietnamese journalist Huy Duc recalled decades later regarding the People's Army's casualties, "No units emerged intact. Some companies existed only on paper, because they had just a couple of soldiers still alive" (Ward 2017, 292). According to the official Vietnamese Communist history, Tet was "a great strategic victory" that shook America's "will to commit aggression" and triggered "a decisive turning point in the war." However, even it conceded, "We had somewhat underestimated the capabilities and reactions of the enemy and set our goals too high" (Military History Institute 2002, 223–224).

Despite the heavy losses incurred by North Vietnam's army, the war continued to enjoy the support of the country's people. The generally low morale of South Vietnam's forces, the corruption of that country's leadership, and the rising desire by the United States to exit the war ensured eventual victory for the People's Army. Years later, a North Vietnamese veteran, Bao Ninh, recalled volunteering in 1969 at age 17. "I was sure that the Vietnamese people would defeat any aggressor, and that we would reunify our country," he insisted. After three months of boot camp, where he was drilled in the use of AK-47s and rocket-propelled grenades, Ninh marched south down the Ho Chi Minh Trail and into combat against South Vietnamese and U.S. forces. Even after Vietnamization and the American withdrawal began, "the fierceness of the war did not diminish in the slightest," he continued, recalling that a "single B-52 attack or artillery barrage could level a mountain, fill a river with mud, turn a rain forest to ash" (Ward 2017, 461–462).

The Paris Peace Accords signed in January 1973 by U.S. Secretary of State Henry Kissinger (1923–) and North Vietnam's Le Duc Tho (1911–1990) provided for America's pullout from Vietnam but did not end the war. North Vietnam had no intention of observing the cease-fire mandated by the accord and continued to push forward. Without the threat of U.S. air strikes, the People's Army constructed a paved highway inside South Vietnam on which convoys of tanks, trucks, and heavy artillery moved in broad daylight (Ward 2017, 527). The central committee in Hanoi debated again between patience and aggression, and once more, Le Duan won the argument. This time, however, he also won the war.

On March 13, 1975, the North Vietnamese army launched an all-out assault on the South, and the southern army crumbled fast. On March 29, South Vietnam's second-largest city, Da Nang, fell. Less than a month later, South Vietnam's president, Nguyen Van Thieu (1923–2001), resigned and prepared to flee. The U.S. embassy began to organize the evacuation of Americans and key South Vietnamese allies. On April 30, with photographers on hand to snap a North Vietnamese tank as it crashed through the gates of Thieu's former palace, the communists took Saigon, ending a war that began 30 years earlier when Ho took arms against the French. By this time, the People's Army of Vietnam had been honed into one of the world's most dangerous combat forces. It would prove its merit again before the end of the decade by fending off an assault from communist China and defeating the Khmer Rouge in neighboring Cambodia.

At the same time that North Vietnam developed its army in preparation for toppling the Saigon regime, the U.S. military prepared itself for a new kind of war, in places such as Vietnam, that the military's more farsighted officers anticipated. Under the encouragement of President John F. Kennedy, the U.S. Army upgraded its Special Forces (Green Berets) and dispatched units to Indochina to hold the front lines against communist threats. Meanwhile, the army's experimental 11th Air Assault Division at Fort Benning, Georgia, tested the capacity of helicopters to ferry light infantry and supplies, evacuate the wounded, and provide mobile gunnery support for combat operations. In 1965, the unit was reflagged as the First Cavalry Division (Airmobile) to draw upon the storied heritage of the army's cavalry regiments. It was not the first time the U.S. Cavalry transitioned to new forms of military technology.

The cavalry was long celebrated in pulp fiction and Hollywood movies for its role in "winning" the western United States. The legend reflected the reality of its mission. The cavalry's speed and mobility made it essential for garrisoning and policing the vast frontier throughout the 19th century. However, traditional cavalry had little role in the mechanized warfare of the 20th century. By the dawn of World War II, the U.S. Cavalry was being refurbished with light tanks, armored cars, and trucks, but horse-mounted troopers still engaged in a final charge against the Japanese in the Philippines (1942).

It was no coincidence that many GIs referred to the jungles of Vietnam as "Indian country." More so than in World War II or Korea, those in the U.S. Cavalry were expected to perform missions in Vietnam similar to their horse-bound predecessors. When deployed to South Vietnam, the First

Cavalry Division (Airmobile) was equipped with several types of helicopters to facilitate its role as mobile artillery and infantry, including UH-1 Iroquois gunships armed with machine guns, grenade launchers, and rockets; more lightly armed UH-1 transports; and twin-engine CH-47 Chinook cargo helicopters carrying payloads of over 7,000 pounds and equipped with vertical cargo hooks like those that lifted the patrol boat in *Apocalypse Now*.

Not unlike during the Indian Wars of the late 19th century, the U.S. Cavalry in Vietnam was able to move rapidly against a fast-moving enemy and reinforce widely separated bases. However, at the Battle of Ia Drang, the cavalry was not confronted by roving bands of fighters but the 320th, 33rd, and 60th regiments of the North Vietnamese army. They had been sent into South Vietnam's Central Highlands, under command of General Chu Huy Man (1913–2006), with an eye toward cutting the South in half. Chu's forces initiated hostilities at the close of the monsoon season in October 1965 with an attack on Plei Mei, a base for Montagnard tribesmen fighting the communists under the leadership of a small U.S. Special Forces detachment (Woodruff 2000, 68). They were beaten back by airpower and reinforcements but succeeded in drawing U.S. forces deeper into the countryside. Two weeks later at Ia Drang, the North Vietnamese army and the air cavalry met for the first time. Both sides were eager to test their tactics and measure the capacity of their enemy.

DESCRIPTION AND HISTORICAL CONTEXT

Most impressions of the Battle of Ia Drang (November 14–18, 1965) as seen in *We Were Soldiers* originated in Joseph Galloway's UPI dispatches and the award-winning article he wrote a quarter century later that became the basis for the book he authored with Harold G. Moore. That book drew from the memories of many surviving participants in the battle, including several North Vietnamese veterans. It remains the definitive account of events on the battlefield, and its sense for the ferocious fighting that occurred in "the Valley of Death," as GIs called Ia Drang, is supported by other recollections by veterans recorded over the years. The historicity of the movie is best judged by reference to the book. As Galloway put it, the film was 80 percent accurate. Moore put the number lower, at 60 percent, possibly for the way the screenplay dwelled on him (Newman 2008).

Moore was largely silent about his personal life in *We Were Soldiers Once ...And Young*, but the screenplay sought to paint a picture of him as a good husband and father, a good-humored but authoritative commander, a man of religious faith, as well as a scholar able to read French-language accounts of that country's war in Indochina. The single reference Moore makes in the book to his home life is conveyed in the film when his wife, Julie, assumes responsibility for delivering condolences from the Defense Department to the widows of fallen members of her husband's command. As in the film, the telegrams were haphazardly brought to the widows' homes by Yellow Cab drivers before she chose to become the bearer of bad news for the sake of providing empathy and maintaining a sense of community (Moore and Galloway 1992, 323–324). In the aftermath of the fumbling that occurred in the early months of combat in Vietnam, the U.S. military established compassionate processes to notify the families of fallen servicemen (Hipps 2015).

Starting with the opening scene, in which a French unit is wiped out in a bloody 1954 ambush in the Ia Drang Valley, the strictly military aspects of the film are dramatized from actual events mentioned in the book. The young Vietminh guerrilla leader depicted in the 1954 battle, Nguyen Huu An (1926–1995), returned to later command North Vietnamese forces in the 1965 battle. In the second scene, set at Fort Benning 10 years after that first Battle of Ia Drang, the transformation of the U.S. Army's historic cavalry regiments into airmobile units, capable of moving quickly in an unconventional war, is neatly summarized (Moore and Galloway 1992, 10–11, 43).

In the interest of containing the Moore-Galloway book into a cinematically effective two-hour narrative, many individual episodes from the Battle of Ia Drang are omitted or trimmed and some individuals are combined into composite characters. Although the movie shows Galloway as green but eager, arriving in the midst of battle after hitching a ride into Ia Drang on a helicopter, in reality, the young reporter had already tasted combat. As Moore recalled, "When he hooked up with us, he carried on his shoulder an M-16 rifle" and entered Ia Drang along with the First Battalion, hoping for a story, before the shooting began (Moore and Galloway 1992, 31–32). The film's dramatic structure also resulted in underplaying much of the context for the battle that occupies most of the screen time, including the battle for Plei Mei, where Galloway arrived as a reporter but became a combatant manning a machine gun.

The sequence of battle events in *We Were Soldiers* largely follows Galloway's account. On November 14, Moore's First Battalion, Seventh Cavalry Regiment, touched down in Ia Drang on a landing zone chosen in advance for its size and topography. An enemy scout quickly lured one platoon into the bush. Their commander, Second Lieutenant Henry Herrick (1941–1965), and several of his men were killed in the ensuing ambush. Sergeant Ernie Savage took charge of the survivors and called for artillery support for his unit, which entered U.S. Cavalry lore as "the Lost Platoon." The movie's depiction squares with Savage's recollections. "The bullets were clipping all around us, hitting men and trees and cutting the grass," he said. "On the radio, we were being told to hang on because help would be awhile getting to us. But after a bit, we realized that we had held on, we'd managed, and we just figured, 'Well, we're going to make it.' And we did" (Ayres 1992).

Unlike the French patrol destroyed in a similar ambush at nearly the same location 20 years earlier, the United States possessed enormous resources in aircraft and artillery. Without that support, it's likely that the greatly outnumbered First Battalion would have met a similar fate. They totaled around 450 men. The North Vietnamese threw 4,000 soldiers into the fray.

On November 15, helicopters arrived with reinforcements and ammunition as U.S. artillery pounded suspected enemy positions. Despite the firepower, Moore's men were often pinned down and always in danger of being overrun. The North Vietnamese commander, An, ordered his forces to continue their assault in the face of heavy casualties.

As shown in the film, one of the critical challenges facing Moore in the Ia Drang Valley was the isolation of individual platoons surrounded by superior numbers of North Vietnamese regulars. Part of the problem, as explained in the book, resulted from Herrick's decision to pursue the enemy into the bush, leaving other platoons exposed to attack from entire North Vietnamese units. According to Savage, "We lost contact with everybody." As Moore recalled, "more than five hundred determined [enemy] soldiers was boiling down the mountain" toward his separated and pinned-down platoons in "the swirling kaleidoscope of a fast-developing battle" (Moore and Galloway 1992, 70, 72). His description of the chaos was rendered vividly in We Were Soldiers, which departed from the strictly linear series of engagements normally depicted in Hollywood war movies to suggest the simultaneous action occurring at different points on the battlefield.

Those battle scenes are riveting. Many were shot while crouching on the ground, accentuating the scrunched position of view from soldiers under fire. "You have to understand that in our area the elephant grass was chest-high; once you hit the dirt your world was about as big as a dining-room table," said Specialist 4 Jack Smith (Moore and Galloway 1992, 252). In directing those scenes, Randall Wallace said he was "informed or inspired by battlefield footage" (Blackwelder 2002).

The troopers under Moore's command were well trained and disciplined and fought bravely, but as the film shows, they almost certainly would have been forced to withdraw, if they weren't annihilated, without the support of artillery from a nearby firebase and, eventually, a massive deployment of airpower. The air strike that finally broke the enemy attack, including bombs dropped from B-52s, arrived after Moore ordered his forward air controller to signal Broken Arrow, code for U.S. forces in danger of being overrun. "The cannonade was awesome to see, and its thunder was a symphony to my ears," Moore wrote. The "fearsome napalm canisters" enveloped the jungle in towering clouds of flame, and the film accurately registers Moore's description of "the constant close-in noise of rifles, machine guns, and exploding grenades and mortar shells" (Moore and Galloway 1992, 75).

The enemy was repulsed, yet pinpoint accuracy was impossible under the conditions of Ia Drang. The bombs fell close to American perimeters, killing GIs. In a chapter titled "Friendly Fire," Moore described the use of colored smoke grenades to mark his positions for the incoming helicopter gunships and fighter bombers. True to his account, the film shows how "the smoke and dust hanging over the battlefield" made it "ever more difficult" for pilots "to pick out our lines" (Moore and Galloway 1992, 159). In one scene, napalm canisters are dropped too closely to the American positions, exploding and killing or severely wounding several men. Galloway attempts to help a wounded soldier whom he befriended earlier in the film, only to be faced with the gruesome effects of napalm on human flesh. Despite the mistake, Moore is shown encouraging and rallying Charlie Hastings, the first lieutenant calling in the strikes, telling him, "You're keeping us alive. You forget about that one." Despite terrible losses, An continued sending his troops forward until they were broken by fire from air cavalry helicopter gunships led by Major "Snake" Crandall. Alerted that his lines have finally broken, An hurriedly retreats from his underground headquarters. Although he lost the Battle of Ia Drang, An later rose in rank and prominence throughout the Vietnam War. In 1975, he raised North Vietnam's flag over Saigon's presidential palace after the city fell to his troops.

We Were Soldiers doesn't stint on showing casualties, not only the enemy dead and wounded but also among the Americans. In some scenes Moore towers above the battlefield, bullets whizzing harmlessly around him like Robert Duvall's Colonel Kilgore in *Apocalypse Now*; in another scene, a wounded GI speaks of "dying for my country" as he expires. With those few exceptions, the combat scenes in *We Were Soldiers* are presented with grim realism and without the dramatic flourishes that often characterize Hollywood war movies. The depiction of the wounded evacuated by helicopter is handled as efficiently as in real life. The probability of serious and life-altering injuries is acknowledged. More than 250 American soldiers were injured.

In the movie and the book, Moore was pointedly critical of the Lyndon B. Johnson administration's policy of 12-month deployments in Vietnam for officers and enlisted men. "Those who had survived and learned how to fight in this difficult environment" went home carrying their experience with them. "Replacing them was an army of new draftees, which in due course would be replaced by newer draftees. The level of training drifted ever lower," he wrote (Moore and Galloway 1992, 343).

We Were Soldiers concludes with a voiceover recrimination, "No honor guard to welcome them home," and the sight of Moore, decades later, scanning Panel 3–East of the Vietnam Veterans Memorial where the names of the 234 Americans who died at Ia Drang are inscribed. The film is less nuanced than Moore's own reflections on his homecoming. "The country that sent us off to war was not there to welcome us home. It no longer existed," he wrote, commenting on the social and political upheaval triggered by the Vietnam War. He understood that many "of our countrymen came to hate the war we fought" but chastised only those who were unable "to differentiate between the war and the soldiers who had been ordered to fight it" (Moore and Galloway 1992, xix).

CONCLUSION

We Were Soldiers presents its subject in a different light from any of the major Vietnam War films that preceded it. Unlike *The Green Berets*, it does not justify America's involvement in the war, and unlike movies subsequent to *The Green Berets*, it refuses to castigate the U.S. intervention. The disillusionment apparent in *Coming Home, The Deer Hunter, The Boys in Company C, Apocalypse Now,* and *Platoon* is seemingly contradicted in *We Were Soldiers* by the disciplined camaraderie of the Seventh Cavalry and the commitment of its troopers to the fight. However, in its portrayal of American soldiers in Vietnam, *We Were Soldiers* is neither more nor less accurate than the aforementioned films but reflects on an earlier phase of the war when U.S. combat troops had first arrived. It was a time when patriotism was undimmed, orders were unquestioned, drug use was rare, and the incapability of the South Vietnamese regime was not yet fully apparent. A year after the events of *We Were Soldiers*, in 1966, Moore became aware that there were no effective "follow-on Vietnamese government programs to reestablish control" in areas where the United States had defeated or pushed back the communists. Usually within one week after American forces departed from a village, the North Vietnamese and Vietcong were back in control (Moore and Galloway 1992, 343).

FURTHER READING

Ayres, B. Drummond, Jr. "Veterans' Journal: Back to a Valley of Death, With Love." *New York Times,* November 10, 1992.

Blackwelder, Rob. "Wallace 'Soldiers' On: Braveheart Writer Tackles the First Battle of Vietnam in his Ambitious War Film Starring Mel Gibson." SPLICEDwire, February 5, 2002. http://splicedwire.com/02features/rwallace.html

Bodard, Lucien. 1967. *The Quicksand War: Prelude to Vietnam.* London: Faber and Faber.

Boyles, William, Jr. "Remember the '60s?: The War: We Were Soldiers Once . . . And Young." *Los Angeles Times,* December 13, 1992.

Butler, Karen. "Interview of the Week: Mel Gibson." United Press International, February 28, 2002. https://www.upi.com/Interview-of-the-week-Mel-Gibson/74491014921053/

Denby, David. "Good Guys: 'We Were Soldiers' and '40 Days and 40 Nights.'" *New Yorker,* March 11, 2002.

Ebert, James R. 1993. *A Life in a Year: The American Infantryman in Vietnam, 1965–1972.* Novato, CA: Presidio Press.

Ebert, Roger. "We Were Soldiers." *Chicago Sun-Times*, March 1, 2002.

French, Philip. "We Were Soldiers." *The Guardian*, March 10, 2002.

Galloway, Joseph L. "Vietnam Story." *U.S. News & World Report*, October 29, 1990.

Hipps, Tim. "Vietnam-Era Events Featured in Today's Soldier Show Inspired Changes to Notification Process in '65." U.S. Army, April 20, 2015. https://www.army.mil/article/146617/vietnam_era_events_featured_in_todays_soldier_show_inspired_changes_to_notification_process_in_65

Hollywood.com. n.d. "'We Were Soldiers': Mel Gibson Interview." http://www.hollywood.com/general/we-were-soldiers-mel-gibson-interview-57163641/

Kirkus Reviews. "We Were Soldiers Once . . . And Young," September 1, 1992.

McAlister, John T., Jr. and Paul Mus. 1970. *The Vietnamese and Their Revolution*. New York: Harper & Row.

Military History Institute of Vietnam, translated by Merle L. Pribbenow. 2002. *Victory in Vietnam: The Official History of the People's Army of Vietnam, 1954–1975*. Lawrence, KS: University Press of Kansas.

Moore, Harold G., and Joseph L. Galloway. 1992. *We Were Soldiers Once . . . And Young—Ia Drang: The Battle That Changed the War in Vietnam*. New York: Random House.

Newman, Rick. "The Story Behind 'We Were Soldiers Once . . . And Young': Joe Galloway's Award-Winning Account of a Bloody Vietnam Battle Became a Book and a Movie." *U.S. News & World Report*, May 16, 2008.

Reporting Vietnam Part One, 1959–1969. 1998. New York: Library of America.

Schwarzbaum, Lisa. "We Were Soldiers." *Entertainment Weekly*, February 28, 2002.

Scott, A. O. "Early Vietnam: Mission Murky." *New York Times*, March 1, 2002.

Ward, Geoffrey C., and Ken Burns. 2017. *The Vietnam War: An Intimate History*. New York: Alfred A. Knopf.

Woodruff, Mark. 2000. *Unheralded Victory: Who Won the Vietnam War?* London: HarperCollins.

Chapter 9

The Quiet American (2002)

The Quiet American is set in 1952, two years before the French defeat at Dien Bien Phu by communist forces led to their withdrawal from Vietnam. France was still determined to achieve victory and received military aid from the United States as part of America's Cold War strategy of containing communism. In the opening scene, Thomas Fowler (Michael Caine, 1933–), the Saigon correspondent for the London *Times*, is brought to French police headquarters, where he is shown the body of Alden Pyle (Brendan Fraser, 1968–), a CIA agent posing as an economic aid adviser, who had been stabbed and dumped into the Saigon River. The police inspector suspects that Fowler knows more about Pyle's death than he lets on but adds with a shrug, "Those Americans are causing a lot of trouble for us." The inspector has no interest in pursuing the investigation.

The rest of the film is a flashback, beginning with Fowler's encounter with Pyle. They become friends, although Fowler is troubled not only by what he regards as Pyle's foolish meddling in Vietnam but also by the American's interest in marrying Phuong (Do Thi Hai Yen, 1982–), Fowler's mistress and Pyle's love interest, and bringing her to America. Pyle pretends to be working on a project to promote better eye care for the Vietnamese, but Fowler grows suspicious. When the London *Times* threatens to recall him to England, Fowler arranges to visit a war zone hoping to find a good story. While accompanying a French patrol, he comes upon a Roman Catholic village whose inhabitants have just been slaughtered. The French deny responsibility, and Fowler thinks the atrocity doesn't bear the marks of the communists. He is surprised to find Pyle at the site, dressed as a Vietnamese peasant and insisting that he is there to promote glaucoma eradication.

NGO DINH DIEM (1901–1963)

Ngo Dinh Diem became America's primary point man in Vietnam as French rule unraveled, and he emerged as president of the Republic of Vietnam (South Vietnam) after the 1954 Geneva Accords split the country in half.

Diem was a faithful Roman Catholic, a minority religion in Vietnam. He worked in the colonial administration but resigned in 1933, complaining that France lacked sincerity in bestowing greater self-rule in Vietnam. As a member of the traditional elite surrounding the court of imperial Vietnam, Diem was offered a cabinet post by Bao Dai when the Japanese installed him as puppet emperor in 1945. He refused, and then turned down a position in Ho Chi Minh's Republic of Vietnam. Diem saw himself as a leader, not a follower.

From 1950 through 1953, Diem lived in exile in the United States, where he astutely cultivated journalists, politicians, and Catholic leaders. The newly elected Senator John F. Kennedy championed him. By the end of 1953, he became Bao Dai's prime minister and bided his time, realizing that the emperor could not survive without French support. In the aftermath of the Geneva Accords, Diem installed himself as president and received generous military and economic assistance from the United States.

The communist rebellion against his regime proved uncontainable. Diem failed to win popular support for his authoritarian and corrupt regime and antagonized many groups, including Buddhists, who charged him with favoring the Catholic minority. By 1963, the United States lost confidence and did not interfere when he was overthrown by his own military. President Kennedy regretted the death of his old friend but survived him by only 18 days before his own assassination.

Back in Saigon, Fowler encounters a parade by forces loyal to General Thé, a onetime supporter of France who now heads his own anticommunist nationalist movement. When he arranges to interview the renegade general at his headquarters near the Cambodian border, Fowler finds Pyle once again. In Saigon, Fowler observes Pyle at the scene of a bloody terrorist bombing on the streets, which the United States blames on the communists. Eventually, Fowler discovers that Pyle is responsible for shipping a plastic substance to the general's supporters, allegedly to make eyeglass frames. In reality the plastic is the material for explosives like those used in the bombing on the Saigon streets. Disgusted by Pyle's hypocrisy and his encouragement of terrorism, and jealous over the impending loss of Phuong, Fowler arranges through his assistant, Hinh (Tzi Ma, 1962–), to have Pyle killed by communist assassins.

Despite a preview showing of *The Quiet American* on September 10, 2001, in which the audience gave the film positive reviews, Miramax withdrew the film from circulation after the September 11, 2001, terrorist attacks in New York City, Washington, DC, and Shanksville, Pennsylvania, concerned that the film's message was too anti-American for the time (Thompson 2002). The knee-jerk response Miramax feared never occurred when the studio finally released *The Quiet American* to art house cinemas in major U.S. cities on November 22, 2002, where it found appreciative audiences and received praise from critics.

Based on the novel by British author Graham Greene (1904–1991), *The Quiet American* drew from Greene's 1951–1955 sojourn in Vietnam as a correspondent for the American magazine *The New Republic*. He fell in love with the country, comparing his experiences to drinking "a magic potion, a loving cup" (Greene 1980, 121). The novel drew controversy from the onset and was banned in South Vietnam for its criticism of the country's anticommunist nationalists (Falk 1984, 134). Prominent critic A. J. Liebling (1904–1963) attacked *The Quiet American* in the *New Yorker*, and the film reportedly infuriated the Central Intelligence Agency (CIA) (Porter 1981, xxiii). With his authorization, Greene's daughter sold film rights for *The Quiet American* to Hollywood. A film version released in 1958 by United Artists and produced, directed, and cowritten by Joseph L. Mankiewicz turned the novel's theme on its head. Instead of a critique of ill-informed American intervention in Vietnam, Mankiewicz transformed *The Quiet American* into a triumphal tale of democracy rising in Southeast Asia with American aid. The novel's protagonist, a jaded British correspondent in Saigon, became the villain.

Greene responded with good humor, saying that Hollywood "overbid its hand" in paying for the rights and that the scrambled movie version of his story "will make only more obvious the discrepancy between what the State Department would like the world to believe and what in fact happened in Vietnam" (Greene 1957).

The version of *The Quiet American* released in 2002 adhered more closely to the spirit of Greene's novel. Written by Christopher Hampton and Robert Schenkkan and directed by Australian filmmaker Phillip Noyce (1950–), who had enjoyed Hollywood success with *Patriot Games* (1992) and *Clear and Present Danger* (1994), *The Quiet American* was filmed on location in Saigon and elsewhere in Vietnam.

The Quiet American became something of a passion project for Caine, who was described in the British press as "bullying" Miramax's owner Harvey Weinstein into purchasing the film and pushing for its release despite its "apparent anti-American slant," which was "considered tricky after September 11" (Bradshaw 2002). Miramax turned a modest profit on its $5 million investment on the film and was pleased by its good reviews. The *Chicago Sun-Times*'s Roger Ebert gave *The Quiet American* five stars, calling it "a film with a political point of view" but commending it because Fowler and Pyle "lose sight of that, in their fascination with each other and with the girl. A question every viewer will have to answer at the end is whether a final death is the result of moral conviction, or romantic compulsion" (Ebert 2003). The *New York Times* praised the film for maintaining a tone of weariness and resignation and wondered whether Fowler's and

Pyle's "feelings for Phuong are meant to reflect their countries' different but equally patronizing attitudes" toward Asia. "Where Fowler, ever the detached journalist, affects indifference to the Vietnamese struggle, Pyle is a meddling anticommunist zealot who has no qualms about helping foment resistance to Communist forces by funneling weapons to a ruthless Vietnamese warlord" (Holden 2002).

For his role as Fowler, Caine received nominations for an Academy Award and a Golden Globe for Best Actor and won an award from the London Film Critics Circle.

HISTORICAL BACKGROUND

The Quiet American unfolds against a complicated backdrop of political intrigue and uncertainty in Vietnam. As World War II (1939–1945) concluded, Ho Chi Minh's (1890–1969) Vietminh movement seized the initiative, declaring an independent Republic of Vietnam and gaining sway over parts of the country, including its largest cities, Saigon and Hanoi. Their uncontested dominance was short-lived. While weighing the fate of postwar Europe, the victorious Allied leaders meeting at Potsdam took up the subject of Vietnam. Courting French support in Europe, the Soviets were happy to allow France to regain possession of Vietnam as well as neighboring Laos and Cambodia, and it supported a plan of temporary occupation by other foreign powers to secure order in Indochina. Loathe to witness the demise of any empire, the British supported the initiative, and while the United States had issued ringing declarations during the war for the freedom of all nations, the fate of Vietnam was not an immediate priority.

As a result, the nationalist army of Chinese leader Chiang Kai-shek (1887–1975) swept in from the north and British troops occupied the southern half of Vietnam. The Chinese and British suppressed the Vietminh where possible in preparation for a return to French control. As early as September 1945, an expeditionary force landed in Saigon under General Philippe Leclerc (1902–1947), who had liberated Paris from the Nazis at the head of Free French forces the summer before. Leclerc "was not possessed by the illusion that Western military force could indefinitely control" the situation and began negotiating with the Vietminh (McAlister 1970, 18). The general became only the first French official to step through a revolving door of administrators whose short tenure mirrored the political instability at home.

Talks continued between France and the Vietminh with neither side defining their terms in the same way. In March 1946, France recognized Ho's Republic of Vietnam as a free country with a separate government, a separate legislative body, and separate finances within the Indochinese Federation and the French Union. However, the degree of freedom was always in dispute as was the boundary of the newly formed Vietnamese Republic.

The French established a separate republic with limited self-government in Cochin China, as they called the southernmost part of Vietnam, leaving Ho with an uncertain autonomy over the north. The French Union could have grown into a fraternity of nations similar to the British Commonwealth but was widely regarded as a screen behind which the French hoped to regain their prewar position in the world (Shaplen 1966, xiii).

Unlike the British, who understood by then that the old order broken by World War II could never entirely be reassembled and were willing to let go of India rather than fight to hold onto it, the French, who suffered the humiliation of wartime occupation, were determined to pay any price to restore their former grandeur. "The colonial mystique was too inextricably wound up with what France thought itself to be," wrote Paul Mus (1902–1969), a French scholar and adviser to his country's administration in Vietnam (McAlister 1970, 20–21). Pressures from the left wing of French politics resulted in only cosmetic changes. France no longer had a minister of colonies but a minister of overseas France.

On May 31, 1946, Ho arrived in Paris, where he was accorded the dignity of a head of state. Something of a Francophile despite his condemnation of the country's colonial policies, Ho still proposed Vietnam's membership in the French Union and guarantees of French economic interests in the country but received no satisfactory response regarding independence. The French "wave flags for me, but it is a masquerade. We will have to fight," he told an American journalist (Ward 2017, 20). The fighting began in earnest in November 1946 after Vietminh and French officials wrestled for control of customs collection at the northern port of Haiphong. To teach Ho a lesson, a French warship shelled the city, killing 6,000 civilians (Shaplen 1966, 57).

One month later, the French military launched a concerted assault on Ho's headquarters at Bac Kan, near the Chinese border, dropping paratroops into the jungle and sending armored columns to cut off his retreat. The troops had orders to take Ho dead or alive, but by some reports he slipped away an hour before they arrived. He became "a being wrapped in mystery, and never did the French manage to track him down;" according to legend, he was always on the move, changing his resting place every night (Bodard 1967, 13–14). To subdue the rebellion, the French eventually marshaled forces totaling half a million men, including units of the regular army, the Foreign Legion, and colonial troops from Morocco, Algeria, Tunisia, and Senegal. The United States lavishly armed the multiethnic army, but it failed to uproot the enemy from the countryside. As early as 1945, Mus, after meeting Ho, declared that the French would reoccupy much of Vietnam "but they would not be able to establish any dependable means of exercising authority over them" (McAlister 1970, 24). His warning went unheeded.

As fighting continued, the French tinkered with political arrangements, setting up the Associated State of Vietnam. Its chief of state, Emperor Bao

Dai (1913–1997), descended from the Nguyen dynasty that had been forced to accept French "protection" in the 19th century. Bao Dai's checkered career included a stint as puppet emperor of Vietnam during the final months of Japanese occupation and a term as counselor of state to Ho's Vietnamese Republic. Living in comfortable exile in Hong Kong, he was coaxed out of retirement with some reluctance. France's "Bao Dai formula" was grounded on the hope that the emperor could rally a significant percentage of Vietnamese and became a viable alternative to Ho, but the equivocating Bao Dai made too many concessions to be credible as a strong national leader. The French severely limited his authority, remaining the real rulers of those parts of Vietnam they were able to secure, chiefly the cities and fortified positions in the countryside. "At their disposal the French had everything that should be on the surface," wrote French war correspondent Lucien Bodard (1914–1998). "The Vietminh, on the other hand, were just underneath everything, present in everything that was hidden" (Bodard 1967, 15).

In 1950, the Soviet Union and communist China recognized Ho's regime as the legitimate government of Vietnam and provided him with greater amounts of arms. Vietminh units underwent training in Chinese camps. During that year, the French suffered a string of embarrassing defeats as fortresses in Vietnam's north fell to the communists.

As the situation on the battlefield worsened, the French continued political negotiations to define the relations of the Associated State of Vietnam as well as Cambodia and Laos with each other and the French Union. While France conceded greater autonomy to the national governments of Indochina, it insisted on "rights of observation" and "intervention" in almost all areas, including economic policy, foreign trade, and internal security. The Pau Agreements, named for the French city where the negotiations occurred, "were more liberal than anything the French had offered before," according to Saigon-based American correspondent Robert Shaplen (1917–1988) but still left the Vietnamese feeling themselves as second-class citizens (Shaplen 1966, 77).

Although France's campaign to hold Vietnam was increasingly denounced at home as *la sale guerre* (the dirty war), casualties mounted, and an increasing number of politicians in Paris contemplated a withdrawal from Indochina, the new French commander in chief, General Jean de Lattre de Tassigny (1889–1952), who arrived in Vietnam at the end of 1950, briefly reinvigorated his nation's military position. General de Lattre was a dynamic figure, a Gallic equivalent to America's Douglas MacArthur. He dismissed the idea that the conflict was a colonial war and recast it as a theater in the Cold War. France was in Vietnam, he insisted, "to save it from Peking and Moscow." Aside from words designed to buttress U.S. support in the name of anticommunism, de Lattre's bold tactics delivered setbacks to the Vietminh. Through 1951, he inflicted many defeats on communist forces and forced them to retreat before he returned to Paris at year's end, dying from cancer. Had de Lattre continued, he might have bought France time to negotiate a more agreeable settlement to the war, but the chance of victory was almost nonexistent (Shaplen 1966, 82–83). Like his predecessors, de Lattre was unable to put a believable Vietnamese face on the French war. Bao Dai inspired no confidence among his people, and the French found no better alternative.

The war dragged on indecisively through 1953 with the Vietminh unable to advance on Vietnam's cities and the French unable to dislodge them from the countryside. In Paris, French Prime Minister Joseph Laniel (1889–1975) announced his willingness to "perfect" the independence of Vietnam, Cambodia, and Laos by conceding greater authority to the governments of those states. Bao Dai was heard to say, "What's the matter with the French—they're always giving us our independence. Can't they give it to us once and for all?" (Shaplen 1966, 93).

While the French signaled their willingness to participate in international talks on the future of Vietnam, they tried to improve their bargaining position through a decisive military victory. The new French commander in Indochina, General Henri Eugene Navarre (1898–1983), spoke of seeing victory "like the light at the end of the tunnel" (Ward 2017, 26). To reach that end, he planned to lure the Vietminh into a conventional pitched battle at the fortress of Dien Bien Phu in the northwestern corner of Vietnam, where he could crush the enemy with artillery and air power. He chose his location poorly, unheeding of the advantage the jungle-covered hills above the base gave to the Vietminh, able to rain shells down on the French, and the persistent cloud cover that obscured targets by air. As the battle turned against it, France tried to persuade the United States to intervene with strategic air strikes, possibly involving a tactical atomic bomb, but President Dwight D. Eisenhower (1890–1969) refused to commit to another Asian war after achieving an uneasy settlement in Korea.

On May 7, 1954, Dien Bien Phu fell to the Vietminh. On May 8, Ho's representatives met in Geneva, Switzerland, with diplomats from France, Great Britain, the United States, the Soviet Union, and communist China to negotiate an end to the war. The Geneva Accords, signed on July 21, 1954, provided for the French withdrawal from Indochina and the temporary partition of Vietnam into a northern zone governed from Hanoi by Ho and a southern zone with a pro-Western administration in Saigon. The agreement called for an internationally supervised election to reunify the country under one democratically elected government. The voting never took place, canceled against the backdrop of mutual suspicion between north and south, leading to war.

DEPICTION AND CULTURAL CONTEXT

The Quiet American was the first significant Vietnam War feature film actually shot in the country. The movie's realism benefited from recognizable settings in Saigon neighborhoods that had changed little since the former capital fell to the communists and became Ho Chi Minh City. *The Quiet American* maintains the decadent feel of the decaying, tropical colonial city as experienced by the era's expatriate journalists who basked in Saigon's opportunities for pleasure amid the war.

As an Australian correspondent posted to the city during the 1950s recalled, "To sit and drink one's *aperitif* on the terrace of the Continental Palace Hotel in Saigon was to replicate the reassuring comfort of the cafes and bars along the Champs Elysees." He remarked on the vast network of casinos, opium dens, and brothels that are the backdrop to many scenes in *The Quiet American*, including the largest institution of vice, the Grande Monde casino, run by "a vicious quasi-military group of Vietnamese gangsters," the Binh Xuyen. Their chief, Le Van Vien (aka Bay Vien) (1904–1972), was an eccentric criminal who kept a tiger and a python for pets (Osborne 2000, 156, 184). Bao Dai gave Vien the rank of major general and incorporated the Binh Xuyen into the Vietnamese National Army in exchange for a percentage of profits from vice; from within the army, they engaged in a twilight struggle against pro-American nationalists (Bodard 1967, 112).

The accuracy of the film's exotic and dangerous milieu was underwritten by the screenplay's overall adherence to the novel, where many details were drawn from the author's own experience as a Saigon correspondent. He was, for instance, witness to more than one terrorist bombing on the city's streets (Greene 1968, i). As shown in the film, the correspondent witnessed scores of civilians killed or maimed as they sat in cafés or went about their business. He could as easily have been a victim. The bombings were not aimed at military targets but were intended to sow fear and diminish confidence in the country's governing authorities.

Greene was also aware of the double game being played by the United States. By the end of 1950, American support for the French regime in Indochina included a $100 million aid package and a team of 35 military advisers to supervise the dispersion of military gear (Ward 2017, 26). At the same time, the Foreign Service and CIA looked past the French, trying to imagine Vietnam's future as an anticommunist American ally in Asia.

In his dispatches from Vietnam, Greene criticized not only the Cold War objectives behind American aid projects of the sort that Pyle advocated, but the ineptitude of the projects themselves. He wrote scornfully of "the white powder (that nobody tells them is milk and a few wily people may tell them is poison for their babies)" thrown away by wary Vietnamese peasants (Greene 1955). In the film, Pyle works with a corrupt Vietnamese businessman to import plastic into the country for the ostensibly benign purpose of making frames for eyeglasses. Fowler discovers that the plastic is really material for making bombs.

Fowler first encounters Pyle on the terraces of the Continental Palace Hotel, a popular meeting place for foreigners in Saigon, a city where

electricity and telephones worked sporadically and all deals were negotiated in public places and fueled by strong drink (Boadard 1967, 71). Fowler
sticks to the credo of journalists who report only what they see; in his first
conversation with Pyle, he claims to have no point of view on the war. Nevertheless, Pyle probes Fowler for insights, especially on why the French have
proved unable to defeat the Vietminh. Pyle seemed shocked when Fowler
told him that Ho would win any free election held in Vietnam, an opinion
most historians came to share (Ward 2017, 31). Pyle was among the idealists
in the U.S. Foreign Service who "wanted to make a difference" for colonial
people as he schemed to contain the spread of communism. Then as now,
CIA officers such as Pyle operated out of U.S. legations under cover of cultural, economic, or other diplomatic assignments.

Pyle inherited a line of thought that had evolved rapidly in the years following World War II. Even before the war had ended, the United States set
forth a pair of objectives that would prove hard to harmonize. On June 22,
1945, the State Department's Paper on Postwar Policy Toward Asia and the
Pacific called for "increased freedom for the Far East and the maintenance
of the unity of the United Nations," that is, France and Great Britain. The
paper identified the Philippines, which the Americans governed beginning in
1936 as a self-administering commonwealth lacking only control over foreign policy and defense, as a model for the future of Europe's Asian colonies
(Porter 1981, 24–25).

Although Vietnam made few headlines in the American press during the
late 1940s, the distant country generated a flurry of paperwork within the
U.S. government. On September 17, 1945, an Office of Strategic Services
(precursor to the CIA) report called Ho "our friend of the forest" and recognized that he "seems to be enthusiastically supported by the majority of the
population" (Porter 1981, 34–35). They were overruled by Acting Secretary
of State Dean Acheson (1893–1971), who identified Ho as a communist and
declared that the least desirable eventuality would be the establishment of a
"Moscow-oriented state" (Porter 1981, 54). The problem moving forward
was finding an alternative to Ho. As early as June 14, 1947, the U.S. con-
sul in Saigon told Acheson that he doubted whether "an obviously French
created regime, centered around the person of Bao Dai, would succeed"
(Porter 1981, 65).

A July 1, 1949, State Department report for the National Security Council
finally spelled out the policy that real-life counterparts to Pyle would seek.
The only "constructive solution" to the impasse in Vietnam "depends on the
French yielding their claims to sovereignty to a native regime," the report
stated. Failure to do so would mean victory for Ho's communists. "It would
be necessary for us, working through a screen of anticommunist Asiatics, to
endure, however long it takes, the triumph of Indochinese nationalism over
Red imperialism" (Porter 1981, 81). As in the film, the Americans were seeking a "third force," neither French nor communist.

Pyle had thrown his support behind a character who existed in real life, General Trinh Minh Thé (1920–1955). As depicted in the film, Thé was anti-French though tolerated by them and was one of several anticommunist leaders funded by the United States. Thé was born in Tay Ninh province, the center of a newly born religion called Cao Dai composed from elements of Buddhism, Taoism, and the theosophy that trickled into Vietnam with the French colonists. The faith's founder, Le Van Trung (1876–1934), was an elected member of Indochina's colonial council who was critical of French policy yet urged cooperation (Hoskins 2012, 4). After World War II, the Cao Dai became a center of anticommunist opposition and fought with brutal efficiency against the Vietminh, but their support was localized and they never achieved widespread backing across the country (Bodard 1967, 31–32).

Thé became the Cao Dai's most prominent figure on a national level after forming a militia called the Lien Minh. His forces were implicated in the terrorist bombings in Saigon conveniently blamed on the communists that found their way into Greene's novel. The CIA's top agent in Saigon, Major Edward Lansdale (1908–1987), actively armed and supported Thé, but this occurred slightly later than the film's 1952 time frame. After South Vietnam's independence in 1953, the Lien Minh were incorporated into the new national army. On May 3, 1955, Thé was assassinated. Some said he was killed by the communists while others blamed the French or the country's new president, Ngo Dinh Diem (1901–1963), who saw the general as a rival (Blagov 2001, 99–102).

Many details in *The Quiet American* were drawn from reality, including the danger faced by Fowler and Pyle when they ran out of gas on the road to Saigon from Thé's headquarters near the Cambodian border. "You were never to stop on any road, above all at twilight," wrote French correspondent Lucien Bodard, recalling the hazards of travel through countryside filled with communist guerillas. "Anyone immobile on the road was condemned, given over to the men in black: in a few minutes they would rise out of the landscape, close in and kill" (Bodard 1967, 83). The guard tower where Fowler and Pyle took refuge was typical of the brick structures built at intervals along Vietnam's highways. Ten to 12 feet high, the guard towers had a hole for an entrance and a room at the top reached by a ladder. They were manned by pro-French Vietnamese militia, ill armed and vulnerable, as seen in the film, to nightly attacks by the Vietminh (Bodard 1967, 19).

The Quiet American's female lead, Phuong, was a familiar character in Saigon observed by Greene during his sojourn in the city. There were many attractive young women like her, who worked as paid dancers at posh nightclubs and were mistresses to foreigners. Poverty and opportunity bred prostitution at the cash-and-carry level of bordellos as well as the more discrete arrangement enjoyed by Fowler. The film doesn't focus on the "vast, wide-spreading wretchedness" of Saigon's impoverished population of 2 million but gives a vivid sense of a city that "swarmed with murder committees" and "a whole world of killers, terrorists, gunmen, bomb throwers and illegal tax gatherers" (Bodard 1967, 75). A man with Fowler's connections would have no trouble arranging for Pyle's assassination, whether with the Vietminh or the underworld. In real life as in the film, corpses were routinely found floating in the river and canals. Each morning brought many more to the surface.

The Quiet American's criticism of American foreign policy might have made it vulnerable to attack during the patriotic wave that swept across the United States in the days following 9/11. At least in the short term, few Americans wanted to openly contemplate how the hatred fueling that attack might have been linked to their country's engagement with rogue foreign elements similar to those critiqued in the film. Parallels can be drawn between U.S. initiatives in Vietnam and Afghanistan, the base from which 9/11 was planned. In both cases, the United States cultivated dubious local forces in a war against the threat of global communist expansion. Not unlike the various nationalist groups that received American support in Vietnam, the diverse bands of *mujahedeen*, armed and encouraged by the United States, included leaders willing to commit any atrocity in their bid for power. Al Qaeda had its roots in the American-backed Islamic struggle against the Soviet-backed communists in Afghanistan (the Soviet-Afghan War lasted from 1979 to 1989).

The Quiet American is skeptical about the shortsighted American policy in Vietnam already taking shape in the last years of French rule. Pyle is depicted as idealistic yet duplicitous, wedded to the idea that the ends of thwarting communism justify almost any means and committed to executing ill-conceived programs intended to win support among the Vietnamese people. Given his unflinching support for an anticommunist militia guilty of mass murder, he becomes the film's villain. The cynical, weary Fowler serves as its antihero.

CONCLUSION

The Quiet American is alone among major motion pictures to render an accurate impression of American intrigue in Vietnam in the final years of French rule. During the time frame of the movie, American strategists did not foresee an active role for U.S. troops but endeavored to find a strong local leader who, supported by American guns and money, could withstand the onslaught of the communists and ultimately defeat Ho. However, they were never able to identify a Vietnamese leader capable of building widespread support and sufficient loyalty among his people to turn the tide.

FURTHER READING

Blagov, Serguei A. 2001. *Caodaism: Vietnamese Traditionalism and its Leap into Modernity*. Hauppauge, NY: Nova Publishing.

Bodard, Lucien. 1967. *The Quicksand War: Prelude to Vietnam*. London: Faber and Faber.

Bradshaw, Peter. "The Quiet American." *The Guardian*, November 28, 2002.

Ebert, Roger. "The Quiet American." *Chicago Sun-Times*, February 7, 2003.

Falk, Quentin. 1984. *Travels in Greenland: The Cinema of Graham Greene*. London: Quartet Books.

Greene, Graham. "Last Act in Indo-China." *The New Republic*, May 9, 1955.

Greene, Graham. Letter to the London *Times*. January 29, 1957.

Greene, Graham. 1968. "Dedicatory Note." *The Quiet American*. New York: Bantam Books.

Greene, Graham. 1980. *Ways of Escape*. London: Bodley Head/Penguin.

Holden, Stephen. "A Jaded Affair in a Vietnam Already at War." *New York Times*, November 22, 2002.

Hoskins, Janet Alison. 2012. *What Are Vietnam's Indigenous Religions?* Kyoto: Center for Southeast Asian Studies.

McAlister, John T., and Paul Mus. 1970. *The Vietnamese and Their Revolution*. New York: Harper & Row.

Osborne, Milton. 2000. *The Mekong: Turbulent Past, Uncertain Future*. New York: Atlantic Monthly Press.

Porter, Gareth. 1981. *Vietnam: A History in Documents*. New York: Meridian.

Shaplen, Robert. 1966. *The Lost Revolution: Vietnam 1945–1965*. London: Andre Deutsch.

Thompson, Anne. "Films With War Themes Are Victims of Bad Timing." *New York Times*, October 17, 2002.

Ward, Geoffrey C., and Ken Burns. 2017. *The Vietnam War: An Intimate History*. New York: Alfred A. Knopf.

Chapter 10

Rescue Dawn (2007)

Written, directed, and coproduced by acclaimed German filmmaker Werner Herzog (1942–), *Rescue Dawn* was "inspired" by events in the life of Lieutenant Junior Grade Dieter Dengler (1938–2001), a U.S. Navy pilot and an American prisoner of war in Vietnam. Dengler was among a small number of American POWs who managed to escape during the war. Gibraltar Entertainment financed *Rescue Dawn*, which Metro-Goldwyn-Mayer released on July 4, 2007, in major North American cities and elsewhere later that month.

Rescue Dawn presents a simplified narrative of Dengler's experience as recounted in his memoir. The film begins as Dengler is sent on a classified mission overflying North Vietnam to bomb targets in neutral Laos. He pilots a fighter bomber from the USS *Ranger*, an aircraft carrier in the Gulf of Tonkin, The objective of the raid is to cut the Ho Chi Minh Trail, the network of jungle roads through Laos used by the North Vietnamese to supply communist forces in South Vietnam. Dengler is shot down and eventually captured by the Pathet Lao, the local communist movement backed by North Vietnam.

After being tortured by his captors, he turns down the opportunity for release, refusing to sign a statement denouncing "U.S. imperialism." Dengler is brought to a prison camp he will share with two other American POWs. U.S. Air Force helicopter pilot Duane W. Martin (1940–1966) and Eugene DeBruin (1933–?), a pilot for Air America, a Central Intelligence Agency–run airline that ran supplies to anticommunist groups in Southeast Asia, have already been imprisoned for many months. Held with them are three Asian employees of Air America, Y. C. Tou, Procet, and Phisit Inharathat. Dengler convinces his reluctant fellow prisoners to join him in a daring escape. Splitting from the other captives, Dengler and Martin fashion a raft and try to reach the Mekong River and float from there to Thailand, but they are foiled by a waterfall. Martin is killed by Laotian villagers, but Dengler is spotted by U.S. helicopters and rescued. Taken to a hospital in Da Nang, South Vietnam, he is debriefed by U.S. government agents but spirited out of the facility by visiting shipmates who return him to the *Ranger*. He is given a hero's welcome.

At first glance, Herzog seems an unlikely filmmaker to direct a movie about Vietnam, but in fact he made two films about Dengler's unique wartime experience. Herzog's early reputation was based on artful German productions such as *Aguirre, The Wrath of God* (1972), an epic about a party of doomed conquistadors pushing up the Amazon River cited by director Francis Ford Coppola (1939–) as "a very strong" influence on *Apocalypse Now* (1979) (Peary 2007). After 1980, Herzog turned to documentary filmmaking. Drawn to Dengler's story, which he discovered through the former POW's memoir, *Escape from Laos* (1979), Herzog made a documentary on Dengler and his wartime captivity, *Little Dieter Needs to Fly* (1997).

The director felt a personal connection with his subject. Both men were boys in the last years of Nazi-ruled Germany who eventually found careers in the United States. The peculiarity of Dengler's background, especially the origins of his interest in flying and the irony of where flying brought him, may have appealed to the director's "dark, inquisitive humor" (Thomson 2010, 443). Dengler knew he wanted to be a pilot after his childhood home in the Black Forest was hit by an Allied fighter bomber near the end of World War II (1939–1945). "I was captivated by those sleek-looking planes," he wrote, "and I could not imagine anything in the world more exciting than to fly one of them" (Dengler 1979, 3). As a U.S. Navy flier, he piloted a Douglas A-1 Skyraider, a propeller-driven plane similar to the one that destroyed his home, and was shot down and imprisoned after dropping bombs on unseen targets in the jungle.

Much of *Little Dieter Needs to Fly* was shot in Thailand and Laos, where Dengler revisited the places of his confinement and escape. Herzog restaged some scenes from *Escape from Laos* using local villagers as cast. As film critic Roger Ebert put it, Herzog was "willing to push beyond documentary fact in his quest for underlying truth." Herzog said that a documentary that does nothing more than point a camera at its subject "can only reach the surface of what constitutes truth." He admitted that he "made up some of the incidents in the documentary" in order to find a fuller picture of a man in jeopardy from the quirks of his own personality—why should he want to become like the man who destroyed his childhood home?—who went on to survive unfathomable cruelty (Ebert 2017, 110, 140).

A decade after *Little Dieter Needs to Fly*, Herzog returned to the subject of Dengler's captivity with *Rescue Dawn*. According to the director, "When I met Dieter, I had the feeling this was a very big epic story with a character larger than life. But since it took quite a while to get the money together

MIA (MISSING IN ACTION)

Nearly a half century after the U.S. combat mission in Vietnam ceased, the POW-MIA flag is a reminder of the scars left by the war on the American public. The black-and-white banner bears the legend "You Are Not Forgotten" and features a silhouette of a face with a guard tower behind him. The flag is flown over many public buildings and is sometimes seen over private businesses. It received official recognition by the U.S. Congress despite the government's position that there is "no compelling evidence" behind the assertion that American prisoners remain alive in Southeast Asia.

Every war has had its "unknown soldiers" missing or unidentified after the carnage of battle. Some 78,000 U.S. service people were unaccounted for after World War II and 8,000 after the Korean War. The numbers listed as missing in action from the Vietnam War are relatively modest and amounted to 1,611 as of 2017. The MIA issue has been promoted by the National League of Families of American Prisoners and Missing in Southeast Asia, a lobbying group that originated among service wives during the war. Interest was fanned through unconfirmed reports of American prisoners by refugees fleeing communist oppression in Southeast Asia in the 1970s. None was ever verified. After North Vietnam released its U.S. POWs in 1973, the only missing American to surface was accused of collaborating with the enemy and was dishonorably discharged after he returned.

The Vietnamese communists have been accused of using access to the remains of missing servicemen as a bargaining chip in the negotiations that led to normalizing relations between the United States and the Socialist Republic of Vietnam in 1995. However, the communist regime has cooperated with U.S. authorities, granting access to battlefield sites and archives, even as hundreds of thousands of Vietnamese remain unaccounted for.

OPERATION IVORY COAST

Despite several attempts, no American prisoners were able to escape captivity from prisons in North Vietnam. The United States mounted at least one commando raid in an effort to free captives. Operation Ivory Coast (November 21, 1970) was a joint operation by the U.S. Army and Air Force. Over 50 Green Berets landed at night by helicopter at the Son Tay POW camp, located 23 miles west of Hanoi. Working with aerial reconnaissance photographs, U.S. intelligence believed that more than 60 American prisoners were kept at the camp. Training for the operation involved Green Beret assaults on a replica of the camp.

The analysis by U.S. intelligence proved to be outdated. The POWs had been moved several months earlier to another camp, and the American raiders found an empty facility. Although it was accounted as a failure, Operation Ivory Coast was a brave endeavor in the face of tens of thousands of North Vietnamese troops stationed nearby and for the skill in which the raid was executed. The mission freed no prisoners but resulted in a reorganization of America's military intelligence agencies.

for the feature, we did the documentary first" (Murphy 2007). The second film took the form of a Hollywood war picture and was cast in the mold of such classic World War II POW films as *The Great Escape* (1963) in which prisoners devise elaborate plans to outwit their captors and flee their camp. Herzog cast a bankable Hollywood star, Christian Bale (1974–), in the role of Dengler. Dengler's fellow American captives were portrayed by Steve Zahn (1967–) as Duane Martin and Jeremy Davies (1969–) as Gene DeBruin. Zach Grenier (1954–) played Dengler's squadron leader and Toby Huss (1966–) a fellow navy aviator. Among the Asian actors cast in Laotian, Thai, and Vietnamese roles, Cambodian-born Francois Chau (1959–) was best known to American audiences. He played the communist provincial chief who tries to convince Dengler to denounce American aggression in Southeast Asia.

Rescue Dawn was deemed a financial failure at the time of its release for falling short of recouping its $10 million investment during its run in U.S. theaters. However, it became profitable through home video rentals and sales. The largely favorable publicity *Rescue Dawn* attracted from critics helped the film find audiences in the years after its release. In an era when veterans are accorded great respect regardless of politics, viewers were attracted to *Rescue Dawn* for endowing a veteran from an unpopular war with the valor accorded fighting men in World War II.

The film also benefited from the realism of its setting and believability of its acting. Writing in the *Chicago Sun-Times*, Ebert noted, "We can almost smell the rot and humidity. To discuss the power of the performances by Bale, Zahn and Jeremy Davies (as another POW) would miss the point unless we speculated about how much of the conviction in their work came from the fact that they were really doing it in the hellish place where it was really done." As for whether *Rescue Dawn* had a patriotic message, Ebert wrote: "Not by intention. It is simply the story of this man" (Ebert 2007). The *New York Times* criticized *Rescue Dawn* for its "disappointingly conventional" ending, despite its basis in fact, but added, "For the most part, though, 'Rescue Dawn' is a marvel: a satisfying genre picture that challenges the viewer's expectations" (Seitz 2007).

HISTORICAL BACKGROUND

Dengler was shot down while on a mission over Laos, a country that remained obscure to the American public throughout the Vietnam War despite the strategic importance it was given by many in the U.S. government. Laos was "the key to the entire area of Southeast Asia," Dwight D. Eisenhower (1890–1969) reportedly told John F. Kennedy (1917–1963) on the day before the latter's 1961 inauguration (Rochester 1998, 28).

Laos had been a French protectorate administered, like Vietnam and Cambodia, as part of Indochina. "French rule rested lightly on Laos," and the colonial administration faced few problems with the Laotians or the Hmong and other minority tribes dwelling in the country's highlands (Hamilton-Merritt 1993, 19). The land the Laotians called "the Kingdom of a Million Elephants under the White Parasol" was at peace until the last months of World War II when the Japanese, after occupying Indochina, encouraged local nationalists to move against the French. After the war, France reasserted authority, but Laos was swept up by Ho Chi Minh's (1890–1969) communist insurrection in neighboring Vietnam. Ill-treated for centuries by both the Vietnamese and the Laotians, the Hmong supported the French, who admired them in turn for their "speed, toughness, and endurance" (Hamilton-Merritt 1993, 31). Later on, the Hmong were listed among the United States' most reliable allies in the Vietnam War.

As Japan surrendered in September 1945, ending World War II, the United States established a clandestine presence in Laos through agents of the Office of Strategic Services (OSS), the forerunner to the Central Intelligence Agency (CIA). The OSS fanned the fire of Laotian nationalism in tandem with the Vietminh and ethnic Vietnamese whom the French brought to the country generations earlier. The communist Pathet Lao party, its name meaning "Land of the Lao," originated in this period. From the beginning, the Vietminh acted as "advisers" to the Pathet Lao, a role North Vietnam continued to play in years to come. Other principal players emerged at this time in the struggle for Laos that continued for 30 years. Chief among them were Prince Souvanna Phouma (1901–1984), who married a French woman and maintained affection for his former colonial rulers, and his half brother, Prince Souphanouvong (1909–1995), married to a Vietnamese woman who supported the Vietminh. The country's Laotian aristocracy numbered fewer than 20 families and, although linked by marriage and other ties, precipitated an ongoing civil war in which family leaders sought foreign support, whether from Vietnamese communists, France, or, before long, the United States (Stuart-Fox 1997, 60–64).

France initially smashed the uprising by nationalists and communists and proclaimed the Kingdom of Laos as a self-governing state within the French Union. Much like Vietnam, the arrangement granted only limited local authority and kept the levers of power in French hands. The demands of Laotian nationalism were not met (Stuart-Fox 1997, 67–68). The situation became more confused after the French withdrew combat forces from Laos as part of their pullout from Indochina after the Geneva Accords (1954). As prime minister, Souvanna Phouma cast himself as neutral, even while receiving aid from France and the United States. Fearing that he might incline toward the communists, the CIA supported a right-wing coup in 1960, led by Prince Boun Oum (1911–1980) and General Phoumi Nosavan (1920–1985). Souphanouvong fled to North Vietnam while Souvanna

Phouma backed a 1961 countercoup, led by a paratroop commander, Captain Kong Le (1934–2014). Kong Le fervently advocated Laotian neutrality but "gravitated reluctantly into an alliance with the Pathet Lao and accepting aid from the Soviet Union" as the United States sent Green Berets and air transports to back Phoumi Nosavan (Rochester 1998, 31).

North Vietnam took advantage of the chaos and solidified the Ho Chi Minh Trail, running under the jungle canopy inside the Laotian border, to ferry supplies for the Vietcong into South Vietnam. Spurred by international diplomacy, culminating in the Geneva Conference on Laos (1962), Boun Oum, Souvanna Phouma, and Souphanouvong signed a pact, ostensibly ending the Laotian civil war. Souvanna Phouma returned as prime minister of a coalition government, but like virtually every treaty signed in Indochina after World War II, the agreement had little effect. The Pathet Lao gained control over the country's provinces along the North Vietnamese border by the mid-1960s. The North Vietnamese army supported them even as Hanoi continued to claim it had no troops in Laos. Souvanna Phouma relied more and more on U.S. aid to check the communists (Rochester 1998, 31).

The situation was sufficiently well understood for the *New York Times* to issue a January 24, 1965, editorial headlined "The 'Twilight' War in Laos." However, that twilight conflict was eclipsed in the American media and public imagination by the more extensively covered war in South Vietnam. U.S. strategy in Laos involved no combat troops, and the United States denied any military role in the country aside from training and supplying the Royal Lao Army. The U.S. Air Force and Navy air raids over Laos were dubbed "armed reconnaissance" flights. While flying one such flight on February 1, 1966, Dieter Dengler was shot down.

The CIA stepped up its activities in the country, flying supplies to pro-Western forces via Air America and providing "other forms of paramilitary assistance," including efforts to "cultivate the native population" (Rochester 1998, 277). An unsigned editorial in the June 17, 1968, *U.S. News & World Report*, "Reds Heat Up Laos," noted the conspicuous presence in the country's capital, Vientiane, of "husky young Americans who, as a local resident puts it, 'aren't in the Peace Corps.'"

Perhaps the most significant American role in the Laotian civil war was the CIA-trained and armed "Secret Army," a guerilla force recruited from Hmong tribesmen under the leadership of General Vang Pao (1929–2011). Many American pilots shot down over Laos were more fortunate than Dengler for being rescued by Vang Pao's men. At his height, Vang Pao commanded some 40,000 fighters in a seesaw set of battles against the Pathet Lao and North Vietnamese (Stuart-Fox 1997, 142–143). "Vang Pao, remembering the French abandonment of the Hmong, repeatedly asked his U.S. advisors for assurances that the Americans intended to stay and fight and not abandon them to their enemies" (Hamilton-Merritt 1993, 105).

Any promises made by Americans on the ground in Laos were nullified by negotiations behind closed doors half the world away. The discussions between U.S. Secretary of State Henry Kissinger (1923–) and North Vietnamese diplomat Le Duc Tho (1911–1990) decided the fate of Laos and Cambodia, even if neither of Vietnam's neighbors was given much consideration. The Paris Accords (1973) ending the U.S. military role in Vietnam resulted in the American withdrawal from Laos. The country had long been a piece on a chessboard of global politics that Kissinger was willing to concede in order to concentrate on other moves. The United States ceased to support Vang Pao with arms and air strikes from bases in South Vietnam and Thailand. Air America and the remaining U.S. military advisers left Laos even as thousands of North Vietnamese troops remained. By some accounts, the Richard M. Nixon (1913–1994) administration pressured Souvanna Phouma into signing an ill-advised, ultimately suicidal peace pact with the Pathet Lao (Hamilton-Merritt 1993, 324–325).

Without the support of North Vietnam, the Pathet Lao were unlikely to have succeeded. Their core membership was small, and they mobilized support mainly through a combination of fear and resentment of foreign influence despite their own reliance on foreigners (Stuart-Fox 1997, 164–165). Laos's capital, Vientiane, fell to the Pathet Lao in the spring of 1975, weeks after the North Vietnamese captured Saigon. Their triumph appeared to fulfill Eisenhower's prophecy of the fate of Indochina, the "falling domino principle," in which the loss of one nation to communism would quickly trigger the fall of its neighbors (Ambrose 1984, 236–237). Laos's leading political figures survived the communist triumph but had no real power. Souvanna Phouma served as an "adviser" to the regime who was trotted out at diplomatic functions; Souphanouvong became figurehead president of the Lao People's Democratic Republic.

Although the scale of violence fell short of Cambodia's killing fields, the Pathet Lao were determined to purge all opponents, especially the Hmong. Sympathetic CIA agents and U.S. military officers arranged for the evacuation of Vang Pao and some of his followers to Thailand. By 1978, Vang Pao and some 30,000 Hmong, most of them Secret Army fighters and their families, were allowed to settle in the United States. A second wave of Hmong immigrants were allowed into the United States in 1980. Many thousands were also settled in France and French Guiana in South America (Romero 2008).

Those who remained in Laos were spared no brutality by their new communist overlords. As early as May 9, 1975, a Pathet Lao newspaper proclaimed that the tribe would be exterminated "to the last root" (Santoli 1986, 156). The Hmong were subjected to a genocidal assault that included mass executions, airborne attacks with a Soviet-made chemical agent dubbed "yellow rain," and relocation to "seminar camps" where "reeducation" consisted of forced labor and torture. Thousands fled to squalid

United Nations–run refugee camps in Thailand, where they waited for opportunities to immigrate. Some remaining bands of Hmong continued to fight a guerilla war in their homeland. In 2007, an investigation by the Federal Bureau of Investigation (FBI), Operation Tarnished Eagle, resulted in the arrest of Vang Pao and several of his followers for a conspiracy to overthrow the Pathet Lao. A retired California National Guard lieutenant colonel and a former state senator from Wisconsin with ties to the Hmong community were also implicated (McBride 2007). As the leading lobbyist for Hmong issues in the United States, Vang Pao had many supporters in Congress. Charges against him were eventually dropped.

DESCRIPTION AND HISTORICAL CONTEXT

Both Lyndon B. Johnson (1908–1973) and Richard M. Nixon hoped that airpower would bring the enemy to its knees, or at least to the negotiating table. The first air raid campaign, Operation Pierce Arrow, in August 1964, resulted in the first capture of a U.S. pilot shot down over North Vietnam. The naval aviator, Lieutenant Junior Grade Everett Alvarez Jr., remained in captivity for nine years. The purpose of the raids, which continued through the end of the war, was to degrade North Vietnam's military and transportation network, weakening its ability to support communist forces in South Vietnam. The raids were soon extended to communist sites in Laos. Inevitably, civilian targets were hit. The air war was a dangerous assignment for the aircrews involved. Of the hundreds of U.S. POWs held during the Vietnam War, most were airmen whose planes were downed by enemy forces, usually by groundfire from Soviet-designed rockets or artillery but sometimes in dogfights with the North Vietnamese air force.

Most U.S. POWs were held in prisons and camps inside North Vietnam where they were often kept in isolation, subjected to beatings and torture, and fed meager rations. The North Vietnamese obeyed the Geneva Convention (1929 and 1949), a set of international accords governing the treatment of POWs, only when it suited them. Alvarez was told that he was a criminal, not a POW, because the United States was waging an undeclared war against North Vietnam. Sometimes American prisoners were able to send and receive letters and sometimes not. Some International Red Cross packages were delivered, giving the POWs soap, canned goods, chocolate, toothpaste, and instant coffee. Other packages were withheld. As shown in *Rescue Dawn*, there were usually long gaps between delivery. In the film, labels from American canned goods, delivered more than a year earlier, are displayed on the wall as reminders of home. Occasionally, POWs were marched through crowds of civilians who pummeled and punched them in anger over the damage caused by air raids (Ward 2017, 178–179). In the film and in his memoir, Dengler was given the same option as POWs held in

North Vietnam. He was offered better treatment or the possibility of release if he signed a confession condemning U.S. policy in Vietnam. Like Dengler, most POWs refused, but several prisoners did sign statements or make propaganda broadcasts on Radio Hanoi (Ruane 2017).

Although Dengler's experience was part of a wider pattern of communist behavior toward prisoners during the Vietnam War, his capture and escape were unique in many respects. No more than two dozen Americans are known to have been taken prisoner in Laos, and only one other POW, Navy Lieutenant Charles Klusmann, managed to escape. His treatment at the hands of the Pathet Lao was considerably milder than what Dengler and other survivors reported, possibly because Klusmann flew a reconnaissance plane and was not on a combat mission. Klusmann was interrogated repeatedly and kept in solitary confinement but nevertheless was given blankets, fresh clothes, toiletries, playing cards, and even a copy of William Makepeace Thackeray's novel *A Shabby Genteel Story*. He escaped along with a pair of Laotian captives and made his way through the jungle to a Royal Lao army base (Rochester 1998, 54–57).

Unlike Klusmann, who had the benefit of eyewitnesses, Dengler was greeted with a measure of skepticism by the U.S. government after his account was assessed. "Hallucinations suffered during the last days of his escape and large doses of medication taken afterward to relieve a serious malaria condition may have impaired his memory," wrote the Defense Department's chroniclers of Vietnam-era POWs. "Defense intelligence officers have had difficulty evaluating Dengler's extraordinary story" (Rochester 1998, 48). At moments in his own narrative, Dengler wondered whether he might be hallucinating. "What if it was only a dream?" he asked when he saw the fighter bomber that spotted him in the jungle and radioed for a rescue team. "What if I was making all of it up in my mind?" (Dengler 1979, 202).

The story Dengler told in *Escape from Laos* and repeated in its essentials in *Rescue Dawn* has little corroboration aside from the U.S. government's verification of the fellow prisoners mentioned in his account. Eugene DeBruin was an American cargo handler on a C-46 transport plane owned by Air America. After his plane was shot down over Laos on September 5, 1963, DeBruin was captured along with the four Asians mentioned in *Escape from Laos*. Radio operator To Yik Chiu was a Hong Kong resident, and the three other crewmen were Thai, their names given in the official account as Pisidhi Indradat, Prasit Thanee, and Prasit Promsuwan. The Pathet Lao branded them as criminals and threatened "a people's trial," a propaganda ploy also used by North Vietnamese officials to emphasize the "criminality" of the POWs. The Pathet Lao proposed direct talks with the United States regarding the Air America crew, but "negotiations never developed, and the history of the five prisoners from this point is inexact," according to the official U.S. report (Rochester 1998, 47–48).

The sixth companion mentioned by Dengler, U.S. Air Force Lieutenant Duane Martin, was captured after his helicopter was downed on September 20, 1965. His three crewmates were taken by the North Vietnamese and held in Hanoi for the remaining years of the war. Martin initially evaded pursuers but soon fell into the hands of the Pathet Lao (Rochester 1998, 48).

The only other supporting account concerns the end of Dengler's narrative and appeared after *Rescue Dawn*'s release. *Hero Found* (2010) was written by a shipmate on the USS *Ranger*, Bruce Henderson (1946–). Henderson witnessed Dengler's return after his rescue on July 20, 1966, and fleshed out some details left sketchy in *Escape from Laos*. However, Henderson, like Herzog, relied on Dengler's memory as the primary source for his material. There were no surviving or available witnesses from Laos. As Dengler remarked in the epilogue of his memoir, Martin was awarded the Distinguished Flying Cross posthumously, and according to rumor, Phisit "is today somewhere in Thailand." DeBruin and the three other Asian POWs "have never been heard of again. The story is over" (Dengler 1979, 211).

In trimming Dengler's memoir for a two-hour feature film, Herzog made several decisions designed to enhance its appeal as a Hollywood movie. Dengler spoke English with a heavy German accent, but Bale spoke his parts in flat American tones. Herzog did not want Dengler's ethnicity to distract from the story's American character.

Rescue Dawn depicts Dengler's bombing mission, the groundfire that crippled his plane, and his dangerous crash landing in a marshy field more or less as written in *Escape from Laos*. In the movie, Dengler hides briefly in the bush and tries unsuccessfully to signal U.S. aircraft passing overhead with a piece of mirror reflecting the sun. He steals food from a peasant hut but is soon seized at a watering hole by loincloth-wearing Pathet Lao guerillas. He is brought into a nearby village with wrists tied with rope and is tortured. Dengler is then brought before the communist provincial chief; he pretends to be a German national but is not believed and is asked to sign a statement condemning "imperialist aggression against the peace-loving working class" of Laos. He refuses and is brought to the camp where he meets Martin, DeBruin, and the other captives. The book depicts a more detailed and complicated journey, a two-week odyssey of incidents including an encounter with Buddhist monks, hostile as well as friendly incidents with Laotian villagers, and the necessity of taking cover in a cave with his Pathet Lao captors during a U.S. air raid (Dengler 1979, 17–53).

For the sake of compressing the story into a screenplay, Herzog depicted Dengler and his fellow prisoners in only one camp. In Dengler's memoir, they were moved from place to place, much like reports from other American captives of the Pathet Lao. There were seven prisoners in Dengler's camps but only six in *Rescue Dawn*. Omitting one character allowed Herzog to better focus on the other six. The broadest liberty Herzog took with the narrative was in casting Dengler as the central figure among the POWs, giving the flier more credit than he gave himself. *Rescue Dawn* shows Dengler devising the picklock that the prisoners used to unlock their manacles after the guards went to sleep at night, but the picklock had already been fashioned before he arrived. More important, *Rescue Dawn* depicts him as the leading figure in encouraging and planning their escape, contradicting the impression given in *Escape from Laos* that it was a group effort (Dengler 1979, 94, 100, 113). Herzog was concerned with having only one primary hero and one story to tell.

As with many aspects of *Rescue Dawn*, the escape scene is a condensed and dramatized version of Dengler's account in *Escape from Laos*. However, there is nothing improbable about the prisoners' plan, which involved striking at a time of day when guards inevitably set down their guns and ate their meal. Seizing their weapons, they gun down their captors, sparing only the kindest among them, a Pathet Lao they nicknamed Jumbo. The POWs then fled in two groups, with Dengler and Martin sticking together. The two Americans looked for a river and built a raft hoping the current would take them to the Mekong and eventually to freedom in Thailand. However, the unforeseen obstacle of a waterfall impedes their journey and Martin is killed by Lao villagers, possibly in anger over the increasing damage caused by U.S. air raids as implied in the screenplay. Dengler is eventually spotted and rescued by American aircraft.

At *Rescue Dawn*'s conclusion, Dengler is "rescued" a second time. Flown to a military hospital in Da Nang, he is kept in seclusion, guarded by black-suited U.S. agents. The agents are determined to keep Dengler under wraps for fear of exposing his secret bombing mission in Laos, but he is snatched away by his shipmates from the *Ranger* and smuggled back to the carrier. The scene is suggested in *Escape from Laos*, where Dengler writes that after several days in Da Nang, "someone came to my room, packed me up, and raced with me out of the back door." He remembered being hidden under a blanket, hustled onto a navy plane, and flown to the *Ranger*. "My own buddies had kidnapped me from Da Nang," he recalled (Dengler 1979, 205–206).

The reality may have been slightly less dramatic. From his arrival at the Da Nang hospital, Dengler was questioned by Naval Intelligence officers under a cloak of secrecy that proved difficult to maintain. Reporters were sniffing around after Dengler's rescue was leaked to the press. The *Washington Post* reported Dengler's escape "from a Communist prison camp" following "a harrowing 23-day trek through the Southeast Asia jungle." The *Post* added, "Reliable sources said that he was downed and imprisoned in neighboring Laos" and that it "is U.S. policy not to admit that it has bombed North Vietnamese troops moving south along the Ho Chi Minh trail in neutralized Laos" (Norris 1966). A congressional delegation had just arrived in Da Nang and might have wanted to ask questions. To prevent more details of the covert Laotian campaign from being made public, the navy's

Commander in Chief Pacific (CINCPAC) ordered Dengler onto a plane and rushed back to the *Ranger*, where he could be questioned out of sight. The hero's welcome he was given in the movie mirrored the reality of the warm greeting Dengler received on the carrier (Henderson 2010, 234–236).

Many of the various situations and conditions in which U.S. POWs found themselves are accurately represented in *Rescue Dawn*. At some point, many American prisoners in North Vietnam, as well as those smaller numbers held in Laos, and by the Vietcong in South Vietnam, were exposed to the harsh "jungle terrain, a monsoonal climate marked by extremes of damp chill and oppressive heat and humidity, primitive sanitation meager nourishment, exposure to tropical diseases" as recounted in the film (Rochester 1998, 10). No POWs returned with happy memories, yet the degree of degradation and deprivation they experienced often varied from time to time according to the temperament of their captors. Those differences were spelled out more clearly in *Escape from Laos* than in the abbreviated version of *Rescue Dawn*.

Several other cases of U.S. captives in Laos can be examined for comparison. At least one American prisoner of the Pathet Lao, Charles Duffy, identified as "a civilian with the U.S. mission" in the country, may have died "after suffering a series of illnesses, dehydration, exposure, and a general deterioration of health" similar to Dengler's experience (Rochester 1998, 31, 33). Army Major Lawrence Bailey (1923–2015), captured in 1961 by the Pathet Lao but released in 1962, reported being treated for his injuries in a field hospital staffed by North Vietnamese (Rochester 1998, 33–34). North Vietnam's army exercised a high degree of influence if not always control over the Pathet Lao. North Vietnamese regulars in green fatigues and pith helmets appear in *Rescue Dawn* and are more evident in *Escape from Laos*. Dengler's relief in encountering them—"their military training showed"—was in contrast to the Pathet Lao, those "lackadaisical and ignorant Laotians" depicted in the film as little better than bandits (Dengler 1979, 81, 137). The escape by Dengler and his companions was triggered by the fear that their Pathet Lao guards, themselves suffering from dwindling rations as a result of the vigorous U.S. air war against supply lines, were planning to kill them. Had they survived longer in the camp, the POWs might have been turned over to the North Vietnamese and taken to Hanoi, as happened to nine Americans captured by the Pathet Lao (Rochester 1998, 281).

Other U.S. prisoners reported ill treatment from the Pathet Lao like that shown in *Rescue Dawn*. Rifles were fired at Dengler and his fellow captives, sometimes to frighten them and sometimes with the intention to wound. They were trussed up like animals, their legs confined to wooden stocks at night, forcing them to endure the degradation of incontinence (Rochester 1988, 42–44). Regardless of doubts over the details shown in *Rescue Dawn* or recalled in *Escape from Laos*, the overall impression given of resilience in the face of cruel captivity is accurate. Imprisonment in North Vietnam was bad, yet, in the aftermath of Dengler's rescue, "stories of Laotian barbarism toward captured Americans would become so widespread that U.S. pilots commonly elected to avoid going down in Pathet Lao territory even if it meant nursing a crippled aircraft into North Vietnam" (Rochester 1998, 57). The roll of Americans listed as missing in action (MIA) from the Vietnam era include more than 200 fliers lost over Laos, claimed by the harsh terrain or impetuous violence by Pathet Lao guerillas.

Throughout the war, the American public was aware that some of its servicemen had been captured. Given the small number of captives in the war's early years, the POW issue remained marginal and was sometimes associated with North Vietnamese propaganda. In November 1965, the Vietcong released Sergeant George Smith (1940–) and Sergeant Claude McClure (1940–) in conjunction with the March on Washington for Peace in Vietnam, one of the early mass protests against the war. Nguyen Huu Tho (1910–1996), chairman of the National Liberation Front, as the Vietcong called itself, termed their release a "response to the friendly sentiments of the American people." Upon their safe delivery in Cambodia, Smith and McClure received a congratulatory telegram from Students for a Democratic Society, a left-wing American antiwar group. Both soldiers insisted that they had been well treated and that the United States "has nothing to gain from the war in Vietnam." The U.S. Army claimed they had been "brainwashed" (Allen 2009, 13).

The fate of the POWs had been politicized from early on as "opponents of the war publicized their plight to encourage an end" to U.S. involvement while the war's supporters "insisted that any lessening of resolve would abandon them to the enemy" (Allen 2009, 4). The most notorious use of POWs as propaganda tools occurred during antiwar activist Jane Fonda's 1972 visit to North Vietnam. Speaking on Radio Hanoi, she claimed to have met seven U.S. POWs shot during air raids. "They are all in good health," she claimed, explaining that she conversed with them at length and "exchanged ideas freely," including their alleged opposition to America's role in the Vietnam War, without considering the role of North Vietnamese coercion (Hershberger 2006, 28).

However, the enduring significance of the POWs as a political issue was initiated in 1969 by the Nixon administration. Some of his advisers saw concern over the prisoners as a way to shift domestic public opinion into channels other than the antiwar movement that was shutting down campuses and filling city streets across America. While Americans had been aware since at least 1965 of POWs, the administration successfully brought the issue to the forefront. However, not everyone was happy with the way the POWs were turned into "a virtual cult," according to *New Yorker* staff writer Jonathan Schell (1943–2014). He complained, "The wounded, the dying, and the dead went virtually unnoticed" as "attention was focused on the prisoners of war" (Schell 1976, 231). Schell's opinion may have been uncharitable, but he identified the emotional engagement the issue had with many middle-class Americans whose support for the prisoners was displayed by wearing "POW bracelets," metal bands bearing the name and rank of Americans captured or missing in Southeast Asia. The unprecedented attention given the POWs may have resulted in part, as a U.S. government report conceded, because they "were mostly officers, and glamorous aviators at that, which added to their media celebrity" (Rochester 1998, vi).

Five hundred and sixty-six POWs were returned by Hanoi as part of Operation Homecoming. They arrived home in the months following the Paris Peace Accords (January 27, 1973) that ended the U.S. combat role in the Vietnam War, and were lionized. Many Americans saw them as symbols of pride and patriotism in light of U.S. failure to win the war. By contrast, most of the troops returning from their tour of duty in Vietnam saw no parades in their honor and received the gratitude of their nation belatedly as passions over the war finally cooled.

CONCLUSION

In writing and directing *Little Dieter Needs to Fly* and *Rescue Dawn*, Herzog was less concerned with getting the details correct than with painting a vivid picture of Dengler's physical and mental state, his duress and courage, during his captivity and escape. As Herzog explained, "We are into illumination for the sake of a deeper truth, for an ecstasy of truth, for something we can experience once in a while in great literature and great cinema." He added, "If you're purely after the facts, please buy yourself the phone directory of Manhattan. It has four million correct facts. But it doesn't illuminate" (Murphy 2007).

Working with those intentions, Herzog crafted a film that resonated with audiences for focusing on a heroic human experience during a war that continues to darken the memory of many Americans. Dengler's "story of unending optimism, innate courage, loyalty and survival against overwhelming odds remains our brightest memory of our generation's war" (Henderson 2010, xix).

FURTHER READING

Allen, Michael J. 2009. *Until the Last Man Comes Home: POWs, MIAs, and the Unending Vietnam War*. Chapel Hill, NC: University of North Carolina Press.

Ambrose, Stephen. 1984. *Eisenhower: The President (1952–1969)*. New York: Simon & Schuster.

Dengler, Dieter. 1979. *Escape from Laos*. San Rafael, CA: Presidio Press.

Ebert, Roger. "Rescue Dawn." *Chicago Sun-Times*, July 12, 2007.

Ebert, Roger. 2017. *Herzog by Ebert*. Chicago: University of Chicago Press.

Hamilton-Merritt, Jane. 1993. *Tragic Mountains: The Hmong, the Americans, and the Secret Wars for Laos, 1942–1992*. Bloomington, IN: Indiana University Press.

Henderson, Bruce. 2010. *Hero Found: The Greatest POW Escape of the Vietnam War*. New York: Harper.

Hershberger, Mary. 2006. *Jane Fonda's Words of Politics and Passion*. New York: New Press.

McBride, Jessica. "Cloak & Dagger," *Milwaukee Magazine*, October 29, 2007.

Murphy, Mekado. "Werner Herzog Is Still Breaking the Rules." *New York Times*, July 1, 2007.

Norris, John G. "U.S. Names Pilot in Mystery Escape." *Washington Post*, July 27, 1966.

Peary, Gerald. 2007. "Francis Ford Coppola," geraldpeary.com, http://www .geraldpeary.com/interviews/abc/coppola.html, retrieved December 7, 2018.

"Reds Heat Up Laos." *U.S. News & World Report*, June 17, 1968.

Rochester, Stuart I., and Frederick Kiley. 1998. *Honor Bound: American Prisoners of War in Southeast Asia, 1961–1973*. Washington, DC: Historical Office/Office of the Secretary of Defense.

Romero, Simon. "From a Hinterland, Hmong Forge a New Home." *New York Times*, December 21, 2008.

Ruane, Michael E. "Traitors or Patriots? Eight Vietnam POWs Were Charged with Collaborating with the Enemy." *Washington Post*, September 22, 2017.

Santoli, Al. 1986. *To Bear Any Burden: The Vietnam War and Its Aftermath in the Words of Americans and Southeast Asians*. New York: Ballantine.

Schell, Jonathan. 1976. *The Time of Illusion*. New York: Alfred A. Knopf.

Seitz, Matt Zoller. "A Vietnam P.O.W. Story, Tangling with the Vines of Convention." *New York Times*, July 4, 2007.

Stuart-Fox, Martin. 1997. *A History of Laos*. Cambridge: Cambridge University Press.

Thomson, David. 2010. *The New Biographical Dictionary of Film*. New York: Alfred A. Knopf.

Ward, Geoffrey C., and Ken Burns. 2017. *The Vietnam War: An Intimate History*. New York: Alfred A. Knopf.

Bibliography

The Vietnam War produced a shelf of books before the end of America's involvement, and in the years since, the shelf has grown into a library. The list below is not comprehensive but includes books that were sources for *The Vietnam War on Film* plus several works that significantly shaped historical and popular understanding of the conflict. In addition, the bibliography includes key sources for the films explored in *The Vietnam War on Film*, the movies that have done as much if not more than any book to engrave the war in memory.

Adkins, Bennie G. 2018. *A Tiger Among Us: A Story of Valor in Vietnam's A Shau Valley*. Cambridge, MA: Da Capo Press.

Allen, Michael J. 2009. *Until the Last Man Comes Home: POWs, MIAs, and the Unending Vietnam War*. Chapel Hill, NC: University of North Carolina Press.

Ambrose, Stephen. 1984. *Eisenhower: The President (1952–1969)*. New York: Simon & Schuster.

Appy, Christian G. 1993. *Working-Class War: American Combat Soldiers and Vietnam*. Chapel Hill, NC: University of North Carolina Press.

Appy, Christian G. 2015. *American Reckoning: The Vietnam War and Our National Identity*. New York: Viking.

Baskir, Lawrence M., and William A. Strauss. 1978. *Chance and Circumstance: The Draft, the War, and the Vietnam Generation*. New York: Alfred A. Knopf.

Bergerud, Eric M. 1993. *Red Thunder, Tropic Lightning: The World of a Combat Division in Vietnam*. Boulder, CO: Westview Press.

Bliss, Michael. 1985. *Martin Scorsese and Michael Cimino*. Metuchen, NJ: Scarecrow Press.

Bodard, Lucien. 1967. *The Quicksand War: Prelude to Vietnam*. London: Faber and Faber.

Bowden, Mark. 2017. *Hue 1968: A Turning Point of the American War in Vietnam*. New York: Atlantic Monthly Press.

Brinkley, Douglas. 2004. *Tour of Duty: John Kerry and the Vietnam War*. New York: HarperCollins.

Browne, Malcolm W. 1965. *The New Face of War*. New York: Bobbs-Merrill.

Caputo, Philip. 1977. *A Rumor of War*. New York: Holt, Rinehart and Winston.

Clodfelter, Michael. 1976. *Pawns of Dishonor*. Boston: Branden Press.

Coles, Robert. 1971. *The Middle Americans*. Boston: Little, Brown and Co.

Coppola, Eleanor. 1979. *Notes*. New York: Simon and Schuster.

Cowie, Peter. 2014. *Coppola*. Milwaukee: Applause Theatre & Cinema Books.

Cronkite, Walter. 1996. *A Reporter's Life*. New York: Alfred A. Knopf.

Davidson, Bill. 1990. *Jane Fonda: An Intimate Biography*. London: Sidgwick & Jackson.

Deeley, Michael, with Matthew Field. 2009. *Blade Runners, Deer Hunters and Blowing the Bloody Doors Off: My Life in Cult Movies*. New York: Pegasus Books.

Dengler, Dieter. 1979. *Escape from Laos*. San Rafael, CA: Presidio Press.

Dittmar, Linda, and Gene Michaud, editors. 1990. *From Hanoi to Hollywood: The Vietnam War in American Film*. New Brunswick, NJ: Rutgers University Press.

Dougan, Clark, and Samuel Lipsman. 1984. *A Nation Divided: The Vietnam Experience*. Boston: Boston Publishing Company.

Downs, Frederick. 1978. *The Killing Zone: My Life in the Vietnam War*. New York: W. W. Norton.

Ebert, James R. 1993. *A Life in a Year: The American Infantryman in Vietnam 1965–1972*. Novato, CA: Presidio Press.

Ebert, Roger. 2017. *Herzog by Ebert*. Chicago: University of Chicago Press.

Falk, Quentin. 1984. *Travels in Greenland: The Cinema of Graham Greene*. London: Quartet Books.

Fall, Bernard. 1994. *Street without Joy: Indochina at War, 1946–1954*. Mechanicsburg, PA: Stackpole Books.

Fitzgerald, Frances. 1972. *Fire in the Lake: The Vietnamese and the Americans in Vietnam*. Boston: Little Brown.

Fonda, Jane. 2005. *My Life So Far*. New York: Random House.

Greene, Graham. 1968. *The Quiet American*. New York: Bantam Books.

Greiner, Bernd. 2009. *War without Fronts: The USA in Vietnam*. New Haven, CT: Yale University Press.

Guiles, Fred Lawrence. 1982. *Jane Fonda: The Actress in Her Time*. Garden City, NY: Doubleday.

Halberstam, David. 1965. *The Making of a Quagmire*. New York: Random House.

Halberstam, David. 1972. *The Best and the Brightest*. New York: Ballantine Books.

Hamilton-Merritt, Jane. 1993. *Tragic Mountains: The Hmong, the Americans, and the Secret Wars for Laos, 1942–1992*. Bloomington: Indiana University Press.

Hasford, Gustav. 1980. *The Short-Timers*. New York: Bantam Books.

Hayslip, Le Ly, with Jay Wurts. 1989. *When Heaven and Earth Changed Places: A Vietnamese Woman's Journey from War to Peace*. New York: Doubleday.

Helmer, John. 1974. *Bringing the War Home: The American Soldier in Vietnam and After*. New York: Free Press.

Henderson, Bruce. 2010. *Hero Found: The Greatest POW Escape of the Vietnam War*. New York: Harper.

Herr, Michael. 1978. *Dispatches*. New York: Alfred A. Knopf.

Herr, Michael. 2000. *Stanley Kubrick*. New York: Grove Press.

Hersh, Seymour M. 2018. *Reporter: A Memoir*. New York: Alfred P. Knopf.

Hershberger, Mary. 1998. *Traveling to Vietnam: American Peace Activists and the War*. Syracuse, NY: Syracuse University Press.

Hershberger, Mary. 2006. *Jane Fonda's Words of Politics and Passion*. New York: New Press.

Jeansonne, Glen, and David Luhrssen. 2014. *War on the Silver Screen: Shaping America's Perception of History*. Lincoln, NE: Potomac Books.

Just, Ward S. 1968. *To What End: Report from Vietnam*. Boston: Houghton Mifflin.

Kagan, Norman. 2000. *The Cinema of Stanley Kubrick*. 3rd ed. New York: Continuum.

Karnow, Stanley. 1997. *Vietnam: A History*. New York: Penguin.

Kissinger, Henry. 1979. *White House Years*. Boston: Little, Brown.

Kissinger, Henry. 2003. *Ending the Vietnam War: A History of America's Involvement and Extrication from the Vietnam War*. New York: Simon & Schuster.

Kovic, Ron. 1976. *Born on the Fourth of July*. New York: McGraw-Hill.

Kremer, Daniel. 2015. *Sidney J. Furie: Life and Films*. Lexington, KY: University Press of Kentucky.

Levison, Andrew. 1975. *Working-Class Majority*. New York: Penguin Books.

Logevall, Fredrik. 2012. *Embers of War: The Fall of an Empire and the Making of America's Vietnam*. New York: Random House.

Mao Tse-Tung. 1967. *Quotations from Chairman Mao Tse-Tung*. Peking: Foreign Language Press.

Mason, Robert. 1983. *Chickenhawk*. New York: Viking.

McAlister, John T., and Paul Mus. 1970. *The Vietnamese and Their Revolution*. New York: Harper & Row.

McMaster, H. R. 1997. *Dereliction of Duty: Lyndon Johnson, Robert McNamara, the Joint Chiefs of Staff, and the Lies That Led to Vietnam*. New York: HarperCollins.

McNamara, Robert S., with Brian VanDeMark. 1995. *In Retrospect: The Tragedy and Lessons of Vietnam*. New York: Random House.

Military History Institute of Vietnam, translated by Merle L. Pribbenow. 2002. *Victory in Vietnam: The Official History of the People's Army of Vietnam, 1954–1975*. Lawrence, KS: University Press of Kansas.

Mole, Robert L. 1970. *The Montagnards of South Vietnam: A Story of Nine Tribes*. Rutland, VT: Charles E. Tuttle.

Moore, Robin. 1965. *The Green Berets*. New York: Crown.

Nicosia, Gerald. 2001. *Home to War: A History of the Vietnam Veterans Movement*. New York: Crown Publishers.

Nolan, Keith William. 1990. *Into Cambodia: Spring Campaign, Summer Offensive, 1970*. Novato, CA: Presidio Press.

Nolan, Keith William. 1991. *Operation Buffalo: USMC Fight for the DMZ*. Novato, CA: Presidio Press.

Oberdorfer, Don. 2001. *Tet! The Turning Point in the Vietnam War*. Baltimore: Johns Hopkins University Press.

O'Brien, Geoffrey. 1995. *The Phantom Empire: Movies in Mind of the Twentieth Century*. New York: W. W. Norton.

O'Brien, Tim. 1990. *The Things They Carried*. New York: Houghton Mifflin.

Osborne, Milton. 2000. *The Mekong: Turbulent Past, Uncertain Future*. New York: Atlantic Monthly Press.

Pitzer, Dan. 1985. "The Release" in *To Bear Any Burden: The Vietnam War and Its Aftermath in the Words of Americans and Southeast Asians*, edited by Al Santoli. New York: E. P. Dutton.

Porter, Gareth. 1981. *Vietnam: A History in Documents*. New York: Meridian.

Prados, John. 1995. *The Hidden History of the Vietnam War*. Chicago: Ivan R. Dee.

Riordan, James. 1995. *Stone: The Controversies, Excesses, and Exploits of a Radical Filmmaker*. New York. Hyperion.

Roberts, Randy, and James S. Olson. 1995. *John Wayne American*. New York: Free Press.

Rochester, Stuart I., and Frederick Kiley. 1998. *Honor Bound: American Prisoners of War in Southeast Asia, 1961–1973*. Washington, DC: Historical Office/Office of the Secretary of Defense.

Santoli, Al, editor. 1985. *To Bear Any Burden: The Vietnam War and its Aftermath in the Words of Americans and Southeast Asians*, edited by Al Santoli. New York: E. P. Dutton.

Schell, Jonathan. 1976. *The Time of Illusion*. New York: Alfred A. Knopf.

Schumacher, Michael. 1999. *Francis Ford Coppola: A Filmmaker's Life*. New York: Crown.

Shaplen, Robert. 1966. *The Lost Revolution: Vietnam 1945–1965*. London: Andre Deutsch.

Shawcross, William. 1979. *Sideshow: Kissinger, Nixon, and the Destruction of Cambodia*. New York: Washington Square Books.

Sheehan, Neil. 1988. *A Bright Shining Lie: John Paul Vann and America in Vietnam*. New York: Vintage Books.

Sheehan, Neil, Hedrick Smith, E. W. Kenworthy, and Fox Butterfield. 1971. *The Pentagon Papers: The Secret History of the Vietnam War*. New York: Bantam Books.

Shepherd, Donald, and Robert Slatzer, with Dave Grayson. 1985. *Duke: The Life and Times of John Wayne*. New York: Doubleday.

Shulimson, Jack, Leonard A. Blaisol, Charles R. Smith, and David A. Dawson. 1997. *U.S. Marines in Vietnam: The Defining Year, 1968*. Washington, DC: History and Museums Division, Headquarters U.S. Marine Corps.

Simpson III, Charles M. 1983. *Inside the Green Berets: The First Thirty Years*. Novato, CA: Presidio Press.

Sorley, Lewis. 2011. *Westmoreland: The General Who Lost Vietnam*. Boston: Houghton Mifflin Harcourt.

Southworth, Samuel A., and Stephen Tanner. 2002. *U.S. Special Forces: A Guide to America's Special Operations Units*. Cambridge, MA: Da Capo Press.

Stanton, Shelby L. 1985. *Green Berets at War: U.S. Special Forces in Southeast Asia 1956–1975*. Novato, CA: Presidio Press.

Stuart-Fox, Martin. 1997. *A History of Laos*. Cambridge. Cambridge University Press.

Suid, Lawrence H. 1978. *Guts & Glory: The Making of the American Military Image in Film*. Reading, MA: Addison-Wesley.

Terry, Wallace. 1984. *Bloods: An Oral History of the Vietnam War by Black Americans*. New York: Random House.

Thomson, Dave. 2008. *"Have You Seen...?": A Personal Introduction to 1,000 Films*. New York: Alfred A. Knopf.

Thomson, David. 2010. *The New Biographical Dictionary of Film*. New York: Alfred A. Knopf.

Thorne, David, and George Butler. 1971. *The New Soldier*. New York: Collier.

Toplin, Robert Brent, editor. 2000. *Oliver Stone's USA: Film, History, and Controversy*. Lawrence, KS: University of Kansas Press.

Turse, Nick. 2012. *Kill Anything That Moves: The Real American War in Vietnam*. New York: Metropolitan/Henry Holt.

Useem, Michael. 1973. *Conscription, Protest, and Social Conflict*. New York: Wiley.

Ward, Geoffrey C., and Ken Burns. 2017. *The Vietnam War: An Intimate History*. New York: Alfred A. Knopf.

Wayne, Aissa, with Steve Delsohn. 1991. *John Wayne: My Father*. New York: Random House.

Westheider, James E. 2007. *The Vietnam War*. Westport, CT: Greenwood Publishing Group.

Westmoreland, William C. 1976. *A Soldier Reports*. Garden City, NY: Doubleday.

Wintle, Justin. 1991. *The Vietnam Wars*. New York: St. Martin's Press.

Wolf, Tobias. 1994. *Pharaoh's Army: Memories of the Lost War*. New York: Alfred A. Knopf.

Index

About the Author

DAVID LUHRSSEN is author of *Secret Societies and Clubs in American History*, *Mamoulian: Life on Stage and Screen*, and *Hammer of the Gods: Thule Society and the Birth of Nazism*, as well as coauthor of several books, including *The Encyclopedia of Classic Rock*, *Elvis Presley: Reluctant Rebel* and *A Time of Paradox: America Since 1890*. He is a contributor to *100 People Who Changed 20th Century America*, *Women at War*, *American National Biography Online*, and the *New Grove Dictionary of Music and Musicians* and has written for *Historically Speaking*, *History Today*, the *Journal of American History*, and other publications.

Luhrssen received graduate and undergraduate degrees in history from the University of Wisconsin-Milwaukee and taught at the Milwaukee Institute of Art and Design and Milwaukee Area Technical College. He is managing editor and film critic for Milwaukee's weekly newspaper, the *Shepherd Express*, and has written about music and film for *Billboard*, the *Milwaukee Journal*, and other newspapers and magazines. He is also a regular commentator on film for Milwaukee's NPR affiliate.

Printed in the USA
CPSIA information can be obtained
at www.ICGtesting.com
LVHW012128141223
766281LV00005B/382